HOW TO GET
A FEDERAL JOB

HOW TO GET A FEDERAL JOB

A Guide to Finding and Applying for a Job with the United States Government Anywhere in the United States

Krandall Kraus

Facts On File Publications
New York, New York ● Oxford, England

This book is lovingly dedicated to Cletus Kraus, my father, the perfect civil servant.

HOW TO GET A FEDERAL JOB
A Guide to Finding and Applying for
a Job with the United States Government
Anywhere in the United States

Copyright © 1986 by Krandall Kraus
Updated 1989

Library of Congress Cataloging-in Publication Data

Kraus, Krandall.
   How to get a federal job.
   1. Civil service positions—United States. I. Title.
JK716.K69 1986   353'.00023   85-29187
ISBN 0-8160-1224-5 (HC)
ISBN 0-8160-1532-5 (PB)

Printed in the United States of America

10 9 8 7 6 5 4 3

Composition by Facts On File/Maxwell Photographics Inc.

Contents

List of Appendixes

Preface

This book came about as the result of the suggestion of many friends and acquaintances whom I have assisted in getting jobs with the federal government. As a manager, supervisor, and chairperson of countless Rating Panels—the panels that score federal job applications—I found I was able to put together a federal job application so that regardless of the job being applied for, the person scored among the top five applicants, generally getting an interview. In one year eight people came to me for assistance with their applications. All eight got job interviews and seven got the jobs they were applying for. When I looked at that track record, I figured

my friends were right: I should write a book telling people the tricks of successfully filling out a government job application form.

But it's not enough to know how to fill out the application. You have to know what jobs are available with the United States Government and where and how to look for them. This book will tell you what kinds of jobs the government has to offer, how to find the job you are best suited for, and—most important of all—how to successfully apply for the job you want. I can practically guarantee you an interview if you follow the suggestions in the following pages. After that, you're on your own.

Acknowledgments

The author wishes to acknowledge the invaluable assistance of Andre Laventure, Ben Dailey, Marjorie Baer, Deloris Gainer, Lucy Vecera, George Thuronyi, and the Library of Congress. Without their assistance, advice, and encouragement, this book could not have been written.

Introduction

Conventional wisdom tells us that when Democrats are occupying the White House it is an extremely good time to look for a job with the federal government, for Democrats are more inclined to create public jobs in order to ease unemployment. However, according to some federal personnel officials, there are plenty of jobs to be had even during a Republican administration—if you know how and where to look.

Let me begin by dispelling the most common misunderstanding about jobs with the federal government. Nearly everyone thinks that if you work for Uncle Sam you are going to have to move to Washington, D.C., because that's where all the jobs with the federal government are located. Nothing could be further from the truth. According to the most recently available statistics published by the Office of Personnel Management, there are 353,000 jobs located in the nation's capital; however, federal jobs throughout the rest of the country total a whopping 2,902,000. And there are 562,962 federal employees working for the government outside the United States as well (Appendix A). These are civilian jobs only and do not include military personnel. So if you are in the market for a federal job, you may not need to look any further than your own community. See Appendix A for a state-by-state breakdown of federal civilian jobs.

There's a lot about applying for a federal job that the general public doesn't know. It's not exactly scandalous. It doesn't make for an exposé. But it is shameful, because what the government doesn't tell you can and will hurt you if you depend upon it to help you get a job, as I once did.

During a brief period of unemployment several years ago—which didn't seem very brief at the time—I decided to go after a federal government job. I knew two things: first, I was tired of being pushed around by tyrannical company presidents who held my security in their over-lunched jowls and could chew me up and spit me out on a whim at any time; and second, my friends who had government jobs seemed to spend most of their time at birthday parties, farewell parties, welcome-to-the-office parties, and the secretary-transferred-to-another-agency parties. I decided that I, too, was due for a party. Was I in for a surprise.

I began my search with mixed emotions, for as I trudged from one government personnel office to another I remembered my father ranting about government workers being lazy, overpaid, and underworked. Never mind that he was himself a government worker. He was a "good" worker. The rest were bums. Nevertheless, I decided I would have to risk bearing the weight of my father's scorn.

I was living in Washington, D.C. at the time, and someone told me about the Federal Job Information Center at 1900 E Street, N.W., in the Office of Personnel Management (OPM). (This is not to be confused, by the way, with the Federal Information Centers operated by the General Services Administration.)

All I had to do, according to my friend, who was a government worker himself, was to fill out an application and receive a "GS rating" from them.

Ninety-five percent of all white-collar federal jobs are rated according to the General Schedule (GS). A job's GS level is an indicator of that job's level of responsibility, minimum educational and experience requirements, and salary range. People, too, are rated, or certified, by OPM as being qualified—or "eligible," in government jargon—to hold jobs at certain GS levels; hence the need for me to obtain a GS rating. If a person is rated at a GS-11 level, for example, then that person can apply for any job the government has open at the GS-11 level or lower for which he or she is qualified.

According to my friend, the Federal Job Information Center would make my application available to every government agency in town. All I would have to do was sit back and wait for the calls to come pouring in. Jobs would be mine for the choosing.

So I went to the job center, obtained my packet of forms, spent an entire afternoon filling them out, mailed them back, and waited. Lucky for me I don't sit still easily. I kept looking for jobs on personnel office bulletin boards at the individual agency offices and found one posted at the Library of Congress that seemed right for me. I applied and was hired.

Four months after starting my job with the Library I received a letter from OPM assigning me a government ID number. It said I *might* be eligible for a GS-9 or GS-11, depending upon what the particular job was, and warned me in no uncertain terms that this was NOT A NOTICE OF RATING! That was the last I ever heard from OPM. It was February 1980.

I've learned a lot since then about applying for—and getting—a job with the federal government. I've also learned that all that talk about civil servants being overpaid and underworked is just talk. I've never worked harder in my life and I can count the office parties on one hand.

I had reason to return to the Job Information Center recently to gather information for this book, and what I found was even more appalling than what awaited me six years ago as an unsuspecting, hopeful member of the ranks of the unemployed.

The room where the Job Information Center in Washington is housed is cavernous. One entire wall is a long counter with eight windows where, at one time, staff members answered questions and distributed information. Now there is only one woman handing out forms and pamphlets.

This particular day the line of people extended from her station at the far end of the counter down one wall, halfway down another wall, and around the half-filled bulletin boards where job announcements were posted behind glass doors.

As I took my place in line I read over the jobs posted on the bulletin boards. "Biological and Agricultural Technician, GS-4/9, closed. Guard, GS-3/4/5, closes January 22. Junior Federal Assistant, GS-4, closes February 1." It occurred to me that it was April 7.

There were all kinds of people in line. Secretaries, servicemen, a psychologist, a management analyst who had just moved from Seattle. Even an attorney. The woman at the counter answered their questions in her official, evenly cadenced monotone and handed out publications and forms she selected after patiently but unexpressively listening to their plaintive hard luck stories.

There was a notice posted on the counter. "Due to severe cutbacks in government funds only one Personal Qualifications Statement (job application form) will be given out per visit."

What were they talking about? There must have been at least five hundred sitting on the shelf in the administrative section next door to my office at the Library. (Later, on my way home, I stopped at two other government agency offices and was offered a fistful of forms at both places.)

After fifty-five minutes of waiting I arrived at the counter. The woman, seemingly knowledgeable and trying to be informative, if not helpful, told me that of the five topics on which I requested information—Professional Administrative Career Appointments (PAC), the Mid-level Register, the Senior Executive Service, the Merit Pay System, and general information about getting a federal job—she could supply printed materials concerning two.

The Office of Personnel Management spent an estimated $2,216,000 on printing and reproduction in Fiscal Year 1984, but it could only give me one job application form per visit and provide me with printed information on two of the five things I need to know about in order to apply for a government job.

As I waited for the woman to gather my forms I recalled my father berating his fellow civil servants each evening, and for the first time I could relate to his frustration with the system.

When I got home, I pried the loafers from my tired feet and looked over what they had given me. First, there was a list of jobs available in the Washington, D.C. area during the months of April, May, and June. But the pamphlet doesn't indicate which agencies are filling these jobs.

Twelve of the forty-one jobs were closed; twenty-three referred me to something called the "current General Notice," but there was no explanation of what that was; two said "apply directly to agency" (remember, they hadn't identified the agencies); three were closed. The rest of the information the woman gave me constituted the Mid-Level Packet. The packet contained several forms and something that hadn't been there four years before:

a sheet of questions and answers titled, "You Say I Don't Get a Rating?" It looked like someone had demanded some answers. I read anxiously.

Q. What has happened to my application?
A. The information . . . has been entered into a computer record . . . and placed into our application referral file.
Q. Will I get a score or rating?
A. No.
Q. How do I know if I am qualified?
A. You can make a fairly accurate determination . . . by carefully reading the announcement.
Q. How soon will my name be referred?
A. Your chances of being referred depend on . . .
Q. Do you maintain a list of vacancies for which I may apply?
A. No.
Q. I have just seen a federal agency's announcement for a position in which I am interested. Since you have my application, will I automatically be considered?
A. Not necessarily.
Q. I submitted an application to an agency in response to a job announcement and was told that the selecting official has requested that I be certified by OPM. Will they be able to hire me?
A. It depends.

After reading this question and answer sheet, one might be tempted to ask, "Why should I go to OPM in the first place?" A good question. My answer is simple: "Don't!"

My experience, and the experience of everyone I know in and out of government, has led to one conclusion: If you want a job with the federal government, apply directly to the agency you want to work for. It's easier—although not always easy, especially if you don't talk their language, are not familiar with the regulations concerning hiring federal workers, or have not prepared the proper paperwork. The remainder of this book will provide you with the information you need in all three of these areas. Chances are that if you apply for a federal job without this information, you will become just another number in the vast computer data files of the Office of Personnel Management and, like me, six years later, still be waiting to be called by some government agency for a job interview.

1

The Pros and Cons of Working for the Federal Government

Federal workers are just like any other workers: they love and hate their jobs. But my experience has been that federal workers love and hate their jobs for reasons quite different from those of their fellow laborers in the private sector. What I'm going to attempt to do in this chapter is tell you why you might want to be a civil servant. Then I'm going to give you a couple reasons why you might not want to. You should consider both sides carefully—even talk to some people who work for the federal government. I think you will find they will confirm the things I say here. I also think you will find that they enjoy the challenge of their work and find a reasonable amount of satisfaction in working "for the public good."

Working in the government, you may get some on-the-job training, you will definitely learn how to work within a system, and you may be fortunate enough to work with some very dedicated people. Most federal workers take their jobs very seriously, in spite of the obstacles and the seeming endlessness of the work. Should you decide at some point in your career to move out of government service, there are plenty of businesses in the private sector that are eager to hire people who have worked within the government, especially if those people know something about government contracting or government programs related to a company's business interests.

A LARGE JOB SPECTRUM FROM WHICH TO CHOOSE

Few people realize the variety of jobs available with the federal government. We

1

usually think of government workers as mailmen, the White House staff, and bureaucratic office workers in general. However, chances are that the very job you perform right now is one you could be doing within the federal government. Just look at this small random sampling from the hundreds of positions available with your Uncle Sam.

Air Conditioning	Police Officer
Mechanic	Community Planner
Animal Caretaker	Economist
Asphalt Worker	Recreation Specialist
Baker	Typist
Carpenter	Computer Operator
Cook	Zoologist
Electrician	Soil Conservation
Elevator Operator	Specialist
Gardener	Radio Operator
Janitor	Accountant
Laundry Worker	Physical Therapist
Machine Tool	Dentist
Operator	Physician
Painter	Lawyer
Pipefitter	Nurse
Rigger	Safety Engineer
Sandblaster	Real Estate
Tractor Operator	Appraiser

STEADY, SOLID PAY

It is commonly held that pay for federal workers falls far below pay in the private sector. Annual studies show that people who work for private companies performing the same jobs as government workers earn more money. However, statistics are a funny thing; you can prove almost anything with them if you juggle them enough.

If we put aside the statistics and look at the facts, we might find something different from what is commonly believed. Let's start by looking at the actual pay scale for federal workers as of January 1989. The lowest salary (Grade 1, Step 1) is $10,213. The highest (Grade 18, Step 1) is $86,682. The middle of the schedule (Grade 9, Step 1) is $23,846. Most federal jobs start at Grades 3 or 5,

$12,531 and $15,738, respectively. Not bad, considering that Grade 3 jobs are mostly file clerks and mailroom helpers.

There is something else to consider: the annual cost of living increase combined with a regularly scheduled pay raise for satisfactory performance, which is given annually, biannually, or triannually, depending upon how many years you have been in your job (see Chapter 2).

Workers in the private sector may make more money initially, but there is no guarantee that they will receive a raise every year. On the contrary, pay raises in the private sector usually depend solely on company profits. Not so in the federal government. At the beginning of each fiscal year (October 1) an automatic cost of living increase goes into effect. Granted, it varies, depending upon the President and the Congress, but it is usually no less than three percent and has gone as high as 9.4 percent during the Carter administration.

Add to that the salary increase you earn if you achieve a satisfactory performance rating and you can come away with a sizable pay raise.

GENEROUS LEAVE (VACATION)

Each federal worker earns from ten to twenty-six days of Annual Leave (vacation days) per year, depending upon length of service. (Ten for newcomers, twenty-six for veterans of fifteen or more years.) Also, there are ten federal holidays with pay and twelve days of Sick Leave per year. Any Annual Leave not used carries over from year to year up to a maximum of 240 hours (thirty work days). After you reach 240 hours you must "use or lose" the excess hours of Annual Leave. This is at least as good as the private sector, and the length of service for earning leave is usually much shorter than it is if you are working for a private company.

Sick Leave accumulates for as long as you work for the government, and while you are not paid for Sick Leave that you do not use, you can count it toward retirement as you approach that time. For example, a colleague of mine at the Library of Congress is retiring this year after forty-two years of service. He has accumulated over 3,500 hours of Sick Leave and, had he chosen to, he could have retired two years early and received the same retirement pay because of the vast amount of Sick Leave he had accumulated.

Another benefit to consider is that if you leave your federal job you will be paid for all the Annual Leave you have accumulated but not used up to that point. If you transfer to another agency, you take your leave hours with you to the new job *along with your seniority*.

TRANSFER POTENTIAL

The possibility for relocating anywhere in the United States is excellent, since Uncle Sam has regional and area offices throughout the United States. Even if your particular agency doesn't have offices in an area where you would like to live, chances are that some other government agency does, and you merely have to watch for an opening and apply.

FAIRNESS

Federal laws and regulations, along with better and better organized workers' bargaining units (unions), assure fair treatment and equality on the job. It is simply not possible for your boss to call you in and tell you to be out by the end of the day. It isn't even possible for her to tell you to be out in two weeks without plenty of documentation as to why. There is a strict procedure requiring several notices and warnings—all of which must be put in writing and sent through the infamous government bureaucracy—that must be followed before a worker can be terminated. Even then, if you belong to a union, you can count on a lengthy appeals procedure. One appeals procedure I know of lasted two years, was decided in favor of the employee, and resulted in the employee being promoted, transferred, and given back pay.

JOB SATISFACTION

In spite of the fact that federal workers have in recent years been labeled by some politicians as what's wrong with the government, civil servants work as hard and dedicate themselves as tirelessly to their tasks as do workers in the private sector. They realize that without their efforts many people in this country who depend on the government would be left out in the cold. There is often a great sense of fulfillment in being part of a system that feeds the hungry, shelters the homeless, provides medical assistance for the sick, Brailles and records books for the blind and physically handicapped, plants trees and maintains parks and seashores, protects our country's wildlife, and watches over the safety of all its citizens.

Although subject to much political debate, civil servants seem to understand that the issue of government workers' salaries costing the taxpayers too much is just politics and that the functioning of the nation and the welfare of its people depend largely on federal workers carrying out their daily tasks. In time of fatigue, restlessness, or boredom, this knowledge of the importance of their work keeps them going.

But working for Uncle Sam is not always a bed of roses. Like most other jobs, federal jobs have their liabilities. After all, that's why we call a job "work."

THE RED TAPE MENACE

By far the most radical adjustment one has to make in moving from the private to the public sector is dealing with the strangling amount of red tape that one finds within any bureaucracy. There are reasons for having so many procedures within the government, the most understandable being that of public accountability. Since federal workers are spending taxpayers' money, it is important that it be spent wisely and that all of it be accounted for.

There is more than a grain of truth in the public sentiment that the federal government could be run more efficiently. How to accomplish that has eluded even the best and the brightest federal managers; yet in spite of this, government workers continue to give their best day after day and the work of the federal government does get done.

One of the unspoken requirements for any federal job is patience. It is why current and former government employees tend to be favored when they apply for a government job. The selecting official figures that anyone who is familiar with all the procedural red tape and still finds it challenging and rewarding to work within the system is the kind of employee who will be productive. Anyone who enjoys the challenge of making a large organization effective and efficient will love working for the federal government.

THERE'S MORE WORK WHERE THAT CAME FROM

In order to make this leviathan government function, millions of people work to accomplish what seems like an endless number of tasks. It is difficult at times to feel like you have accomplished anything, for in the bureaucracy, as in a large corporation, what you accomplish often takes place somewhere beyond your observation. All you see is the paper you push, the forms you fill out, the invoices you process. The government is the biggest factory of all, producing invisible goods that in the eyes of its critics—and that includes nearly every citizen in the country—are seldom adequate.

Yet it is these same men and women who make possible all the luxuries, privileges—even rights—that are so commonly taken for granted: the maintenance of public highways, safe travel to foreign countries, the movement of the mails, national and international communications networks, public libraries, parks, and seashores, the public health. There is virtually no facet of our daily lives that isn't at some point affected by a civil servant somewhere in the maze of the federal bureaucracy doing his or her job. And in order to accomplish these

things and see that they continue to be accomplished, an endless amount of work is generated.

FEDERAL WORKERS CAN'T STRIKE

It should be remembered that federal employees are forbidden by law to strike. As a result, a number of employee bargaining organizations have been formed that work diligently to negotiate solid contracts with management in order to avoid the kinds of situations that result in worker walkouts. A job seeker should investigate the unions available to him at the agency where he is applying for a job. It is rare that mediators are not able to work out solutions to problems that arise between management and the unions, and strikes are virtually unheard of in the government.

Summary

It is not difficult to see that the assets outweigh the liabilities in working for the federal government, so long as you are patient and can cope with being part of a huge corporation, which is all the federal government really is—the largest business in the world. But unlike a business in the private sector, its work is vital to the very lives of the citizens of this country. Without the accomplishment of the most seemingly insignificant task within this huge organization, a child somewhere might not have the school lunch that provides him with the majority of his daily nutrients, a senior citizen would not receive her Social Security check in time to pay her winter heating bill, or a town along the Gulf Coast hit by a hurricane might not get the help it needs to rebuild demolished homes.

Perhaps these are some of the reasons why civil servants work so hard and keep working—it may have something to do with compassion and love of country. Whatever the reason, our nation couldn't function for long without them.

2
How the System Works (or Doesn't Work)

There are three common misconceptions about working for the federal government.

First, government jobs are all cushy. In the sixteen years I have been a working adult, I've worked for a college, a West Coast consulting firm, and a graphic design company; I've served as a consultant for the White House and a mid-level manager at the Library of Congress. Without a doubt, my government jobs demanded more of me than any I have ever held.

Second, government jobs are difficult to get. Correction: government jobs are difficult to find out about. During nearly any given week in 1988, more than 2,800 jobs were available with the federal government. The trick is finding out about them. After that, the key to a successful application lies in correctly and completely filling out the tedious and in-timidating Personal Qualifications Statement —otherwise known as the Standard Form 171.

Finally, and most insidiously, there is the belief that when a government hiring freeze is imposed by the administration, no federal jobs will be available until the freeze is lifted. When Ronald Reagan entered the White House in 1980, there were 3,076,646 jobs in the civil service system. By the end of 1987, civil service positions totalled a whopping 3,817,962.

NON-COMPETITIVE HIRING AUTHORITY

This is partially due to what the Office of Personnel Management (OPM) calls "Non-

Competitive Appointing Authorities." These "authorities" allow an agency to hire new employees without announcing or "posting" the position, thus sidestepping the law and eliminating the opportunity for the general public and other civil service workers to compete for the job based upon their qualifications. These authorities are usually adopted for certain highly specialized types of jobs or for special types of people, such as legal trainee jobs, which are filled by law students, and positions filled by severely handicapped persons. Many of these positions have "not-to-exceed" dates, meaning the job must end after a specified period of time has passed, usually one year.

These appointing authorities include some interesting categories, such as the Presidential Management Intern Program, Nuclear Regulatory Commission employees, the White House staff, and employees of the Office of the President.

OPM will quickly point out that most of these hiring authorities do not allow for conversion to career or career-conditional (i.e., permanent) status, meaning that the appointments must be ended after the designated time period has elapsed. This gives the impression that a person having completed the job obtained through the Non-Competitive Appointing Authority would have to go through all the regular bureaucratic procedures for finding and applying for a federal job, just as though he or she had no federal work experience.

What really happens, however, is that the employee—watching the job openings posted every day on the bulletin board of the personnel office where he is working at this temporary job—finds a job vacancy in his particular field (clerk-typist, engineer, welder, contract manager, etc.) and applies for it. With the year's experience gained in this non-competitive appointment, that applicant's chances for getting the job are greatly enhanced.

An extremely important point to note is that once you have been in a federal job for a minimum of one year, you are eligible to apply for a similar job at the next highest grade level. So, for example, let's say you were hired under a Non-Competitive Appointing Authority to work in an office as a Clerk-Typist at the GS-4 level for a period not to exceed one year. In your eleventh month you check the bulletin board in your agency's personnel office and see that a job has been posted for a Clerk-Typist at the GS-5 level. By the time you submit your application and the job closes, you will have had one year's experience as a GS-4 Clerk-Typist, which makes you eligible to apply for a GS-5 Clerk-Typist position. You see what has happened? Without ever going through the red tape and long wait of the normal competitive procedures of applying for a federal job, you have been given a temporary position "non-competitively"—i.e., without competing with the hundreds of other people who are looking for clerk-typist jobs with Uncle Sam. More importantly, you will be applying for the position as someone who has a full year's experience with the federal government. That sets you way above all those people who will apply for that job but who have only worked in the private sector, because the tendency is to hire people for government jobs who have experience with the government.

PERMANENT CIVIL SERVICE STATUS

Of course, the average citizen has never heard of these Non-Competitive Appointing Authorities. Most of us are under the impression that the best way to find employment with the federal government is to apply directly to OPM. After all, this is the agency that is the caretaker of all government jobs; these are the people who certify us as eligible for holding government jobs, thus opening that golden door to achieving "permanent civil service status," which carries with it so many important benefits. After three years of satisfactory performance in a federal job—during which you are classified as a "career-conditional" employee—you are awarded "permanent status" with the federal civil service. Once you have achieved "status," you are eligible to apply for jobs whether there is a job freeze in effect or not. Also, you are protected by volumes of civil service legislation, making it practically impossible for the government to fire you unless you have committed a felony or have a long record of unsatisfactory performance. This is why permanent status is so eagerly sought and highly treasured among federal workers. It is also why you so often hear that once you get a job with the U.S. Government you are "set for life." While that is not entirely true, there is a great deal of security in the civil service after your three-year "conditional" employment period has passed.

DON'T FILE WITH OPM

Because the Office of Personnel Management is designated as the clearinghouse for all government jobs, we, in good faith, apply for federal jobs through the established channels of OPM.

But when you fill out a Mid-Level Data Sheet and Standard Form 171 and deposit it with OPM, don't expect that the next step is for them to send it on to federal agencies looking for someone with your qualifications. It goes nowhere. That's right—NOWHERE.

Your application is evaluated, and you are sent a form letter (CSC 920X)—usually within ten to twelve weeks—telling you that the processing is complete. Yes, they've done their job; they looked at what you wrote and said you *might* be eligible for some mid-level jobs, depending upon what those jobs are.

They then take your name and some of the information you gave them, like what kind of job you're looking for and the experience you already have, and put it into a computer.

The letter they send you once they have evaluated your application and entered you into their data bank does NOT mean you are eligible for mid-level positions or any particular job. It is NOT a notice of rating. It does mean you are on file with all the other people who are looking for government jobs. And how many is that? Well, in fiscal 1987, for example, OPM processed 731,725 applications. You do the math.

So why bother putting your name there? Why go to the trouble of filling out all those forms and waiting three months to get a form letter back? OPM will tell you that the advantage in doing it is that your name will be there when an agency requests the names of people with your qualifications to fill a job.

But one personnel official laughed when I asked if it was really worthwhile. She told me the chances were slim.

The only time a name gets sent to an agency from OPM is when the agency sends OPM something called an "Eligibles Request and Certification" form. An agency does this when it has decided to fill a position with an outside person—i.e., a non-status or non-civil service applicant, someone who has never held a government job.

They will then send OPM the applicant's SF-171 (application form), an official position description, and the Eligibles Request and Certification Form. OPM will evaluate the application and then rate and rank the candidate in competition with others in the computer file who have similar qualifications and who have expressed an interest in jobs in the same job series.

If the candidate whose application was sent to OPM is found qualified, OPM will certify the person as being eligible to hold the job and return the SF171 along with a "list of eligibles"—that is, names of people who are equally or better qualified to fill that position. These additional names are taken from the computer record that your name went into when you filed all those forms with OPM.

The agency is then required to consider hiring those people whose names OPM sent back and who have a rating higher than the person that the agency requested OPM certify. If there is someone among the new names who is a veteran and who is just as qualified as the agency's original choice, then the veteran must be hired. (This assumes, of course, that these people are still sitting around waiting for the government to call them.) *That's the only time an agency will see your name.* What do you think the odds are?

HIRING UNDER DELEGATED AUTHORITY

A personnel specialist at one agency pointed out that occasionally the person whose application was sent to OPM for certification does not appear on the list that comes back. "Sometimes they find people on the register who are better qualified than the guy you want to give the job to."

What happens then? The bureaucrat smiled. "Well . . . if you really want to hire the person, the first thing you do is cancel the job posting. Then you go looking for loopholes. And there's always one to be found." This maneuver, called "Hiring Under Delegated Authority," is yet another kind of appointing authority that lets an agency hire someone on a non-competitive basis.

Under the Civil Service Reform Act of 1978, federal agencies—in order to alleviate some of the tremendous burden placed on OPM—were authorized to independently recruit and evaluate candidates for job vacancies. What this means is that applicants must file their job applications with the individual agencies—not OPM—in order to be considered for those particular jobs. In other words, an agency may not even have to request that OPM certify someone it wants to hire. All it has to do is hire the person under its "Delegated Authority." So, in the example above, our smiling bureaucrat would simply cancel the job opening for a permanent employee and go ahead and hire the person he wanted to hire in the first place, only on a temporary basis. After a year the agency will post the job again, and the person who held it temporarily for a year will apply for it with a full year's experience performing exactly those duties listed on the vacancy announcement. What outside applicant can beat that?

Still another way, and by far the most popular, is to hire someone on a temporary basis, since a temporary employee can be hired immediately on a non-competitive basis, usually for a period not to exceed one year.

For the bureaucrat who is trying to fill an empty position in his office, the beauty of this law regarding temporary appointments is that the person does not have to be certified by OPM unless the position is above the GS-7 level, so no names of equally qualified persons will be sent to the agency.

This is why one so frequently finds overqualified people working temporary jobs that have low GS ratings. They are biding their time, getting a year's experience, thereby making them eligible to apply for any federal job for which they are qualified at a higher GS level anywhere in the federal system.

PROFESSIONAL AND ADMINISTRATIVE CAREER EXAMINATION (PACE)

People looking for administrative or managerial trainee jobs in the GS-5 to GS-7 range should be aware that OPM has managed to get themselves out of the business of certifying those levels. Prior to 1982, OPM administered the Professional and Administrative Career Examination, or PACE. A person could walk into a Federal Job Information Center and take an exam for a GS rating in the GS-5 to GS-7 range for administrative or managerial positions. After receiving a Notice of Rating, the person was considered eligible for jobs rated at the GS level for which she was found qualified in her field of experience.

It was a quick, efficient way for a job seeker to obtain a GS rating and an easy method for agencies to get non-professional help in a hurry. They could simply call OPM, say they were looking for a secretary or technician or architectural trainee, and OPM would send them a batch of names of people with appropriate qualifications who scored high on the PACE. (This is probably how the misconception arose that OPM handed out GS ratings to anyone who applied, even people seeking mid-level positions.)

All this came to an abrupt halt as a result of a civil action in January 1982, when a U.S. District Court decree required the elimination of the PACE exam and register. Now agencies are required to do their own certification under a new program called PAC (Professional and Administrative Careers).

The bad news is that one personnel official told me the red tape in the new certification process is so menacing that her agency has not certified one GS-5 or GS-7 since the policy came into effect.

"We just don't do it. It would take forever, and it's not worth it. We hire on a temporary basis, or we hire people who already have status. The red tape in this new procedure is a nightmare, even to someone like me. And I've been in government personnel for nearly ten years. I wouldn't touch it."

The most important lesson you can learn from this discussion of how the system operates is this: By being aware of such things as Delegated Appointing Authorities, you can walk into a federal agency office, find a job for which you are qualified, and say directly to the person doing the hiring, "I know you can hire me temporarily without going through a lot of red tape and taking up a lot of valuable time. I'm qualified for the job, so why don't you hire me on a temporary basis through your Delegated Hiring Authority? It will save you time and a lot of paper-shuffling. It will get me a job, which I need. And if you aren't satisfied with my performance, you can always fire me." You might be very surprised at how often that will get you a job, especially if the office is overworked and under-staffed—and what office isn't?

3
The Various Forms of Federal Employment

There are basically two types of jobs the federal government has to offer: Competitive Service Jobs and Excepted Service Jobs.

COMPETITIVE SERVICE

The federal government is required by law to fill the majority of its positions under what is termed Competitive Service. This means that jobs with the government are competed for by qualified applicants and are filled, supposedly, by the most highly qualified people competing for jobs. The criteria for selecting those people are contained in the Selective Service Reform Act of 1978, which established "merit principles" that must be adhered to by government officials when filling a position or taking personnel actions.

These merit principles require, for example, that employees be given equal pay for work of value equal to similar work in the private sector. They also require that the government recruit employees from every segment of American society and that hiring and promotion be carried out on the basis of the ability, knowledge, and skills applicants and employees possess and demonstrate.

One of the most important features of the Reform Act is the dictum that the government shall practice fair and equitable treatment in all its personnel matters without regard to politics, religion, sex, race, color, marital status, age, national origin, or handicapped condition.It also states that Uncle Sam must respect each individual's privacy and constitutional rights. It makes arbitrary personnel actions, favoritism, and political coercion unlawful and protects civil servants from being punished for lawfully disclosing information.

So you can see that there are protections for the employee in the federal government that are rarely available in the private sector. This in itself can make a difference in deciding where you want to work. A great deal of comfort can be taken in knowing that—by law—you cannot be discriminated against by your employer, and that you are protected from the arbitrary and whimsical actions of a ruthless boss.

Very simply, then, Competitive Service jobs are jobs with the government that are filled openly, fairly, and without discrimination from among those applicants who compete with one another according to their abilities, knowledge, and skills.

EXCEPTED SERVICE

The second basic kind of federal job you can obtain is one within the Excepted Service. These jobs are positions that, for various reasons, have been made exceptions to the Competitive Service. They are excepted either by statute or by action of the Office of Personnel Management. There are basically no differences between these positions and Competitive Service positions so far as salary and personnel principles are concerned.

The basic disadvantage to working in an Excepted Position is that you do not accrue civil service seniority and are always outside the system. So, for example, if you worked in an Excepted Position for twenty years and then wanted to apply for a job within the Competitive Service, your application would, technically, be evaluated like all non-government applications. Of course, your abilities, knowledge, and skills would probably be considerable by that time, and your chances of getting at least an interview for the position would be very good.

One advantage to working in the Excepted Service is that you are not directly under the Executive Branch, so certain presidential decrees don't affect you. Reductions in Force (RIF) and job freezes, for example, do not necessarily apply to you unless the agency of

the federal government you are working for chooses to follow the President's lead in enacting such personnel policies.

Some agencies in the Excepted Service by statute are the Library of Congress, the Federal Reserve System, the Federal Courts, the Tennessee Valley Authority, the U.S. Foreign Service, and federal intelligence organizations.

The kinds of positions that are excepted by virtue of Office of Personnel Management action are jobs for which it is felt to be impossible to recruit through normal civil service channels, jobs that are policy-determining, jobs that require a close personal relationship between the employee and the agency head and/or key officials, and jobs that are filled by non-citizens and Veterans Readjustment Appointments. These sometimes require the passing of an examination. Many feel that most such excepted positions are merely bureaucratic ways in which to return political favors after winning an election campaign. They may fall under various "schedules"—Schedule A, Schedule B, and Schedule C—or they may be Non-Career Executive Assignments or Overseas Positions. The Schedule A, B, and C positions are very high-paying jobs; if you are interested in one of these, the best channel for pursuing employment is to contact someone you know who holds public office.

TYPES OF APPOINTMENTS

Within both the Competitive Service and the Excepted Service there are various kinds of appointments that are made. Your appointment, usually dictated by the nature of the position you are filling and the needs of the agency, will fall into one of the following categories.

Non-permanent Positions

There are two types of non-permanent positions within the federal government.

Temporary Appointment

Under this kind of appointment the employee can't be promoted or transferred to another government agency. Also, the temporary employee does not receive standard government benefits such as health insurance, life insurance, etc. In other words, temporary employees do not attain Permanent Civil Service Status, which is only earned after the three-year "conditional" period is up, and only when an employee has been working in a "permanent" position.

Until January 1985, the Office of Personnel Management had allowed agencies to hire temporary employees for a period not to exceed one year with a possible renewal of not more than one year. However, on January 2, 1985, OPM issued a new authority that radically changed that policy. In order to save the government money, OPM greatly broadened government agencies' temporary hiring authority. Whereas previously agencies could only hire people on a temporary basis up to the GS-7 level and only for one year with a maximum renewal of one year, now OPM is allowing agencies to make temporary appointments without OPM approval at the GS-12 level and below (and Wage Grade equivalents). Even more important is the fact that agencies may now renew those temporary appointments in one-year increments for *up to four years.* This turns out to be great for Uncle Sam and not so great for the employee. Since the appointments are for increments of one year or less, the employee is not eligible for health or life insurance or civil service retirement. He/She is covered by Social Security and is eligible for Annual and Sick Leave if the appointment is full- or part-time and is for at least ninety days.

Term Appointment

A term appointment is allowable when a person is hired to work on a particular project that is anticipated to last more than one year, but not more than four years. It is important to note that a term appointment, because it is for more than twelve months, carries full benefits

with it. *Any appointment that is initially made for more than a twelve-month period must carry full benefits.* That, of course, is why temporary appointments are made for no more than one year at a time, even though they can now be renewed for up to four years in one-year increments. Because the appointment has been classified as a Term Appointment, the employee does not earn Permanent Civil Service Status in this job.

Permanent Positions

Career-Conditional Appointment

This is the normal type of appointment that you receive when you are hired for a federal job. What this means is that the employee is actually hired conditionally for a probationary period and that after three years of satisfactory performance he or she will be converted to permanent status. Most jobs with the federal government are classified as Permanent Positions, but in order to protect the government from becoming stuck with an unsatisfactory employee, the employee is classified as Career-Conditional until an adequate evaluation of his or her performance can be made. The federal government protects itself from making a mistake by holding back the awarding of Permanent Status for three full years.

Career Appointment

This status in the federal civil service is usually referred to as "permanent" status. It means that you have worked satisfactorily in your job for a period of three years and you have earned a kind of "tenure" within the system. If, for example, the government finds it necessary to lay off workers, your status as a Permanent or Career employee will protect you—within certain limits—from being affected. Those who only hold Career-Conditional status will be laid off first.

4
The Benefits of Working for Uncle Sam

HEALTH INSURANCE PLANS

As a federal employee, you will be entitled to participate in the Federal Employees Health Benefits Program (FEHB). This plan offers you a choice of health insurance plans and options. The government makes a contribution toward the cost of your premium, and the balance is automatically deducted from your paycheck. Once enrolled, you obtain immediate coverage from the date of enrollment without a medical examination or any restrictions related to age or physical condition. There are conversion policies should you leave government service, and you are entitled to continued protection at no increase in cost after retirement. Your family may continue to be covered after your death.

Uncle Sam pays about sixty percent of the average premium of the six largest health benefit plans but not more than seventy-five percent of the premium for any one plan. In 1985, for example, regardless of which plan was chosen, the government contributed $98.46 per month for a "self only" policy and $215.54 toward a policy that insured the employee and his or her family members.

A variety of plans are offered through the federal government, but there are four basic types of plans available to federal workers:

1. The Service Benefit Plan

This plan is administered by the national Blue Cross and Blue Shield organization and is a government-wide plan that is available to every eligible federal employee. It generally provides benefits through direct payments to doctors and hospitals and certain medical cost reimbursements to individuals.

2. The Indemnity Benefit Plan

This health insurance plan is administered by Aetna Life Insurance Company and is also a government-wide program. It provides benefits by cash reimbursement either to the employee or, at the employee's option, to doctors or hospitals.

3. Employee Organization Plans

Some employee organizations —Government Employees Hospital Association (GEHA), National Association of Letter Carriers (NALC), National Association of Government Employees (NAGE), etc.—sponsor indemnity-type programs. Some of these plans are open to all government workers, while others are available only to certain groups of civil servants. To enroll in one of these plans a federal worker must join the organization that sponsors the plan. This is usually a simple procedure involving no waiting; there is, however, a membership fee at the time of signing up, and some of the organizations require annual dues.

4. Comprehensive Medical Plans

These plans are referred to as HMOs or Health Maintenance Organizations. HMOs differ from conventional health insurance plans insofar as members of HMOs must visit the organization's facilities—usually a local hospital—or a doctor who has agreed to participate with the organization in providing health care services. These plans are usually open to employees who live in a certain geographical area served by the plan. For example, federal workers in Washington, D.C. who belong to the George Washington University Health Plan receive their health care services at the George Washington University Hospital; members of the Kaiser-Georgetown Community Health Plan, Inc., receive their services at Georgetown University Hospital.

Beginning in January of 1989 there were twenty-two plans available to all federal employees anywhere in the world and plans offered to federal workers through local and regional programs in the fifty states, Puerto Rico, and Guam.

The chart in Appendix B shows the twenty-two 1989 FEHB government-wide plans and some of their benefits, along with the monthly premium paid by the federal employee.

CONTINUED ENROLLMENT

Health benefits plans continue to cover you and your family should you transfer from one federal agency to another without a break in service of more than three days. If a federal employee goes on "Leave Without Pay" (LWOP), enrollment can be continued up to 365 days; however, payment of the premiums is the responsibility of the employee during the leave period, since there will be no payroll check from which to deduct insurance premiums. If the employee dies while enrolled for "self and family" coverage, the eligible survivors can continue the enrollment with exactly the same benefits at the same cost as is computed for retired civil servants. Their premiums are deducted from their annuity checks.

Probably the most salient feature of health insurance for federal employees is the extremely wide variety of plans offered and the low cost of the plans to the employees. If an employee decides to change from one plan to another, there is a period—usually the month of November—referred to as "Open Season," during which the employee may change insurance plans. Changes can only be made during the open season.

LIFE INSURANCE

As a government employee, you are eligible also to participate in FEGLI (Federal Employees' Group Life Insurance), although in recent years there has been some dispute as to how economical this plan actually is. Each person must decide for him or herself, and—as with all purchases—it is best to shop around before signing up. In January, 1985, FEGLI worked this way: In order to be covered, you must have what is called the

Basic Life Plan. That means you must enroll for "coverage equal to the greater of (a) your actual rate of annual basic pay rounded to the next $1,000 plus $2,000 or (b) $10,000" minimum. (Nothing in the government is simple.)

For example, if you are beginning a job at the GS-9 level, then your annual basic rate of pay is $21,804. Your "annual basic pay rounded to the next $1,000" is $22,000. You add $2,000 to that for a total of $24,000. FEGLI rates are fifty-two cents per $1,000 monthly (1985). In this case, your life insurance, should you elect to belong to FEGLI, would cost you $12.48 per month.

Compounding the complexity of this formula even more is the new "extra benefit" clause. This clause doubles the amount of life insurance payable if you are age thirty-five or younger. Beginning on your thirty-sixth birthday, the extra benefit decreases ten percent each year until, at age forty-five, there is no extra benefit.

FEGLI is automatically deducted from your paycheck, so you never have to worry about forgetting to pay the premium.

But there are cheaper policies. For example, the League of Federal Recreation Associations, Inc.—to which all or nearly all government agencies belong—offers a life insurance policy to federal employees. If you were a federal employee at the GS-9 level, were forty-five years old, and insured yourself through the League of Federal Recreation Associations plan, you could obtain a $30,000 life insurance policy for $7.75 per month. That's a savings of $56.76 per year over FEGLI. If you were between the ages of thirty and thirty-four it would cost only $3.85 per month, a savings of $103.56 annually. Shop around.

RETIREMENT

There is no more hotly debated or volatile issue in the federal government than that of the Federal Retirement System. Seen as a way to salvage Social Security, many advisors to recent presidential administrations—most of whom were not part of the federal retirement system, since they were presidential appointees hired to serve for no more than four years—have proposed merging the federal system with Social Security, i.e., dumping all the money federal workers have put into their retirement system into the Social Security system. Needless to say, the federal employee unions and labor organizations have fought long and hard to prevent this. So far they have been successful, but even as this book goes to press there are bills before the Congress proposing some restructuring of the federal retirement system so as to merge or include it in the Social Security system (see below).

At present, the retirement law provides optional retirement at age fifty-five with thirty years of service, age sixty with twenty years of service, or age sixty-two with five years of service. Of course, disability retirement is allowed at any age with five years of service and proper documentation of the employee's inability to perform his or her job. There is no longer mandatory retirement at any age except in certain special groups where physical ability is essential to the performance and safety of the job. These groups include law enforcement personnel, firefighters, air traffic controllers, etc.

As with everything else in the government, the formula for retirement boggles the mind. The average annuity is currently based upon the highest three years' salary received during federal employment. The annuity formula allows 1.5 percent of the average salary for the first five years of service, 1.75 percent for the next five years of service, and two percent per year for any remaining service up to a maximum of eighty percent of the average salary.

Example: A woman retires after thirty years of service. Her high three-year average salary comes to $15,000.	
1.50% x $15,000 x 5 years of service	$1,125.00
1.75% x $15,000 x 5 years of service	1,312.50
2% x $15,000 x remaining 20 years of service	6,000.00
Highest Annual Basic Annuity	**$8,437.50**

The woman's basic annuity would be $8,437.50 per year. Of course, this would be adjusted regularly by the Cost of Living Adjustment (COLA) passed each year by the Congress in order to assist people to keep up with the inflation rate. This means that this retired civil servant would begin her retirement with the above amount, and it would gradually increase as the COLA was added to it each year. The COLA is almost based upon the Consumer Price Index (CPI) for the previous calendar year. This COLA is guaranteed. However, certain presidential administrations, when trying to cut the federal budget, may try to cancel or postpone the COLA for retired federal employees in an attempt to save money. Naturally, this sort of move must be approved by the Congress.

Seven percent of an employee's salary is deducted each pay period for retirement. Much more detailed information is available from the Office of Personnel Management, but there is no real reason to look into it until you are part of the federal system—unless you are the type of person who enjoys complex puzzles.

SOCIAL SECURITY

In its move toward merging the federal retirement system with Social Security, the Congress has decreed that all federal employees newly hired after December 31, 1983 will be covered by Social Security and currently will pay 7.05 percent of their salaries in Social Security taxes (FICA). This law also applies to employees with previous federal service (excluding rehired annuitants) if their break in service was a year or more. Certain current federal employees are covered under Social Security after December, 1983. These include:

- most political appointees
- currently sitting federal judges
- Legislative Branch employees who are not covered by the Civil Service retirement system as of December 31, 1983
- All members of Congress, the President and the Vice-President

So, as it stands at the time of the publication of this book, if you were not a federal employee as of December 31, 1983, and you join the government now, you will be covered under the Social Security system, and *not* the federal retirement system. However, these things can always change, especially if there is a concerted lobbying effort to keep alive the federal retirement system. The best way to keep abreast of developments in this area is to watch your local newspapers and network television news.

MEDICARE

As a result of the Tax Equity and Fiscal Responsibility Act of 1982, Medicare was extended to federal employees. Federal employment now counts toward eligibility for Medicare hospital insurance protection and the hospital insurance portion of the Social Security (FICA) tax is deducted from workers' pay. The dollar amount of the biweekly deduction depends upon the amount of the employee's gross biweekly earnings.

Like Social Security eligibility, a specific dollar amount of earnings equals one quarter of coverage. The amount of earnings required for a quarter of coverage will increase automatically each year to keep up with increases in average wage levels nationally.

Like every other worker, the federal employee qualifies for Medicare hospital insurance at age sixty-five if he or she has earned enough quarters of coverage. You can qualify for hospital insurance before age sixty-five only if you become disabled and meet the eligibility requirements of the Social Security disability insurance program. This means you must meet the Social Security definition of disability, have enough quarters of coverage, and be disabled for twenty-nine months or more. You are considered disabled if a severe physical or mental impairment prevents you from working for at least twelve months. The exact number of quarters of coverage needed depends upon your age at the onset of the disability.

Hospital insurance is available at any age for someone needing a kidney dialysis or a kidney transplant for permanent kidney failure, but only if enough quarters of coverage have been earned. Medicare hospital insurance covers in-patient hospital care, in-patient care in a skilled nursing facility, and home health care. For detailed information about services offered and not offered by Medicare, the Social Security Administration publishes a free brochure, "A Brief Explanation of Medicare."

Plans under the Federal Employees Health Benefits Program offer protection against the same expenses as Medicare in what is called a "double coverage" provision. The plan will provide benefits payable under Medicare up to, but not exceeding, one hundred percent of allowable expenses. Even though an employee may receive Medicare benefits, the premium for the FEHB insurance plan he or she subscribes to remains the same. These premiums are calculated with the "double coverage" provision in mind and are therefore lower than they would be without the Medicare plan in effect.

ANNUAL LEAVE

Annual Leave is time off for personal reasons, such as vacation. How much Annual Leave you earn depends upon the number of years you have worked for Uncle Sam. Full-time federal workers with less than three years of federal service earn four hours of Annual Leave per pay period (every two weeks). With three to fifteen years of federal service, workers earn six hours per pay period, and those with more than fifteen years of service earn eight hours. Part-time workers' Annual Leave is calculated in proportion to the number of hours per week they work.

The use of Annual Leave can be a touchy subject. Technically, you have a right to use the Annual Leave you earn and to use it when you want to; however, all Annual Leave must be approved by your supervisor. The supervisor can deny a request for Annual Leave for reasons having to do with the agency's workload, staff shortages, and other such work-related situations. As in all work

situations, there are those who abuse their leave, taking it as fast as they earn it, or having weekly "emergency" situations and therefore needing to take Annual Leave on the same day they request it. Generally, Annual Leave is requested in advance, allowing the work unit supervisor to plan for the absence of a staff member; however, emergency Annual Leave can be granted. Because a serious illness might cause you to use up all of your Sick Leave, it's a good idea to have some Annual Leave you can draw from. While advance Sick Leave can be requested—borrowing on your future Sick Leave—it doesn't have to be granted, and there are limits to the amount of advance Sick Leave that can be given.

Annual leave "carries over" from one year to the next up to a maximum of 240 hours or thirty days. Any leave you have over and above 240 hours is forfeited. In government circles, the excess is referred to as "use or lose," and many people with large amounts of Annual Leave take their "use or lose" hours around Thanksgiving and Christmas.

If you leave your job with the federal government, you will be paid in one lump sum for any Annual Leave you have accumulated—another good reason to save those leave hours.

SICK LEAVE

Sick Leave is earned in much the same way as Annual Leave, except in smaller increments. No matter how long you have been with the federal government, you earn four hours of Sick Leave per bi-weekly pay period, or twelve days per year. Part-time employees earn one hour of Sick Leave for every twenty hours they work.

Sick leave is officially used when:

1. You are ill, injured, pregnant, or confined for medical reasons.
2. You have a contagious disease and your presence at work would endanger the health of others.
3. A member of your immediate family

has a contagious disease and needs your care.

4. You must undergo medical, optical, or dental examination or treatment.

Unlike Annual Leave, Sick Leave may be accumulated indefinitely. One employee who recently retired from the Library of Congress had over 2,000 hours of Sick Leave accumulated. This served him well, since accumulated Sick Leave (in whole month increments) is added to your length of service upon retirement from the federal system, resulting in a larger retirement annuity.

Another difference between Annual Leave and Sick Leave is that when you leave the federal government, you are not paid for accumulated Sick Leave; however, the Sick Leave not used is recredited if you are reemployed with Uncle Sam within three years of leaving a federal job.

COURT LEAVE

If you are called for jury duty or to testify as a witness in a case to which the federal government is a party, you will be paid during the court proceedings, and there is no charge to your leave. However, if you are summoned to testify in a civil suit involving private parties, you must take Annual Leave or Leave Without Pay.

A recent ruling allows for federal employees on jury duty to keep the small fee paid to jurors by the court.

MILITARY LEAVE

Full-time employees who are members of the National Guard or a military reserve unit are entitled to fifteen calendar days of military leave per year without charge to their Annual Leave. You are also paid for these days. If they are called in support of law enforcement—e.g., to restore public order or assist in a natural disaster—they will be paid for up to twenty-two days of military leave.

FUNERAL LEAVE

One of the more interesting and controversial types of leave is Funeral Leave. Attendance at funerals is considered a private matter, and your absence from work to attend a funeral is charged to Annual Leave—with two exceptions: 1) An employee may have up to three days of funeral leave in connection with the funeral or memorial services of an immediate family member who died in military service in a combat zone; 2) A veteran may be given up to four hours of funeral leave to serve as pallbearer or on a firing squad or honor guard at the funeral of a member of the armed services or a veteran.

LEAVE WITHOUT PAY

Leave Without Pay (LWOP) can be granted for any period of time up to a full year. Usually, the longer periods of absence must in some way serve the needs of the agency. Short periods of LWOP are granted to accommodate employees' personal needs when they don't have enough Annual or Sick Leave or prefer not to use their accumulated leave for some reason.

MATERNITY/PATERNITY LEAVE

Women may use Annual Leave, Sick Leave, and Leave Without Pay for absences from work related to pregnancy, childbirth, and infant care. Sick leave may be used for physician's exams, delivery, and recuperation. Annual Leave or Leave Without Pay must be used for any time spent caring for a newborn infant. A father may also request Annual Leave or Leave Without Pay during this time. The needs of the family are weighed against the needs of the agency when paternity leave is requested.

MISCELLANEOUS ABSENCES

There are certain other times when a federal employee may be absent from work without being charged leave. These "excused" absences are categorized as "administrative leave" and include local holidays, time for voting and registering to vote, donating blood, travel between government agencies, etc. The absence of a civil servant without prior approval is recorded as "Absence Without Official Leave" (AWOL). The employee receives no pay for absence recorded in this way, and in certain cases an employee who is AWOL may be subject to disciplinary action.

ANNUAL COST OF LIVING ADJUSTMENT (COLA)

Each year the President proposes and the Congress approves a cost of living adjustment for federal salaries. It varies from year to year, supposedly according to the inflation rate nationwide. However, some people argue that it is also subject to political considerations. For example, in a presidential election year, federal workers might find themselves getting a very sizable cost of living increase from an incumbent President running for a second term of office. A President pledged to cut the federal budget might be more inclined to propose a very small increase. In recent years the cost of living adjustment has ranged from three percent to nine percent. As a rule, this cost of living adjustment takes place at the beginning of the federal government's fiscal year, October 1. Recently, however, President Reagan has proposed—and Congress has approved—making the cost of living increases effective on January 1. Whether this practice will continue remains to be seen.

FEDERAL PAY SYSTEMS

There are four types of pay systems within the federal government.

1. The General Schedule

About half of all government workers are under the General Schedule (Appendix P) for white collar employees. These people serve in administrative, technical, or clerical positions. There are eighteen Grades or levels on this schedule and ten "Steps" within each Grade. The rate of pay on the General Schedule may be adjusted each October by the President and the Congress, according to pay rate changes for comparable jobs in the private sector and a variety of other factors.

Usually new employees begin at Step One in the Grade at which they are hired. The Grade level of the job is always determined by the level of responsibility of the job; strict standards, filling volumes, have been written as guidelines for personnel staff regarding the classification of positions. Once in a while someone may be hired at a step other than Step One, but usually these are people who have worked for the government or who come from a high-level job in the private sector and are forced for some reason to take a position with much less responsibility than they are qualified for. Even in these cases, a lengthy justification must be written by the selecting official who is hiring the person and requesting placement at a step higher than Step One. What this means is that you can try to dicker your way into a higher step once you've been told you have the job, but it's not very likely to happen. Also, if you think you are qualified to be placed at a step higher than Step One, you should mention it to the interviewer at the time of your interview and not bring it up after you have been selected. Asking for more money is not the best way to begin your new government job.

Within-Grade Pay Increases on the General Schedule

Pay increases occur on a regularly scheduled basis according to the type of pay schedule you are on and how long you have been employed at your present level. There is a defined minimum waiting period between Steps on the General Schedule. For employees on Steps 2, 3, and 4, the waiting period is fifty-two weeks; for Steps 5, 6, and 7, it is 104 weeks; and for Steps 8, 9, and 10, it is 156 weeks. At the end of these waiting periods, if the employee is evaluated by his or her supervisor as having worked at an acceptable level during the period, the Within-Grade Increase is approved and the employee's salary increases by the amount designated for that fiscal year. A General Schedule Pay Scale for Fiscal Year 1989 appears in Appendix C.

2. Wage Grade

The majority of federal employees not under the General Schedule are paid under a system commonly referred to as the "Wage Grade" schedule (Appendix Q). These skilled workers are paid under the Prevailing Rate System. Rates of pay for these positions vary in different geographic locations around the country. The salaries for these jobs are determined by the "prevailing rate" for the type of work being done in the area where the job is being performed. A periodic survey is conducted by the federal government to determine what rates are actually being paid around the country by typical employers in each region. A typical Wage Grade salary chart for Fiscal Year 1989 appears in Appendix D.

3. Merit Pay System

Employees of the federal government who are supervisors and/or management officials on the General Schedule at the GS-13, 14, or 15 level are compensated under the Merit Pay System (GM). The salary ranges for the GM are exactly the same as for the GS and, like the GS, are uniform across the nation; however, unlike the worker on the General Schedule, merit pay employees do not advance through their Grades in steps based on longevity and acceptable performance. Their salary increases are directly related to their performance appraisals *only*. Merit employees earn pay increases annually according to their performance appraisals. The appraisals determine by what percentage their salaries will be increased. If performance is rated high enough, the increase can far exceed the value of a single step on the General Schedule.

4. Senior Executive Service

Employees in the Senior Executive Service (SES) are compensated under a system established by the Civil Service Reform Act of 1978. This system (ES) is composed of six levels, the lowest level corresponding to the first step of a GS-16. Rates of pay are determined by individual qualifications, performance, and position requirements.

Regardless of the system under which a citizen's desired position falls, he or she must complete and submit to the agency a Standard Form 171.

THE WORK DAY

In keeping with bureaucratic tradition, there is no simple explanation of the federal workday, because there are several types; by the time you are reading this, there will probably be even further variations. Nevertheless, the basic work schedules are the following three:

Straight Time

Most federal workers work a straight eight hour day, five days per week, Monday through Friday, for a total workweek of forty hours. The hours may vary slightly from position to position (8:30 A.M. to 5:30 P.M.; 9:00 A.M. to 6:00 P.M.). Certain positions require evening and weekend shifts, but most do not.

Flex-Time

Some agencies or organizations within agencies have nontraditional work schedules in which an employee may work a flexible schedule. The most common one allows an employee to arrive at work any time between 6:00 A.M. and 9:30 A.M. and to leave eight hours after arriving, but no earlier than 3:00 P.M. and no later than 6:00 P.M. So, for example, if you arrived at work on Monday at 7:15 A.M., you would leave work at 3:45 P.M. If you then came in on Tuesday at 8:10 A.M., you could leave for home at 4:40 P.M. As a rule, most department supervisors prefer that employees come in at a regular time; i.e., if you choose to come in to work at 7:00 A.M., you do so on a regular basis. This allows for planning and scheduling staff presence in the office, so that there will be someone available at all times to answer phones and respond to inquiries. If everyone on the staff wants to arrive at the same time and it results in the office being empty during certain hours, the supervisor may assign certain staff members regular hours, or the supervisor may request from agency administrative managers that certain positions be exempted from Flex-Time schedules in order to assure that the office is staffed at early morning and late afternoon hours.

Comp-Flex Time

Still another flexible schedule that some agencies allow is Comp-Flex. Under this flexible schedule an employee may choose to work a longer day in order to have one day off per pay period. For example, workers would be allowed to choose the first Friday or Monday of each pay period as their "comp day" or day of "compensatory time." They would work a nine-hour day for eight of the ten days in the pay period, one eight-hour day, and have one day off, so that their total hours in a two-week period would still be eighty hours; but every two weeks they would have one Friday or Monday off in addition to the regular weekend. No matter what work schedule an employee chooses, the hours for every two-week pay period must total eighty.

OVERTIME

Federal employees may be required to work overtime on occasion. If this is necessary, overtime is paid, usually at the rate of "time and a half," or the worker may be given equal time off at another time (compensatory time).

HOLIDAYS

The following holidays are observed in the federal government, and federal employees are given these days off with pay:
New Year's Day, January 1
Martin Luther King's Birthday, the third
   Monday in January

Washington's Birthday, the third Monday in February
Memorial Day, the last Monday in May
Independence Day, July 4
Labor Day, the first Monday in September
Columbus Day, the second Monday in October
Veterans Day, November 11
Thanksgiving Day, the last Thursday in November
Christmas Day, December 25

Federal workers in Washington, D.C. are also given the day off on Presidential Inauguration Day every four years.

If a holiday falls on a Saturday and you do not regularly work on Saturday, you will be given the preceding Friday off. If the holiday falls on Sunday and you do not regularly work on Sunday, you will be given the following Monday off. For federal workers who do not work a regular Monday through Friday workweek, if a scheduled holiday falls on a non-workday, the workday before the scheduled holiday is the day off.

THE SIGN-IN SHEET

Each office has a Sign-in Sheet. All employees are required to sign in and enter on the sheet the time they arrive for work. At the end of the day they must sign out, entering the time departing work. If any Annual Leave, Sick Leave, or administrative leave was taken, an employee must also enter the hours during which it was taken and the total number of leave hours it amounted to, along with the kind of leave taken (Appendix E).

AWARDS

Federal employees may earn various types of awards in the federal service. These awards are usually given for suggestions that save the government money or improve the quality of service a federal agency provides or for outstanding performance.

Quality Increases

When an employee's work is considered by a supervisor to be outstanding, the supervisor may nominate the employee for a Quality Increase. The Quality Increase advances the employee's standing on the General Schedule by one Step within the employee's current Grade. A Quality Increase may be given at any time, but it is most frequently awarded at the time of the annual performance appraisal. When this is the case and the employee is scheduled for a Within-Grade Step Increase anyway, the effect is that of receiving a double raise. So, for example, a worker at Grade 9, Step 2, who receives a Quality Increase at the time of his annual performance appraisal will jump from Step 2 to Step 4. Quality Increases are especially helpful when they are given to an employee who is in Steps 4 through 9 of his Grade, since his waiting period before a Within-Grade Step Increase can be awarded is either 104 or 156 weeks.

Incentive Awards

Every agency of the federal government participates in an Incentive Awards Program. Employees can earn cash or honorary awards for suggestions or special achievements that result in more economical or better service within the agency. The amount of the cash award is determined by a complex formula that takes into account the amount of the savings to the federal government or the degree and range of improvement of government services as a result of the employee's contribution. These awards range from $50 to $10,000.

THE WORK ENVIRONMENT

Federal offices come in all sizes, shapes, colors, and conditions. I have been in plush offices in the Government Printing Office and the Office of the Comptroller of the Currency, and I have worked in a warehouse converted to offices where rat poison had to be placed all along the walls of the building. Uncle Sam, usually through the General Services Administration (GSA), leases office space in what are determined to be the most economical and efficient buildings available.

If you apply for a federal job and get an interview, chances are—unless you are interviewed by phone for a job in a geographical location other than where you are currently living—you will be interviewed in the office where you will work. This will allow you to view the environment, including the neighborhood where the building is located, and to decide if you would be comfortable and efficient working there.

While working in one of the Library of Congress' annexes, I actually had interviewees turn down jobs once they saw the neighborhood, realized they weren't going to be working at the main building on Capitol Hill, or saw that no one had private offices. More times than not in the federal service, offices are simply cubicles separated by partial walls, since this serves the purpose of separating work areas without tremendous expense to the taxpayer.

Another environmental factor you should take into consideration when applying for a government job is equipment. When you go for your interview, take a look around at the kind, quality, and vintage of the equipment being used in the work environment, whether it's in the maintenance department or in an office. Very often, depending upon the agency's internal politics and the budget for "nonrecurring items," equipment may be old or poorly maintained. So long as it is in working condition and safe—which nearly all government equipment is—you shouldn't have any problem.

Remember, every job has its assets and its liabilities, and, as a rule, the assets of a federal job far outweigh the liabilities.

5
Where to Look for Federal Jobs

The first step in obtaining a job with Uncle Sam is to find out what jobs are available with the United States Government. Appendixes P and Q list every job offered by the federal government on both the General Schedule (Administrative and Professional Positions) and the Wage Grade System (Trade and Skilled Labor). Consult these to find the job that most closely matches your aptitudes and/ or experience.

NEWSPAPER ADS

No matter who you are or what kind of job you want, the hardest part of getting a job seems to be finding one. If you talk to "head hunters"—those agencies that make their living by finding people jobs—you will be told that no good job is ever advertised in the newspaper. That has not been my experience. I have known many excellent jobs to be advertised in newspapers, but very often the high-paying professional jobs are not listed in the classified section of the paper; they are placed in the business section of the Sunday edition.

The consulting firm I worked for after leaving the White House always used *The Washington Post* to advertise vacant positions, even top management jobs. Whenever new staff members were needed, the company would place an ad in the newspaper. The federal government also uses that avenue of reaching potential employees. However, not all jobs available with Uncle Sam are advertised in newspapers *or anywhere else in the public domain.* My estimate is that less than one percent of available jobs with the civil service ever get advertised in a publication that the general public reads.

Once in a while, when an agency is hiring a large number of people for a special short-term project or when a very specialized high-level position is vacant, the agency personnel office will place an ad in a local newspaper. But the red tape that has to be chopped through to place an ad and pay for it usually discourages that approach.

When I announced I was leaving my position as Assistant Head of Publications and Media of the National Library Service for the Blind and Physically Handicapped at the Library of Congress, it was decided to advertise the position, because it was a specialized job within the Library. That is to say, if the position were only posted on the Library bulletin boards, there would most likely not have been enough qualified applicants to choose from, since most Library employees are librarians or have a library science background.

It was also decided, however, that there was no need to conduct a national search for applicants, since there are plenty of people in the Washington, D.C. area with publications and public relations credentials. So an ad was placed in the classified section of *The Washington Post* on two consecutive Sundays. The result was that the Library ended up with over one hundred qualified applicants. That means that one hundred were found qualified after extensive screening. Many more than that had sent in applications.

The point here is that the newspaper is a fine place to look for federal jobs, but you will most likely be competing with many applicants for less than one percent of the jobs that are actually available. Your chances might be improved if you look elsewhere—somewhere the general public is not so apt to look.

SPECIALIZED PUBLICATIONS

One place to look is in specialized periodicals—publications that are read only by members of certain professional or skilled trade groups. For example, a person looking for a job as a librarian or library technician might search through periodicals such as *Library Journal*. Someone in search of a position in public relations or public education would do well to check the *Journal of the American Association of Public Relations Professionals*. Naturally, the easiest and least expensive way to do this is to go to your public library, where there is a large collection of current periodicals available to be read at no cost. If your public library doesn't subscribe to such specialized publications, check with the library of a nearby college or university, another excellent resource for information.

Looking through periodicals, whether esoteric journals published for small groups of professionals or the widely read *New York Times*, is a tedious and time-consuming method of tracking down government jobs. Wouldn't it be more efficient to go directly to the source? "Yes," you answer, "but I live two thousand miles from Washington, D.C." Take heart, would-be civil servant. There is an easier, closer solution to the problem. In fact, there are two solutions.

FEDERAL JOB INFORMATION CENTERS

The federal government divides its geographic responsibilities into ten Regions. A breakdown of the fifty states and U.S. territories by these Regions appears in Appendix F. The Office of Personnel Management operates Federal Job Information Centers (FJIC) throughout the country. There is an FJIC located in at least one major city in every region. This office is there for one reason only: to provide information and application forms to citizens seeking employment with the federal government. In addition, some of them provide information regarding vacant positions with city, county, and state governments in their areas. If their budgets allow, they also send out information regarding federal jobs to college and university placement offices so that college graduates looking for jobs after graduation or students seeking summer employment will have that information available.

The Federal Job Information Center is—understandably—one of the busiest of all federal government offices. As a result, it is often very difficult to get through to them on the telephone. And with federal budget cuts and reduced staffing, even visiting the center can result in waiting in long lines for information or application forms.

But as I mentioned in the beginning of this book, the FJIC and OPM are not the best places to look for a job anyway. *It is always best to begin with the individual agency when looking for a federal job.* Nevertheless, there may be a time when you will need to contact the FJIC, if only to obtain an application form. Therefore, a list of Federal Job Information Centers with addresses and telephone numbers appears in Appendix G.

STATE EMPLOYMENT SECURITY OFFICES

Another surprising place to obtain listings of vacant positions with Uncle Sam is your local State Employment Security Office—commonly referred to as the "unemployment office." Most taxpayers don't realize that this office is one of the most useful resources available for finding a job—even a government job. And if the office is run efficiently, like the one in San Francisco, for example, it can prove to be much more helpful than even going to an employment agency, and much less expensive.

All government agencies, including state, county, and city agencies, are required by law to list their available jobs with employment security offices. After all, the government doesn't want high unemployment any more than anyone else. In fact, it is in its own best interest to keep unemployment as low as possible, and so it makes every effort to help people find jobs. One way government does this is by making sure that every employment security office has a copy of all the jobs available within the federal government. So it turns out to be a very good place to look for a government job.

Another fact about these offices that most people don't know is that they are excellent resources for mid-level and top management positions with some companies. The general public has come to think of unemployment offices as places where people go to pick up their unemployment checks, or places where you might go to find a job as a dishwasher, a waitress, or a file clerk. Don't be fooled. The state employment security office not only has those support staff kinds of jobs—and who hasn't waited tables at one point or another and was glad to have the work?—but it also has listings of high-level jobs with certain major companies.

Once, during a job-seeking period in San Francisco, I was sent by the employment security office to an interview with a large California corporation. The job was a senior-level publications position, and when the woman interviewed me for the job she finally interrupted herself and said, "It says here you were referred by the unemployment office. That's a mistake, isn't it?" I told her it was not a mistake. She then remarked that she had never had an applicant for a middle management position referred by that office and wanted to know why on earth I ever went to them to look for a job. I replied, "I'm a taxpayer. That's my employment agency."

The point is, you are a taxpayer and your state Employment Security Office is your employment agency—your *free* employment agency. Use it!

To assist you in your search for a government job, Appendix H lists the major State Employment Security Offices throughout the United States. If you have questions regarding the location of other offices or questions concerning employment with your state government, Appendix I lists the telephone information numbers for each state government.

FEDERAL AGENCY REGIONAL OFFICES

Probably the most efficient and reliable place to look for a federal job is the individual agency offices, for this is where official Vacancy Announcements are posted (Chapter 6) and where the actual hiring takes place. But most people don't even know they exist, let alone where they are located. If you ask an average citizen how to get a job with, for example, the National Labor Relations Board (NLRB), he would probably tell you to contact Washington, D.C.; yet there are thirty-three regional Director's Offices for that agency that can give you direct and immediate information on what jobs are currently available with the National Labor Relations Board, where the jobs are located, and how to apply for them. These NLRB offices exist all over the country, from Tampa, Florida to Peoria, Illinois.

Every federal agency—at least every major agency—has no less than ten regional offices, one in each of the ten federal regions. And these offices hold the postings of every available position in their region for their agency, and sometimes for other agencies as well. A complete list of all federal agency regional offices, including addresses and telephone numbers, appears in Appendix J.

Suppose you have experience, a college degree, or both, in forestry and live in Nederland, Colorado. To find out what jobs are currently available with the National Park Service of the Interior Department in Colorado you would contact the Rocky Mountain Region Office of the National Park Service by writing or visiting them at 655 Parfet Street in Denver or calling them at (303) 234-2500. You might also want to check with the Interior Department's Bureau of Land Management office. In Colorado, that would be at 1037 20th Street in Denver, (303) 837-4325.

Use Appendix J to find these and all other regional offices for each federal agency.

FEDERAL CAREER OPPORTUNITIES

The Federal Research Service, a private company in Virginia, publishes a biweekly magazine that lists virtually every job currently available with the federal government. *Federal Career Opportunities* is available at most public libraries, is usually posted in most federal personnel offices, and can be subscribed to by writing to Federal Research Service Inc., P.O. Box 1059, Vienna VA 22180.

6

The Federal Vacancy Announcement

Of all the possible ways to find out about jobs with the federal government, reading the Vacancy Announcements is by far the best, for the Vacancy Announcement—or Job Posting, as it is sometimes called—will contain the details of the position. As a rule, even when a position is advertised in a newspaper, magazine, or other periodical, applicants will be advised to contact the government agency and request a copy of the Vacancy Announcement for that particular job. Should you come across an advertisement for a job that does not suggest you get hold of a Vacancy Announcement, you should call or write the agency if there is time before the deadline, or Closing Date, and ask them to send you one. This is the *only* source of all the valuable information you will need in order to complete your SF-171.

Each Vacancy Announcement will—or should—contain the following information. (Refer to the Key Announcement in Appendix K.)

1. Identifying Number. This is also frequently referred to as the Announcement Number. It is the number by which this job posting is recorded within the agency. There may be, for example, many jobs currently open for the position of Administrative Assistant, but they may be in several different departments. This number identifies the exact Administrative Assistant job for which you are applying.

2. Announcement Date. This is also referred to as the Issue Date or Opening Date. It is the date the Vacancy Announcement was posted and the job officially became open for the submitting of applications.

3. Closing Date. This is the date by which the agency must receive your application form (SF-171). You should note that the regulations vary from agency to agency. Some offices require that your application be received in their offices by the close of business on the day the announcement closes. Others only require that the application be postmarked by that date. Sometimes you may send a letter, Mailgram, or telegram notifying the agency that you have just been made aware of the position vacancy and that a Standard Form 171 will follow shortly. If you have any doubts that your application will arrive in time, you should contact the hiring office and ask if you must have it in their hands by the closing date or whether having it postmarked by that date will suffice.

4. Position Title, Schedule, Grade, Salary, Job Series, Job Number and Appointment Tenure. Here you will find the official title of the position for which you are applying. Also here is the federal schedule on which you will be placed—e.g., General Schedule, Wage-Grade, etc.—the Grade at which the position is classified, the salary you will be paid to start, and the highest salary you can earn at that Grade level. Other information includes the Job Series this position is classified under according to the Office of Personnel Management, the Job Number this position has been assigned by the agency, and the length of the appointment under this Vacancy Announcement—i.e., whether this is a full-time permanent position, part-time, temporary, etc. This is also where you will learn if this position is part of a career ladder promotion plan. That is, will it lead to better jobs with higher pay, or is it what is considered a "dead-end" job? You can tell this in two ways. Either there will be a statement somewhere on the announcement clearly saying this is part of a promotional ladder plan, or the position will list more than one Grade. For example, instead of listing the job as a GS-09, it will list it as a GS-09/11/13. That tells you that you will begin the job at Grade 09, but that it is planned and budgeted for the person

holding the position to advance to the GS-13 level. How long that takes is usually determined by how well you perform in the job.

5. Organization and Geographic Location of the Position. This tells you which organization or department within the agency you will be working for and where the job is located.

6. Number of Positions Vacant. Some agencies will tell you how many jobs of this nature are being filled at this time. There may be more than one. Sometimes, for example, a department will have an increase in their staffing budget because they have been overworked for a long time, and they may be hiring six new Clerk-Typists. This will tell you if you are competing for one job or for several. The more jobs vacant, the better your chances of getting hired.

7. Area of Consideration. Agencies within the Executive Branch of government will usually state who is eligible to apply for the job. During times of fiscal constraint and federal job freezes no one without civil service competitive status is allowed to apply for jobs in the Competitive Service.

8. Description of Duties. This is a summary of the official description of duties expected and required to be performed by the person holding this position. It tells you specifically what the job entails and the kinds of tasks that you will be expected to perform. It is a key element of the Vacancy Announcement and must be fully understood in order to successfully complete the SF-171. Read it carefully, as you will want to relate the duties of the position for which you are applying to the kinds of things you have done in jobs held in the past.

9. Qualifications. These are the minimum qualifications used to determine an applicant's basic eligibility for a posted position. They are analyzed on an either/or basis. Either you are minimally qualified for the job or you're not. If you meet the minimum qualifications, you are then evaluated according to "Quality Ranking Factors." If you do not meet them, you are eliminated from further competition and notified by letter that you did not make the "List of Qualified Applicants."

10. Educational Requirements. The minimum amount and type of education required to hold this position are stated along with substitutions for the required education. Most of the time within the federal service one can substitute job experience for certain educational requirements. Also, one can very often substitute education for a number of years of job experience. It is not uncommon, for example, for an agency to waive all required job experience in lower level positions if the applicant holds an advanced degree.

11. Quality Ranking Factors. These are the specific knowledges, skills, and abilities upon which your application will be evaluated. These are probably the most important elements within the Vacancy Announcement, for these are the specific items upon which the "score sheet" that will be used to evaluate your application is based. (See Chapters 7 and 8.)

12. Clearances and Tests Required. If security clearances are required, as they are for sensitive positions, this will be stated. If any specialized tests are required, such as typing, clerical, or language tests, that will also be noted on the Vacancy Announcement.

Keep in mind that each agency must list all the above information on its Vacancy Announcements, but each agency has its own format. In Appendix L you will find several examples of actual federal Vacancy Announcements. Study them and see if you can find all the information you would need in order to apply for the job.

HOW TO GET YOUR QUESTIONS ANSWERED

If you come across a position you are interested in applying for, but you have questions about it, you should contact the Personnel Staffing Specialist whose name appears on the posting. This is the person in the agency's personnel office who has been assigned the administrative work for this particular job. He or she will be able to answer all your questions. *It is very important to remember that it is improper to directly contact the departmental office where the job is located, and it is illegal for the selecting official or anyone in a direct supervisory role to discuss a vacant position with an applicant.* Calling the office directly will not help you obtain any additional information, and it may even harm your chances by alienating the selecting official.

If you have questions or concerns regarding your application after you have submitted it, call the Staffing Specialist. This is the only person who will see your application prior to the time it is evaluated for Quality Ranking Factors. It is the Staffing Specialist who screens applications for minimum qualifications, so until such time as your application is forwarded to a Rating Panel or Selecting Official he or she is the only person who can answer your questions anyway.

A NOTE ON TESTS

For certain jobs a test is required. It is not at all like the now-extinct PACE exam, which tested various technical areas. It is more likely to be a typing or clerical test. For an editor/writer position, the hiring agency usually wants an employee who will be able to produce typewritten copy, not handwritten copy that has to be given to a Clerk-Typist to type. That would be a waste of time, effort, and taxpayers' money. In such cases there will be a notice on the Vacancy Announcement that reads something like this:

> **Passing the agency typing test with a minimum net speed of 25 words per minute is mandatory. Agency employees who are not currently in a position requiring typing at 25 words per minute and all other applicants who have not been certified for the required typing speed within the past year must pass the agency typing test or another certified typing test, viz. one administered by another government agency.**

You will have to make arrangements to take the required test. To do this, call the Staffing Specialist listed on the Vacancy Announcement and ask how to go about taking the test. He/she will tell you when and where the test is given, how long it takes, and what procedures you should follow for taking the test(s).

7
The Standard Form 171

The federal job application form is called the SF-171, and in government circles it's called nothing else. You will never hear someone tell you to send in your application. They will always say, "Send us your 171."

The 171 (Appendix L) is a four-page form that asks you to describe who you are, what you have done, and what you want to do. It looks innocuous enough at first glance. Even at second and third glance. It doesn't reveal itself as a true menace until after your fifteenth rejection.

The key that ultimately unlocks the door to getting a job with the federal government is the 171. Don't let anyone tell you anything different. I have seen excellent job candidates not get interviews simply because they filled out their 171 incorrectly. Perhaps it wouldn't be considered incorrect to the world at large, nor to a potential employer in the private sector. But the system works by Uncle Sam's standards and no one else's.

The more qualified you are for a position, the easier it is to get the job, or at least to get interviewed for the job—providing you have properly filled out the Standard Form 171. The 171 asks you to list all the information you would normally put on a resume, but the federal government likes to organize things in its own way. As a result, it will not accept a resume in place of an application for a federal job. You may submit a resume along with your 171 if you like, but you must always submit the 171. It is wise to remember that you can alienate someone by giving him or her too much to read, especially if it's redundant. So generally speaking, the 171 by itself is enough.

One other thing you need to know is that it is always better to submit a separate 171 for each job you apply for, in spite of the fact that you may find six jobs in two weeks that you are interested in. Unless those jobs are in the same job series with very similar job requirements, you need to tailor your 171 to the specific duties listed on the Vacancy Announcement for each job. One of the cardinal rules to remember when applying for a federal job is this: You are writing your 171 according to the Vacancy Announcement as well as according to your qualifications. The trick is to match your qualifications to the Vacancy Announcement language as closely as possible.

Before we look at how to fill out a 171 we need to discuss two very important items and the relationship between them.

QUALITY RANKING FACTORS AND THE FOUR VITAL AREAS

In Chapter 6, "The Federal Vacancy Announcement," we discussed Quality Ranking Factors and learned that they are the knowledges, skills, and abilities considered essential in performing a given job. When a Vacancy Announcement is written, the selecting officer will include the knowledges, skills, and abilities considered essential for the job he or she is trying to fill in the form of Quality Ranking Factors. This means that applicants will be scored according to whether or not they can convince the rating panel that they indeed possess the knowledges, skills, and abilities listed on the Vacancy Announcement.

This is easy enough to understand and can usually be figured out by reading a Vacancy Announcement, which will list the Quality Ranking Factors and ask you to address them in some way on your 171. What is not known by most applicants—including those who are already working for the federal government—is that each Quality Ranking Factor is scored *four times in four separate categories.* I call these categories **the Four Vital Areas.**

These Four Vital Areas are:

**EXPERIENCE
EDUCATION
SELF-DEVELOPMENT
AWARDS AND COMMENDATIONS**

This means that when you are filling out your 171 you must keep in mind not only the

Quality Ranking Factors but also the Four Vital Areas in which you are going to be rated on those factors.

So, for example, if you choose to apply for a secretarial position, and one of the Quality Ranking Factors reads "Knowledge of Office Filing Systems," you must remember to put down all your **experience** with office filing systems (Block 24), any **education or training** you have had dealing with office filing systems (Blocks 29, 30, and 31), anything you have ever done on your own (**self- development**) to increase your knowledge of office filing systems (Blocks 31 and 32), and any **award, commendation, bonus, citation**, etc. you may have received either in school or from an employer for work you did with an office filing system (Block 36).

Memberships in organizations, clubs, etc. are generally considered to be self-developmental kinds of activities (Block 32). Courses taken on your own, even if they are just one- or two-day seminars, are also considered to be self-developmental activities (Block 31).

The "ability to meet and deal effectively with others" is a Quality Ranking Factor frequently found on federal Vacancy Announcements, since it is important to be able to work well with a variety of people in a large bureaucracy. If you find this Quality Ranking Factor on your Vacancy Announcement, remember to include on your 171 all your **experience** in meeting and dealing with various people in any and all of your former jobs.

If it is appropriate, emphasize the fact that you had to work with people at all levels of the organization, from secretaries to the chief executive officer. In other words, show that you can deal with workers at all levels within the organization. Also include the kinds of people you worked with outside the organization, such as sales reps, politicians, travel agents, filmmakers, etc.

List every bit of **education and training** you have had in dealing with people. Include courses in psychology, transactional analysis, supervision, stress management, etc., whether they were taken for credit at a university or junior college, in an adult education program, or even if they were given in-house by one of your former employers.

Don't overlook any **award** you may have received for your ability to get along with others. You may have been voted most likely to succeed in your senior class, or perhaps you were elected student body president or class treasurer. They all show an ability to rally people around you. Put them down on the 171.

If you belong to clubs, organizations, or church or temple groups, say so. This shows you have the initiative and desire to go out on your own and do things with others. It indicates that you like to be involved with people. That means you are more likely to meet and deal effectively with others.

Get the idea? For every Quality Ranking Factor, your job is to show how you excel in that factor in each of four different ways: **experience, education, self development,** *and* awards and commendations. I am saying it over and over because it is the most important message in this book. It means the difference between getting enough points on your application to earn you an interview or not making it into the group of best qualified applicants.

I have seen highly qualified—even the best qualified—people not make it into the top five applicants simply because they didn't know how to put down information the way the government wants to see it.

THE STANDARD FORM 171

Let's take a look at how to fill out the 171 so you get the most mileage out of what you have done in your life—that's right, your whole life, not just the jobs you've held. This section will show you how to score the most points when your application is evaluated. A blank Standard Form 171, which is referred to here appears in Appendix M.

Block 1: Job You Are Applying For

Enter the job title as it appears on the Vacancy Announcement. Also, remember to enter the announcement number to make sure you are not considered for another job with the same title, in case the agency has posted more than one opening.

Block 2: Multiple Listings

Sometimes more than one position will be listed on the same announcement. If that is the case, you need to list the specific job you are applying for. However, when more than one job is listed on an announcement they are always very similar; therefore, it is a good idea to enter the word "open." Very often a personnel staffing specialist will—based upon your qualifications—submit your 171 for consideration for another job if you say you are open to virtually any job for which you are qualified.

Block 3: Social Security Number

Enter your Social Security number.

Block 4: Birth Date

Enter the date of your birth.

Block 5: Name and Address

Enter your name and current address.

Block 6: Other Names Used

This information is necessary only in cases where women have changed names through marriage or divorce and will be on a former employer's records under a name other than the one used on the 171. If this block does not apply to you, enter "N/A" for "Not Applicable." The government likes *every* block filled out, even if it's with the letters "N/A." This tells them that you didn't overlook or ignore it.

Block 7: Sex

This block is optional, and *supposedly* it won't be held against you if you don't fill it out. However, remember you are dealing with human beings, and most of us are, if nothing else, curious about whether we are dealing with a man or a woman. Also, the truth is that some people do have preferences, in spite of the fact that it's against the law. At this point in the process there's nothing you can do about that. It is better to enter the correct information here and deal with possible personal prejudices at the interview. You might be able to change someone's mind. Not filling it out makes you look like a potential troublemaker.

Block 8: Home Phone

Enter your home phone number (including area code).

Block 9: Work Phone

Enter your work phone (including area code) if you have one, but remember that no matter how discreet callers are, if they leave a name and say who they are with, someone in your office will put two and two together. It may be advisable to enter "see cover letter" and then in your cover letter explain that you would rather not be called at work, or that the caller should leave only a name and number and not mention the purpose of the call or where he or she works.

Block 10: Former Federal Service

If you have ever been employed by the federal government, indicate in the appropriate box what kind of appointment you had—i.e., Temporary, Career-Conditional, Career (full-time permanent), or Excepted. Be sure to include the classification series number and the highest grade at which you worked. Also indicate the time period in which you served at your highest Grade. If you have never been a civil servant, then write "N/A" and proceed to Block 11.

Block 11: Current Application Information

If you have previously submitted a 171 to the Office of Personnel Management, enter the information requested. This current 171, if you are submitting it to OPM and not to the individual agency, will replace the old one. If you are applying to an agency and the agency requests a name certification (Chapter 9) from OPM, this 171 will supersede the one previously submitted.

Block 12: Availability for Work

You need only enter the month and year of your availability for work. You can work out more specifics at the interview or after you receive a formal notice of hiring. If you are available right away, enter the word "Immediately."

Block 13: Lowest Pay or Grade

Be careful here. Make certain that the lowest grade level you will accept is not higher than the grade level of the job you are currently applying for. For example, if you are applying for a position as a Research Program Assistant at a GS-7 grade level (GS-303-7), don't enter GS-9 as the lowest grade level you will accept. If you do, you will be considered ineligible for the job. A listing of grade levels and equivalent salaries on the General Schedule as of October 1985 appears in Appendix C.

Block 14: Location

List the appropriate information as it applies to you regarding where you are willing to work. Make sure this answer correctly corresponds to the location of the job for which you are applying.

Block 15: Availability for Part-time Work

Check the appropriate boxes, indicating whether you are available for full-time work only or if you will consider part-time work, and, if you will accept part-time work, the minimum number of hours you will consider. Again, accepting part-time work will enable you to show the agency your stuff.

Block 16: Availability for Temporary Work

Enter the information requested. Remember, temporary work is one of the surest ways to find out about other jobs within the agency and is certainly the best way to show the agency how good you are. If they like you enough, they'll find you a permanent job.

Block 17: Overnight Travel

If you can't tell from the Vacancy Announcement how much travel is involved, you have to play this one by ear, depending upon how much you want the job and how willing you are to travel. Remember, traveling for the U.S. Government is not like traveling for a private company. You are on a strict per diem and anything you spend over and above that amount comes out of your own pocket. Each city has a government rate that ranges from $50 to about $100 per day. Try to live in Honolulu or New York on $100 a day. I have never traveled for the U.S. Government and *not* lost money in the deal. Think carefully.

Block 18: Military Service

Indicate whether you have served in the U.S. armed forces. If you have not, proceed to Block 22.

Block 19: Military Discharge

If you served in the military, indicate the type of discharge you received. If you received a clemency discharge, explain the circumstances in Block 47.

Block 20: Military Retirement Rank

If you retired from or are planning to retire from the military, indicate whether you did/will retire at or above the rank of major or lieutenant commander.

Block 21: Service Data

List here the dates, branch of the military, and serial number for any active duty service you performed.

Block 22: Veteran Preference

Indicate if you are claiming no veteran preference or, if you are, the kind of preference you are claiming.

Block 23: Present Employer Reference

Indicate whether or not your present employer can be contacted for a reference. If you mark the "No" box and the selecting official needs to talk with your employer, you will be contacted first.

Block 24: Experience

There are differing viewpoints on how much to write in the "description of work" sections under the experience block on page two of the 171 and on the Continuation Sheet for Standard Form 171. My experience as a member of Rating Panels varies. If an applicant has read the Vacancy Announcement carefully and has used the right language, there is usually no need for additional pages. By employing the exact language used on the Vacancy Announcement you assure serious consideration of your 171. Most people make the mistake of thinking that if they respond with the same language used on the announcement, the rating panel or evaluator will dismiss the application, assuming that the applicant simply copied down what was on the posting. WRONG! THE RATING PANEL OR EVALUATOR IS PROHIBITED FROM ASSUMING ANYTHING! If the applicant says he has "planned, researched, coordinated, edited, proofread, and monitored production of publications," then the evaluator has no choice but to accept the applicant's word.

Naturally, some discretion is advised in writing the description of work, but don't stray too far from what is being asked for or you might stray right out of an interview.

Block 25: High School Attendance

Indicate whether you graduated from high school and when. If you didn't graduate, enter the highest grade you completed. If you did not attend high school, write "N/A."

Block 26: Location of Your High School

Enter the name and location of the high school you attended. If you did not attend high school, write "N/A."

Block 27: College or Graduate School Attendance

Indicate whether you have attended college or graduate school. If you haven't, proceed to Block 31.

Block 28: College Information

Enter the appropriate information regarding where you went to college, when you attended, the number of completed credits, the type of degree you earned, and when you received or plan to receive it.

Block 29: Major Subjects Studied

List the subjects you studied in college, beginning with your major field of concentration.

Block 30: Chief Graduate Subjects

Enter the subjects you studied in graduate school, beginning with your field of concentration.

Block 31: Related Courses and Training

Enter all training courses you have taken that relate to your profession and/or to the position for which you are applying. To the best of your ability, recall the name of each course, the geographic location where you attended it, the name of the offering organization or school, and the dates you attended. Also indicate how many hours or days you attended. This is an important area, one that most people skim over and lose points on.

Block 32: Special Skills, Accomplishments, and Awards

Enter any special skills or aptitudes you possess. Most importantly, list all the different kinds of equipment you can operate—e.g., word processors, computers, memory typewriters, even sophisticated photoduplicating equipment, forklifts, soldering irons, etc. This is very important, because an applicant who already knows how to use office equipment or other kinds of machinery—depending upon the job you are applying for—is someone who will not have to spend precious time learning how to operate that equipment.

This is also where you list publications, speaking engagements, and memberships in professional societies.

This block is where you get credit for some things you never thought you'd get credit for. Your activities in social groups and professional societies can play a large part in the evaluators' perception of you as someone who takes your career seriously. This will also show them that you can get along well with others and seek people out.

Block 33: Typing Skill

If you type, enter the number of words per minute. Very often, even for nonclerical jobs, typing can be an influencing factor, as it may mean better workflow within a department, since a secretary or clerk-typist will be receiving typed drafts rather than handwritten ones.

Block 34: Licenses and Certificates

List any licenses or certificates you hold, including medical licenses and certificates, driver's license, or special equipment handling certificates.

Block 35: Language Proficiency

Enter information relating to any languages you have proficiency with. Remember not to exaggerate. Most departments filling positions that require language skills conduct part of their interviews in the language(s) in question. Some jobs will require a written test in the language(s). Tell it like it is.

Block 36: Honors, Awards, and Fellowships

Think hard. Did you ever receive any awards, nominations for awards, bonuses, letters of commendation, scholarships, fellowships, invitations to address (or even attend) conferences, outstanding performance evaluations? They are all worth points if they relate to your profession. Something as seemingly meaningless as "Telephone Voice of the Year" while working as a receptionist could earn points in the Vital Area of Awards and Commendations if "Ability To Meet and Deal Effectively with Others" happens to be one of the Quality Ranking Factors on your Vacancy Announcement.

Block 37: References

List here references who are not related to you and who know the quality of your work. These should obviously be people who will give you a good recommendation on a professional level. These are *not* character references. They should be people who actually worked with you at one time and can discuss your capabilities and work habits intelligently.

I've found it helpful to tell the persons whose names I've listed in this section exactly what kinds of jobs I'm applying for and what kinds of things I would like them to stress if and when they are called by a potential employer. Also, a word of caution: Be certain you know what people are going to say. One of my references gave me a terrible recommendation when I applied for my job at the Library of Congress. It wasn't until after I was hired that my new boss told me I should remove her name from my 171.

Note: Be sure you have not listed anyone here who is also listed as a supervisor in the experience sections under Block 21.

Blocks 38 through 46: Citizenship and Legal History

Mark these "Yes" or "No" as appropriate, and give any necessary details in Block 47. Don't be afraid to tell the truth regarding any of these matters. Remember, you are dealing with the government, and eventually, when they run their routine checks, they will find out the truth anyway. Better to have told the truth from the beginning, especially since lying on a 171 can be grounds for dismissal. You would be surprised at how many people don't think twice about hiring those who have been fired from another job or who have a criminal record.

Block 47: Additional Information

This block is used only to elaborate upon or continue answers from another block.

Blocks 48 and 49: Signature and Date

Never sign your original. Only sign photocopies. The original can be kept and updated or revised in its various parts and then duplicated for submission for other jobs. Even though you may tailor your 171 for each job, it is never a good idea to submit your only copy, for you will most likely need to revise just the experience block (21) as you change jobs or increase responsibilities. The majority of the 171 will stay the same. Important: **You cannot submit a copy of your signature when applying for a government job.** You must always sign the copies of your 171, or you will be considered ineligible.

Submitting photocopies of the 171 for jobs is common practice—and common sense. One rarely sees an original 171 in a batch of applications. There are many reasons for this. First of all, if you submit an original it implies that you wrote it specifically for this job, which might suggest that you have exaggerated your credentials. Regardless of the fact that most people tailor a 171 to a specific Vacancy Announcement, it looks better if you submit a copy rather than an original. That way it appears as though this is the standard 171 that you submit for all jobs, and the fact that so much of your experience, education, etc. almost perfectly match the job you are applying for is simply a coincidence. Secondly, if you submit an original, especially one that isn't typed, it appears that you may have just come across this job by accident and filled out a 171 while visiting the personnel office. You want to give the impression that you heard about the job through professional channels and weren't really out looking for a job. All this psychological game-playing may seem unnecessary, but believe me, I have seen some incredible prejudices displayed by members of Rating Panels.

Remember when you fill out your original to leave the following blocks blank:

1. Kind of position (job) you are filing for.
12. When will you be available for work?
13. Lowest pay or grade you will accept.
48. Signature Block.
49. Date.

You will want to fill those in individually on each application, since you will most probably be applying for jobs at various GS levels.

A CASE STUDY

The following example is designed to illustrate the proper way in which to complete the SF-171 by utilizing the language found in the Vacancy Announcement.

The Library of Congress posts a Vacancy Announcement for a Writer-Editor (see Appendix N) and a young woman, Marcie Delich, wants to apply for it. She has sound experience in publications procedures and practices, including editing, proofreading, and production techniques, and she wants to convey that information on her 171 (see Appendix O) in order to gain points in Quality Ranking Factor 1, Knowledge of Publication Practices and Procedures. Here is one way she might consider doing that in Block 24 of the 171:

> I edited and proofread copy for publication in newsletters, magazines, brochures, and various company publications. I also worked with reports and letters from several managers. I was responsible for correcting galleys and page proofs and making sure all publications I was working on were on time. I edited a bimonthly newsletter sent to 7,500 association members. Took some of the photographs and developed them myself. It was my responsibility to see that copy got to the typesetter on time and then made it to the printer by press time. Worked under heavy pressure much of the time.

Keeping in mind the Four Vital Areas—Experience, Education, Self Development, Awards and Commendations—she chose to express the same information this way:

> Responsibilities include: plan, research, write, rewrite, edit, proofread, and monitor production of museum's publications distributed to a readership of nearly 8,000 on an ongoing basis; establish and maintain many production schedules, guidelines, and procedures; work with contractors and subcontractors, including subject specialists, authors, typesetters, designers, and printers; edit rough and finished manuscripts for style, grammar, factual accuracy, readability, and tactfulness in the context of the intended audience; assist with design development of audio-visual programs and television spots.

Let's see why this second paragraph is likely to earn more points from the rating panel.

She has used the language that appears under "Brief Description of Duties" on the Vacancy Announcement to demonstrate her knowledge of publication practices and procedures (Quality Ranking Factor 1). She embellished it just a little and turned a phrase or term here and there so that it does not seem that she simply copied the job description off the Vacancy Announcement. Everything they ask for is included. By saying she "worked with" contractors, rather than "copy got to the typesetter on time," she has touched upon her experience working and dealing effectively with others (Quality Ranking Factor 2).

Notice that our applicant lists only the skills requested on the Vacancy Announcement's description of duties. Since they are not looking for someone to process film, she doesn't put down her ability to work in a darkroom, deciding instead to devote the limited space on the 171 to just what they're asking for.

Notice also how many phrases, words, and terms on her 171 coincide with the language of the Vacancy Announcement:

plan	maintain
research	schedules
write	contractors
edit	typesetters
proofread	printers
publications	subject specialists
guidelines	developing/development
procedures	design/designers
audio-visual	

By using the same language, she conveys to the evaluators that she has exactly what they are looking for. By putting it down in a different order or sequence she doesn't appear to have simply copied the description of duties appearing on the Vacancy Announcement.

Note also a very subtle tactic our applicant uses. The brief description of duties on the Vacancy Announcement lists the following: "Plans, researches, writes, edits, and proofreads publications and informational materials *for blind and physically handicapped users of the Library of Congress free reading program.*"

An astute journalist knows what this means: a targeted audience. The publications are written and prepared for a specialized group of readers; therefore, careful handling of the written material is required. The person hired will have to be socially and politically sensitive to a special interest group—in this case, people who are blind and/or physically handicapped.

To call attention to her capacity in this area, our applicant includes the following in her experience with the Smithsonian Institution: "edit rough and finished manuscripts for style, grammar, factual accuracy, readability, and *tactfulness in the context of the intended audience.*"

Even if the Rating Panel should miss this—and it is very doubtful, since at least one member of the hiring department's staff sits on the panel—the person doing the interviewing will pick it up.

Finally, if we go through the three experience sections (A, B, and C) of Block 24 on our applicant's 171 and list the terms she has included that can be associated with the Quality Ranking Factors on the Vacancy Announcement, we come up with an impressive list:

Quality Ranking Factor 1: Knowledge of publications practices and procedures.

Plan, research, write, rewrite, edit, proofread, monitor production, publications, readership, schedules, guidelines, procedures, subject specialists, authors, typesetters, designers, printers, manuscripts, style, grammar, accuracy, readability, audience, audio-visual, television, advertising, promotional copy, campaigns, public relations, publicity, newsletters, mailings, direct markets, indirect markets, writing, interviewing.

Quality Ranking Factor 2: Ability to work and deal effectively with others.

Work with (contractors, subcontractors, subject specialists, authors, typesetters, designers, printers), assist with, assisting, coordinating, gathering, taking photographs, giving tours, arrangements, answering.

All the terms in the first group relate to publishing activities. Everything in the second group relates to working with people. These are all key "buzz words" that evaluators are familiar with and are looking for in relation to these particular quality ranking factors. Quality Ranking Factor 2, by the way, is a very common one, appearing on many federal Vacancy Announcements.

An important note: **include all the volunteer work you do that relates to your profession**. For example, if you are a bookkeeper and you have contributed your services to your parish church once a week for the past three years, by all means include that in one of the experience sections under Block 24. One of the very finest editors I ever hired for the Library of Congress was a woman whose children had grown and left home and who wanted to go back to work. She had virtually no full-time paid experience in her immediate background. Her 171 consisted of section after section of her volunteer work for local community groups, the PTA, her children's schools—all of it writing and editing, all of it good, sound work, examples of which she brought me. And even though their budgets were extremely limited and most of the work was reproduced off a photocopy or mimeograph machine, it was clear that her writing and editing skills were well developed and that she had been practicing them steadily for fifteen years.

Utilizing the *standard* procedure for filling out a job application, the task of completing the 171 would be done for the average job applicant. But for Marcie, who is now aware of the Four Vital Areas, the job has just begun. The potential employing government agency now knows that she has publications *experience*, but what about the other three vital areas?

Education
Quality Ranking Factor 1

While she was living in California our applicant took a five-day newsletter editing course in a continuing education program offered at San Francisco State College. As it turned out, the course was not all that valuable to her. However, while the course itself may not have been profitable, the very fact that she took it will earn her points for Quality Ranking Factor 1 in the Vital Area of Education (Block 31).

Quality Ranking Factor 2

By mentioning a two-day workshop in Interpersonal Skills that she completed while working for a hospital in Napa, California (Block 31), she also earns points for Quality Ranking Factor 2 in the Vital Area of Education, since the Rating Panel of evaluators will consider this as educating herself in the techniques of meeting and dealing effectively with people. These points may later make the difference between being selected and not being selected for an interview.

Self-Development
Quality Ranking Factor 1

It's not enough to indicate that she took the newspaper editing course (Block 47). By noting that it was during a period of unemployment she will also get credit for Self Development, since this course was not part of her duties on a job and was not paid for by an employer. The point is, she did something to increase her editorial skills *on her own*. By referring to this in Block 47 (space for detailed answers) she will earn still more points for knowledge of publication practices and procedures, this time in the Vital Area of Self-Development.

If the course had been paid for by an employer, as was the Interpersonal Skills workshop, she might indicate that she requested to attend the course and that her employer rewarded her initiative by picking up the tab. By doing this she might earn extra points in the Vital Area of Self-Development, since the course was something she sought out on her own and not something that she was told to enroll in.

By mentioning that she is editor of the newsletter for the American Association of Public Relations Professionals, Chapter 348, she will gain points in the Vital Area of Self-Development, since this is obviously something she does on her own time (Block 32).

Quality Ranking Factor 2

Her very membership in the American Association of Public Relations Professionals earns her points for meeting and dealing with people in her profession *on her own* (Block 32). This outside activity, which involves fraternizing with other people in her profession, is considered to be a form of self-development.

Awards and Commendations
Quality Ranking Factor 1

While working for a Berkeley consulting firm, our applicant received a bonus as a result of having produced twenty-six newsletters one year without a single proofreading error. In Block 36 she lists that bonus and the reason she earned it, and she receives even more points for Quality Ranking Factor 1 in the Vital Area of Awards and Commendations.

Quality Ranking Factor 2

During her last summer of college, while working as an intern at the *Napa Register*, she was selected as liaison between student interns and management. She enters that information now (Block 36), realizing that—as insignificant as it seemed at the time—it will earn her points as a kind of commendation on her "ability to work and deal effectively with others."

Our applicant has now garnered substantially more points than she would have earned had she not been aware of the Four Vital Areas of the SF-171.

Chapter 8 will show you the method the evaluator or Rating Panel uses when scoring a Standard Form 171 once it has been received in application for a position.

8
Evaluating Applications: The Point System

We have seen how your Standard Form 171 should be filled out and submitted to the hiring office, but what happens after it is received? What takes place between the time you turn it in to the personnel office and the time you receive either a phone call to come for an interview or a letter telling you someone else was hired for the job?

THE STAFFING SPECIALIST

After the closing date has passed, the personnel office Staffing Specialist in charge of receiving job applications reviews each 171 to determine which applicants have met the minimum requirements and which have not.

Those who have failed to show that they are minimally qualified are notified by letter that they failed to meet the minimum qualifications. They are told that they have ten days in which to challenge that finding by submitting further evidence of their qualifications. If they do not appeal, they will no longer be considered for the position.

Should you receive such a letter and believe you are qualified for the position, you should immediately contact the Staffing Specialist who sent you the letter and ask what you can do to give evidence of your qualifications.

The letter you receive stating the agency's decision that you are not qualified for the job will be a form letter, and it will explain generally why you were found unqualified, but a call to the Staffing Specialist can usually provide you with a great many more details, especially concerning the kind of additional evidence you should submit to satisfy the qualification requirements. Many people give up at this point, concluding that they simply don't have the necessary credentials for the job. Don't make that mistake! Three of my coworkers at the Library of Congress (a GS-9 and two GS-13s) were found unqualified the first time they submitted applications for the positions they ended up getting. If you can convince the Staffing Specialist that your application should be reviewed again with an eye toward certain qualifications that you point up in a letter, chances are very good that you will be considered for the job. Remember: The people reviewing your application are human, just like you. They have good days and bad; they argue with their spouses and fight traffic on their way to work; sometimes their minds are on other things while they are reviewing applications. If you want another chance at the job, give the Staffing Specialist another chance with your 171. Also remember that most people don't want a fight, so if you are determined enough to resubmit your 171, the Staffing Specialist may review it again, this time looking for a way to qualify you in order to avoid possible further confrontation.

If you have applied for a position and haven't heard anything after an unusually long time, you should remember that one of the things that can delay the hiring process is the appeal of one or more applicants. However, it is not uncommon for the review process in the government to take four to six weeks.

Once the minimally qualified applicants have been selected and any appeals have been heard and decided upon, one of two things will happen. Either a Rating Panel will be convened, or the personnel office Staffing Specialist will rate and rank each application. More times than not, however, applications are evaluated first by a Rating Panel of three agency staff members. But regardless of whether the Staffing Specialist evaluates the 171s or they are given to a Rating Panel, the criteria are the same, the process is the same, and—if the evaluation is performed correctly—the results will be the same.

THE RATING PANEL

When the final group of qualified applicants has been determined, the Rating Panel of three agency staff members is convened. The panel members must hold jobs at Grade levels equal to or higher than the Grade level of the job being filled. Also, the Selecting Official—the supervisor who will be interviewing for the position—is not allowed to sit on the Rating Panel. The panel members are given the applications of everyone who applied for the job, along with a score sheet called an Evaluation Criteria Record, and they are sequestered in a private room until they have finished evaluating each one. With this Record, or score sheet, in front of them, each panel member individually reviews and scores each application, assigning a certain number of points for each item on the Record. After all applications have been scored, the panel compares scores for each individual. In cases where there are wide discrepancies among the points awarded to an applicant by individual members of the panel, the applications in question are looked at again by the panel as a group in case one member overlooked something and didn't award enough points, or in case one panel member misinterpreted some part of the application and awarded too many points.

The three totals for each application are then recorded on a separate form, which will be kept by the Personnel Office for future reference in case there is a question about any individual applicant's score. The three totals are added together and divided by three to arrive at each applicant's average score. This score is then recorded as the applicant's final score. The three applicants receiving the highest average score (or more than three, if there is a tie for third place) are then referred to the Selecting Officer—that is, the supervisor who will be conducting the interview and hiring the new employee. The Selecting Officer then telephones the applicants and arranges for interviews.

EVALUATION CRITERIA RECORD

Every time a job is posted, the Selecting Official is required to forward to the

Personnel Staffing Specialist an Evaluation Criteria Record. This record is actually a score sheet based upon the Quality Ranking Factors (QRF) that apply to the job. Each Quality Ranking Factor is listed on this score sheet and given an assigned maximum number of points that can be earned. Applications are then rated against this score sheet. Applicants earn points for each Quality Ranking Factor up to the maximum number allotted for each one. That is simple enough; anyone applying for a job and reading what the Quality Ranking Factors are would try to show on his or her application that he or she was qualified in each area. However, remember what we learned in Chapter 7 about the Four Vital Areas. It isn't enough to touch upon each Quality Ranking Factor once. *You must address each one in terms of the Four Vital Areas.* This is because the Evaluation Criteria Record, or score sheet, is set up to allow points for *each* Quality Ranking Factor in *each* of the Four Vital Areas.

Let's go back to our example from Chapter 7. First look at the Vacancy Announcement for that position in Appendix N and then review the applicant's 171 in Appendix O.

With those two items in mind, let's now look at the Evaluation Criteria Record that will be used by the panel rating applications for this position.

QUALITY RANKING FACTORS

Factor One: Knowledge of Publication Practices and Procedures—80 Points

Experience—47 points

1. A. Writing and editing material for formal publications such as catalogs, magazines, annotated bibliographies, and newsletters; using and applying rules of grammar as well as rules prescribed in the University of Chicago *Manual of Style* or similar sources; and evaluating manuscript copy for accuracy, organization, appropriateness of subject matter, and general communications effectiveness. 1-14

1. B. Establishing production schedules and preparing production specifications for contracts and purchase orders that include distribution instructions. 1-8

1. C. Directing the work of others to produce publications on deadlines; working on joint or group projects that result in finished publications. 1-8

1. D. Marking copy to specify typographic instructions for photocomposition; proofreading and marking typeset proofs; marking and preparing camera-ready copy for printers. 1-8

1. E. Planning layouts; pasting up mechanicals; sizing illustrations. 1-5

1. F. Operating word processing and/or phototypesetting equipment to prepare finished manuscripts and/or camera-ready mechanicals for publication. 1-4

Education and Training—20 points

1. G. Degree in liberal arts. 1-8

1. H. College coursework in English, literature, journalism, or creative writing. 1-7

1. I. Professional workshops and seminars sponsored by reputable training agencies. 1-5

Awards and Commendations—10 points

1. J. Any award or commendation for the writing, editing, and production of a print or audio-visual product. 1-5

1. K. Any academic honor or fellowship for publications achievements. 1-5

Self-Development—3 points

1. L. Any participation in activities not prescribed by employers or educational institutions that relate to publishing or the publishing field. 1-3

Factor 2: Ability to Work and Deal Effectively with Others—20 Points

Experience—10 points

2. A. Dealing effectively with peers and professional subject matter specialists—i.e., automation experts, engineers, scholars, politicians, technical personnel, bibliographers, etc. 1-5

2. B. Dealing effectively with typesetters, printers, graphic artists, other technical personnel in the publishing field. 1-5

Education and Training—4 points

2. C. Any courses, seminars, training classes conducted by accredited colleges, schools, or training agencies relating to the ability to work and deal effectively with others. 1-4

Awards and Commendations—3 points

2. D. Any award or commendation pertinent to "meet and deal" abilities. 1-3

Self Development—3 points

2. E. Any participation in activities not prescribed by employers or educational institutions that relate to the ability to work and deal effectively with others. 1-3

THE SCORING PROCESS

Let's look at just part of the scoring process in order to better understand how points are assigned and why it is essential for an applicant to address each Quality Ranking Factor in *each* of the Four Vital Areas.

Under Quality Ranking Factor Number One, Knowledge of Publication Practices and Procedures, there are twelve elements or subfactors. For element 1.A., "writing and editing," there are fourteen points that an applicant can receive. Let's see where Marcie will gain points on her application.

In her current job with the Smithsonian Institution she lists as part of her responsibilities "write," "edit . . . for style, grammar, factual accuracy." If we compare that to the language on the Evaluation Criteria Record under 1.A., we see that the panel is going to be looking for "writing and editing," "applying rules of grammar as well as rules prescribed in the University of Chicago *Manual of Style*," "evaluating manuscript copy for accuracy." So she will definitely receive points for her experience at the Smithsonian, since she has used key words from the Vacancy Announcement, such as "writing," "editing," "style," "grammar," "accuracy."

She says on her 171 that while working for Green Associates in Berkeley, California she did "writing" and "editing." She will gain

points for this work as well, for while it is the same kind of work as is listed in Block A for the Smithsonian job, it *increases the amount of time, and therefore the amount of experience,* she has in writing and editing.

Again, at Queen of the Valley Hospital in Napa, she lists "writing" and "editing" as part of her job. More experience, so more points under element 1.A.

In Block 32 of her application she has thought to mention that she is not only a member of the American Association of Public Relations Professionals, but that she is the editor of her chapter newsletter. *This counts as experience in editing.* Don't forget: All experience counts, even volunteer work. She goes on in the same block to state that she has published "various news and feature stories in assorted newsletters and newspapers." This also counts as experience in writing. Remember: Experience does not only mean experience on the job.

By this time Marcie has probably received close to the maximum number of points allotted for experience in writing and editing.

Now, if we go to element 1.B., "Establishing production schedules and preparing production specifications," and compare that with what she has listed as her responsibilities under the three jobs she has held, we find that she has dealt with "production schedules" only at the Smithsonian. However, her work "coordinating mailings to direct and indirect markets" at Green Associates and her supervision of "mass mailings to Napa County residents" may very well be interpreted by the evaluators on the panel as having worked within production schedules in order to achieve mailings by a certain deadline. If so, she will receive more points for element 1.B. for that work as well.

This evaluation process is followed by the evaluators throughout the entire Evaluation Criteria Record, assigning points according to how well each application matches the lists of skills and duties appearing on the Record.

So Marcie has done well under Quality Ranking Factor One *in the Vital Area of Experience,* but that is only one of Four Vital Areas in which she must garner points under the Quality Ranking Factor of Knowledge of Publications Practices and Procedures. Let's look at the other three vital areas and see how she covered those.

If we turn to the Vital Area of Education and Training under Quality Ranking Factor One, we see that Marcie has stated on her 171 that she holds a Bachelor of Arts degree in journalism. This earns her points under element 1.G. on the Evaluation Criteria Record. However, because it is in journalism and because she mentions another eighteen hours of course credit in English, she will also gain points under element 1.H. for having completed college coursework in English and news writing. This is an important point to note, because it is a subtle way to earn points that most people would miss. It is likely that an applicant listing a Bachelor of Arts degree in journalism would not bother to mention eighteen hours college credit in English, assuming that the person or persons evaluating the application would *assume* that anyone majoring in journalism would have to take some English courses. In fact, an applicant with a Bachelor of Arts degree in any field might think that evaluators would assume he or she completed courses in English, but, while certain things stated on an application might be open to interpretation, evaluators *cannot by federal regulation* assume anything. If it isn't there in black and white, you don't get points for it. Evaluators are comparing your 171 with the score sheet; they are not trying to guess what you left out.

Marcie's five-day newsletter editing course, mentioned in Block 31, earns her still more points in the Vital Area of Education and Training under element 1.I. Had she only mentioned her major in journalism, thinking that would be plenty of credentials in "knowledge of publication practices and procedures," she would have lost these valuable extra points—points that may be tie-breaking ones between her and someone else for the number three spot when all the points are tallied.

Her Associated Collegiate Press award in 1974 and her bonus award from Green Associates in 1978 will earn her up to five points under element 1.J—"Any award or commendation for the writing, editing, and production of a print or audio-visual communication." Because Marcie was aware

that points would be given for Awards and Commendations received relating to each Quality Ranking Factor, she listed in Block 36 tuition scholarships in journalism received at Napa College. This will earn her points for "academic honor or fellowship for publications achievements," as stated in element 1.K. under Awards and Commendations for Quality Ranking Factor One. Finally, in the Vital Area of Self-Development, the panel will note that Marcie became a member of the American Association of Public Relations Professionals (Block 32 of the application), that she taught *herself* the Wang Word Processing Course, and that she took the Newsletter Editing course during a period of unemployment, not as a requirement for any job or educational program (Blocks 32 and 47). This will undoubtedly earn her high marks for self-development under Quality Ranking Factor One, Element 1.L.

Points can be racked up just this easily if you read the Vacancy Announcement carefully, study the Quality Ranking Factors, and address them in terms of each of the Four Vital Areas where points will be assigned.

A question is bound to arise in the mind of the reader regarding how many points are awarded for each element on the Evaluation Criteria Sheet. There is no set answer, for there is no set formula. There is a maximum number of points that can be given for each element, as you can see from looking at the Evaluation Criteria Record. But there is no formula that directs the panel of evaluators as to how many points to give, for example, for one course in journalism, how many points to award for two courses, etc.

"But," you say, "that means that each evaluator will score differently. Some high, some low." Yes, that is correct. But remember, in general people are either strict or liberal. There are high scorers and low scorers, just like there are easy teachers and hard teachers in school. So if one of the evaluators is giving applicants the full number of points allowed for having a single class in journalism, he is scoring everyone on the high side. If another evaluator is giving just one point, or even half a point, for each course in journalism, he or she is scoring everyone on the low side. So in the end, when all scores are added and divided by three for the average, it will work out. All of panel member A's scores, which are low, are added to all of panel member B's scores, which are high, and the average results in a ranking that reflects where each applicant fell in the range of each panel member's total rating system.

The bottom line is that a person applying for a position with the federal government has a better chance of being dealt with fairly and honestly and not being a victim of one person's whim, as is often the case in the private sector. There are strict and definite regulations that govern the process that evaluates an applicant's qualifications. But these regulations and procedures cannot help a person if he or she doesn't fill out the application knowledgeably and carefully. That is why being aware of the Four Vital Areas is so essential to successfully applying for the desired job.

9

Federal Employment of
the Handicapped

The Rehabilitation Act of 1973 as amended by Public Law 93-516 and the Vietnam Era Veterans' Readjustment Assistance Act of 1974 require federal agencies to develop and implement affirmative action program plans for employing handicapped individuals. These public laws ensure the hiring of physically and mentally handicapped persons and address the placement, promotion, and retention of these valuable federal employees.

The Office of Personnel Management (OPM) conducts a carefully monitored and enforced program for handicapped applicants through its central office in the nation's capital and in each of its ten regional offices throughout the country. To facilitate the recruitment and placement of handicapped individuals federal agencies are allowed to process handicapped applicants through normal competitive channels, and they may also utilize special "appointing authorities," such as those mentioned in Chapters 2 and 3. Certain special, or noncompetitive, appointing authorities allow an agency to hire someone immediately without going through the competitive procedure, thereby avoiding all the horrendous red tape of the bureaucracy. Handicapped applicants are required to possess only the minimum medical qualifications necessary to safely and efficiently perform the duties of any given position, along with the minimum job requirements.

REASONABLE ACCOMMODATION

Bolstering this mission to employ handicapped citizens is the basic affirmative action concept of "reasonable accommodation." Regulations regarding nondiscrimination in federal employment of handicapped persons require federal agencies not only to recruit, place, and promote handicapped persons, but also to make reasonable accommodation for the known physical or mental limitations of a handicapped applicant or employee. The only exception to this rule is when it can be demonstrated that the accommodation would cause undue hardship for the agency.

Some people feel that the government goes too far in making accommodations for the handicapped employee, but these same people fail to take into consideration that accommodations are made for nonhandicapped employees all the time. Every time an employer institutes a program of in-house training or establishes a flexible work schedule, he or she is being accommodating. Something as simple as allowing for coffee breaks or obtaining a more efficient piece of machinery or equipment is an accommodation to a company's or agency's employees. So a program that equalizes the employment opportunities of those citizens who for one reason or another are handicapped in their attempts to become productive members of the nation's work force is hardly an unreasonable accommodation.

Just like any other accommodation, considerations for handicapped employees must, by law, be given on an individual or case-by-case basis. What is reasonably accommodating for one handicapped employee may not be suitable for another with the same handicap. For example, if a department or agency provides written materials in Braille for a blind staff member, those same materials may not be useful to another blind staff member who does not read Braille. Providing a Kurzweil machine—which reads print material through the use of a synthesized voice—or having another staff member read materials to the blind employee may be the answer to reasonably accommodating that person's needs.

In order to provide handicapped employees the opportunity to attend formal training programs, government agencies are authorized to spend training funds to provide special services, such as interpreters, readers, and Brailling or taping of training course materials. Thus the task of providing reasonable accommodation does not end with recruiting and hiring but is carried on after the employee is on the job.

Reasonable accommodation includes a host of considerations. Test administration methods may be modified by providing Braille materials for the blind or extra time for persons with reading disabilities caused by a mental or physical impairment. Test sites must be accessible to physically handicapped applicants. If they are not, alternate test sites must be established.

When examinations are required for establishing minimum qualifications for a position with the federal government, special arrangements are made to allow handicapped applicants to achieve test results commensurate with their abilities. The objective here is to attempt to eliminate any barriers that would prevent handicapped persons from demonstrating their full capabilities in an examination.

In the work environment itself alterations can make it possible for handicapped individuals to work where they might not otherwise be able to. Rearranging shelves or files, widening aisles to accommodate wheelchairs, using Braille labels, adding special holding devices to desks or chairs for workers with impaired limb movement, and installing telecommunication accessories or telephone amplifiers are examples of modifications that enable the handicapped employee to function at full capacity.

Adjusting work schedules is another way to accommodate handicapped workers. Flexible or alternating work schedules can accommodate mobility-impaired employees who find it difficult, if not impossible, to commute on public transportation during peak traffic periods. Persons requiring therapy or occasional rest periods can benefit from a flexible work schedule also.

In addition, readers and interpreters for the blind and hearing impaired are considered to be within the realm of reasonable accommodation.

The important point to remember here is that all of these methods are not only possible in the public sector, they are required by law.

Each agency has a Coordinator for Selective Placement in its employment office whose job it is to provide detailed information to handicapped applicants. If you are a handicapped individual looking for a position with the federal government, you may want to contact the Coordinator by finding the agency regional office nearest you in Appendix J and writing or calling for more information.

EXCEPTED SERVICE

Having read this far, it should be clear to you that exceptions to the rules are the name of the game in government, and when it comes to hiring handicapped persons these exceptions also apply—as they should. The handicapped applicant would do well to remember those special Appointing Authorities mentioned in Chapter 2. There are two in particular that should be kept in mind and even mentioned to the prospective hiring agency:

The 700 Hour Trial Appointing Authority

This allows an agency to immediately hire a handicapped individual for a period of 700 hours to allow the person an opportunity to demonstrate his ability to perform the duties of the job. Applicants must, however, either meet the minimum qualifications requirements or be certified by a State Vocational Rehabilitation Counselor or a Veterans Administration Rehabilitation Counselor as being capable of performing the duties of the position being applied for. This appointment is a temporary one, but it may lead to a permanent position with the agency.

The Schedule A Appointment

Section 213.3102(u) of the Schedule A Appointing Authority allows for the government to hire on a full time basis a severely handicapped person who has either a) successfully completed a 700 hour trial appointment or b) has been certified directly to a position by a State Vocational Rehabilitation Counselor or a Veterans Rehabilitation Counselor.

After two years of successful performance in the position, an employee who is holding one of these jobs in the "excepted" service may be *noncompetitively* converted to a Competitive Appointment upon the recommendation of the supervisor. That means that after a two-year period working in a job that was given under the special Appointing Authority (without having to compete through normal channels with other nonhandicapped applicants), the person may become a member of the Competitive Service. Conversion to Competitive Service means achieving Competitive Civil Service Status and, therefore, eligibility to apply and compete as an experienced, certified civil service employee for any federal job that is vacant anywhere in the world.

Remember: once the conversion to regular Competitive Status occurs, you are eligible to apply for those jobs that are closed to outside applicants, i.e., people who do not hold civil service status. This means there is virtually no job in the U.S. Government for which you cannot apply and be given serious consideration so long as you meet the minimum qualification requirements.

The very important point of all this technical information is simply this: Just as nonhandicapped persons can walk into the personnel office of a federal agency and be hired on a temporary basis without going through the nightmare of the bureaucracy's red tape, so can a physically or mentally handicapped individual. In fact, it is easier for the handicapped person because the special Appointing Authorities are very clearly spelled out. There can be no doubt that the reason for hiring a handicapped individual is legitimate and that this is not just a case of someone in a position of power within the government trying to give a friend a job.

If you are handicapped and looking for work with Uncle Sam, or if you are assisting a handicapped friend or relative to find a federal job, be prepared to tell the agency that you are familiar with the Special Appointing Authorities and you know that if there is a job open you or your friend or relative can be placed in it immediately for at least a 700-hour trial period, assuming that the minimum qualifications are satisfied.

Appendix A
Federal Civilian Employment:
A Breakdown of the Total Federal
Jobs Available Throughout the
United States

Total, All Areas, 1988	3,817,962
Outside U.S.	562,962
United States	2,902,000
District of Columbia	353,000

FEDERAL EMPLOYMENT BY STATE, 1984

Alabama	59,915
Alaska	13,780
Arizona	33,783
Arkansas	17,940
California	300,785
Colorado	49,328
Connecticut	20,573
Delaware	4,954
Florida	84,783
Georgia	76,928
Hawaii	26,922
Idaho	9,993
Illinois	100,192
Indiana	39,316
Iowa	18,212
Kansas	22,383
Kentucky	35,535
Louisiana	31,906
Maine	8,896
Maryland	129,107
Massachusetts	55,406
Michigan	53,709
Minnesota	28,671
Mississippi	23,760
Missouri	65,516
Montana	11,762
Nebraska	14,937
Nevada	9,149
New Hampshire	15,690
New Jersey	71,666
New Mexico	25,371
New York	153,616
North Carolina	42,821
North Dakota	7,781
Ohio	86,836
Oklahoma	46,495
Oregon	26,992
Pennsylvania	129,065
Rhode Island	9,025
South Carolina	32,519
South Dakota	9,581
Tennessee	58,221
Texas	155,680
Utah	35,443
Vermont	4,396
Virginia	152,737
Washington	62,666
West Virginia	14,955
Wisconsin	25,883
Wyoming	6,550

From the 1985 Federal Personnel Guide. (These statistics do not include employees in the Judicial Branch other than those employed by the Administrative Office of the U.S., Courts, the Central Intelligence Agency, and the National Security Agency.)

Appendix B
Federal Employees Health
Benefits Program Guide and
Comparison Chart

FEHB Plan Comparison Chart - For Benefits Beginning in January 1989
Fee-for-Service Plans

- All plans require you to share costs for covered charges. In addition to the calendar year deductible (see below), other cost-sharing amounts you pay may include coinsurance, copayments and/or inpatient deductibles.

- The calendar year deductible shown is the per person amount. Under a Self and Family enrollment, generally no more than two or three family members, depending on the plan, must meet this deductible. For a few plans, which have established a family deductible, the per person amount shown applies to just one person; the difference between it and the family deductible can be met by any or all of those covered. The calendar year deductible may not apply to every covered charge.

- The amounts of covered charges that plans pay for medical-surgical primary care shown on the next page are maximum amounts. Payments may be affected, however, by certain limitations and conditions, which are described in the plan brochures.

	Plan Name and Option		Enrollment Code			Brochure Number RI	Plan Telephone Number	1989 Monthly Premium Your Share		1989 Biweekly Premium Your Share		Medical-Surgical Primary Care You Pay	
			Plan Code	Self Only	Self & Family			Self Only	Self & Family	Self Only	Self & Family	Calendar Year Deductible	Catastrophic Limit (max. covered out of pocket) person/family
*	ACT		Y3	1	2	72-9	(800) 262-4228	$ 28.14	$ 74.77	$12.99	$ 34.51	$200	$1,500/$3,000
	Aetna (Indemnity Benefit)	High	20	1	2	71-1	(800) 222-3862	168.65	318.70	77.84	147.09	$200	$2,000/$4,000
		Stnd	20	4	5	71-1	(800) 222-3862	66.03	154.01	30.48	71.08	NA	$3,000/$6,000
	AFGE	High	30	1	2	71-2	(800) 424-4308	170.88	311.52	78.87	143.78	$200	$1,500/$1,500
		Stnd	30	4	5	71-2	(800) 424-4308	22.98	49.96	10.61	23.06	NA	$2,500†
	Alliance	High	46	1	2	71-3	(202) 939-6325	68.59	228.58	31.66	105.50	$250	$1,500/$2,500
		Stnd	46	4	5	71-3	(202) 939-6325	20.33	54.75	9.38	25.27	$325	$2,500/$2,500
	APWU		47	1	2	71-4	(800) 222-2798	40.34	78.46	18.62	36.21	$175	$1,500/$1,500
*	BACE		Y2	1	2	72-8	(301) 881-0510	42.83	118.04	19.77	54.48	$200	$1,500/$1,500
	Blue Cross-Blue Shield (Service Benefit)	High	10	1	2	71-5	See Local Phone Book	183.03	378.67	84.48	174.77	$200	$1,500/$1,500
		Stnd	10	4	5	71-5		32.72	68.77	15.10	31.74	$250	$2,500/$2,500
*	Foreign Service		40	1	2	72-1	(202) 833-4910	47.47	139.25	21.91	64.27	$175	$1,500/$1,500
*	GEBA		YZ	1	2	72-2	(301) 688-7912	31.18	85.89	14.39	39.64	$250	$2,000/$2,000
	GEHA		31	1	2	71-6	(800) 821-6136	38.60	73.00	17.82	33.69	$250	$2,000/$2,000
	Mail Handlers	High	45	1	2	71-7	1-800-468-2958	23.74	61.31	10.96	28.30	NA	$2,500/$5,000
		Stnd	45	4	5	71-7	1-800-468-2958	22.97	54.35	10.60	25.08	NA	$2,500/$5,000
	NAGE	High	YJ	1	2	71-8	(800) 424-3707	152.16	369.96	70.23	170.75	$200	$1,500/$2,500
		Stnd	YJ	4	5	71-8	(800) 424-3707	26.77	63.88	12.36	29.48	$250	$2,000/$3,000
	NALC		32	1	2	71-9	(703) 471-1550	61.51	103.13	28.39	47.60	$150	$1,000/$1,000
*	NAPUS		YP	1	2	72-3	(800) 451-4479	88.94	179.75	NA	NA	$200	$700/$1,400
	NFFE	High	YR	1	2	71-10	(800) 262-5233	119.79	283.99	55.29	131.07	$750	$750/$1,500
		Stnd	YR	4	5	71-10	(800) 262-5233	50.93	135.40	23.51	62.49	$250	$1,000/$2,000
	NTEU		YY	1	2	71-11	(202) 785-4411	27.06	61.11	12.49	28.20	$275	$2,250/$2,250
*	Panama Canal Area		43	1	2	72-4	(402) 978-5596	27.66	59.98	12.76	27.68	NA	$1,000†
	Postal Supervisors		YV	1	2	71-12	(800) 950-7727	59.36	158.60	27.40	73.20	$250	$1,500/$1,500
	Postmasters	High	36	1	2	71-13	(703) 683-5585	116.04	247.22	53.56	114.10	$200	$2,000/$2,500
		Stnd	36	4	5	71-13	(703) 683-5585	26.38	64.32	12.17	29.68	$275	$2,500/$2,500
*	Rural Carriers		38	1	2	72-5	(800) 638-8432	67.42	99.58	NA	NA	$250	$1,500/$3,000
*	SAMBA		44	1	2	72-6	(301) 984-1440	40.90	139.17	18.88	64.23	$300	$1,000/$2,000
*	Secret Service		Y7	1	2	72-11	(800) 424-7474	27.92	69.81	12.89	32.22	$200	$1,000/$2,000

* Plans are open ONLY to specific groups

ABBREVIATIONS: ECF — Extended Care Facility   R & C — Reasonable & Customary
HHC — Home Health Care   SA — Scheduled Allowance
NA — Not Applicable

† Per person

Do Not Rely on This Chart Alone - See Plan Brochures for Details

- Most plans require that accidental injury care must be received within a specified number of hours of the injury for the amounts shown to apply.

- The mental conditions inpatient catastrophic limit is the maximum amount of covered out-of-pocket expenses you pay per person per year until the plan pays up to the lifetime maximum; you pay any expenses that exceed it. The lifetime maximum is the amount up to which plans pay per person for covered mental conditions inpatient services.

- While not shown on the Chart, virtually all of the fee-for-service plans provide:
  —Mental conditions outpatient care benefits, which usually have dollar and/or visit limits, and you share costs to these limits.
  —Inpatient and outpatient care benefits for alcoholism and drug abuse, which usually have dollar, day and/or visit limits, and you share costs to these limits.
  —Inpatient and outpatient hospice care benefits, which have a dollar maximum that varies by plan.
  See plan brochures for details.

Medical - Surgical Primary Care — Plan Pays								Mental Conditions — Inpatient Care		Other Benefit Features			
Inpatient Care				Outpatient Care				You Pay	Plan Pays				
Hospital Charges		Physician Charges		Physician Charges		Diagnostic Tests (R & C)	Accidental Injury Care (R & C)	Catastrophic Limit †	Lifetime Maximum †	ECF and/or HHC	Dental Care	Rx Drugs	Chiropractor
Room & Board	Other Hosp. Exp.	Surgeons (R & C)	Other Drs (R & C)	Surgeons (R & C)	Other Drs (R & C)								
100%	100%	80%	80%	80%	80%	80%	80%	$5,000	$25,000	No	Yes	Yes	Yes
80%	80%	80%	80%	80%	80%	80%	80%	$3,000	$50,000	HHC	Yes	Yes	No
70%	70%	SA	SA	SA	SA	SA	75%	$8,000	$55,000	HHC	Yes	Yes	No
100%	100%	100%	80%	100%	80%	80%	100%	$6,000	$50,000	Both	No	Yes	Yes
100%	80%	SA	SA	SA	SA	SA	SA	$5,000	$25,000	ECF	Yes	No	No
100%	100%	80%	80%	100%	80%	80%	100%	$8,000	$50,000	Both	Yes	Yes	Yes
100%	100%	75%	75%	90%	75%	75%	100%	$8,000	$50,000	Both	Yes	Yes	Yes
100%	80%	85%	85%	100%	85%	85%	SA	$8,000	$25,000	No	Yes	Yes	No
100%	80%	80%	80%	100%	80%	80%	100%	$8,000	$50,000	Both	Yes	Yes	Yes
100%	100%	80%	80%	80%	80%	80%	100%	$4,000	$75,000	HHC	No	Yes	No
100%	100%	75%	75%	75%	75%	75%	100%	$8,000	$50,000	No	Yes	Yes	No
100%	80%	90%	80%	100%	80%	80%	100%	$1,500	None	Both	Yes	Yes	No
100%	75%	75%	75%	85%	75%	75%	SA	$10,000	$25,000	Both	Yes	Yes	Yes
100%	80%	80%	80%	85%	85%	85%	100%	$8,000	$50,000	HHC	Yes	Yes	Yes
100%	100%	SA	SA	SA	SA	SA	75%	$5,000	$25,000	No	Yes	No	Yes
100%	100%	SA	SA	SA	SA	SA	75%	$5,000	$25,000	No	No	No	Yes
90%	90%	90%	80%	90%	80%	80%	100%	$7,500	$50,000	Both	Yes	Yes	Yes
75%	75%	75%	75%	75%	75%	75%	75%	$8,000	$50,000	Both	Yes	Yes	Yes
100%	100%	90%	75%	100%	75%	75%	SA	$8,000	$50,000	HHC	Yes	Yes	No
100%	100%	75%	75%	100%	75%	75%	100%	$4,200	$50,000	Both	Yes	Yes	Yes
100%	100%	100%	100%	100%	100%	100%	100%	None	$50,000	Both	Yes	Yes	Yes
100%	100%	75%	75%	75%	75%	75%	100%	$8,000	$40,000	HHC	Yes	Yes	Yes
100%	100%	75%	75%	100%	75%	75%	100%	None	None	Both	Yes	Yes	Yes
100%	80%	100%	SA	100%	SA	SA	100%	None	None	No	Yes	No	Yes
100%	100%	80%	75%	90%	75%	75%	100%	$8,000	$50,000	Both	Yes	Yes	Yes
100%	85%	100%	80%	100%	80%	80%	SA	$8,000	$40,000	Both	Yes	Yes	Yes
100%	80%	SA	75%	SA	75%	75%	SA	$8,000	$40,000	Both	Yes	Yes	Yes
100%	80%	90%	75%	90%	75%	75%	SA	$8,000	None	ECF	Yes	Yes	Yes
100%	90%	100%	80%	100%	80%	80%	100%	$6,500	$50,000	Both	No	Yes	Yes
100%	100%	80%	80%	80%	80%	80%	100%	$4,000	$50,000	Both	Yes	Yes	Yes

The above benefits may be subject to dollar, day and/or visit limits; as well as preadmission approval, precertification, second opinion and/or other requirements. Read the plan brochures carefully.

Appendix C
The General Schedule (GS)
Pay Scale

President's Planned Increase for the
General Schedule Pay Scale—expected to be effective January 1989

Time-in-Grade Step Increases

	ONE	TWO	THREE	FOUR	FIVE	SIX	SEVEN	EIGHT	NINE	TEN
GS-1	$10,213	$10,555	$10,894	$11,233	$11,573	$11,773	$12,108	$12,445	$12,461	$12,780
GS-2	11,484	11,757	12,137	12,461	12,601	12,972	13,343	13,714	14,085	14,456
GS-3	12,531	12,949	13,367	13,785	14,203	14,621	15,039	15,457	15,875	16,293
GS-4	14,067	14,536	15,005	15,474	15,943	16,412	16,881	17,350	17,819	18,288
GS-5	15,738	16,263	16,788	17,313	17,838	18,363	18,888	19,413	19,939	20,463
GS-6	17,542	18,127	18,712	19,297	19,882	20,467	21,052	21,637	22,222	22,807
GS-7	19,493	20,143	20,793	21,443	22,093	22,743	23,393	24,043	24,693	25,343
GS-8	21,590	22,310	23,030	23,750	24,470	25,190	25,910	26,630	27,350	28,070
GS-9	23,846	24,641	25,436	26,231	27,026	27,821	28,616	29,411	30,206	31,001
GS-10	26,261	27,136	28,011	28,886	29,761	30,636	31,511	32,386	33,261	34,136
GS-11	28,852	29,814	30,776	31,738	32,700	33,662	34,624	35,586	36,548	37,510
GS-12	34,580	35,733	36,886	38,039	39,192	40,345	41,498	42,651	43,804	44,957
GS-13	41,121	42,492	43,863	45,234	46,605	47,976	49,347	50,718	52,089	53,460
GS-14	48,592	50,212	51,832	53,452	55,072	56,692	58,312	59,932	61,552	63,172
GS-15	57,158	59,063	60,968	62,873	64,778	66,683	68,588	70,493	72,398	74,303
GS-16	67,038	69,273	71,508	73,743	75,473	76,678*	78,869*	81,060*	82,500*	
GS-17	76,990*	79,556*	82,122*	82,500*	83,818*					
GS-18	86,682*									

*Basic GS pay is limited by public law to the rate for Level V
of the Executive Schedule, which is expected to be $75,000 in January 1989.

Appendix D
The Wage Grade (WG)
Pay Scale

NON-SUPERVISORY (WG)		LEADER (WL)		SUPERVISORY (WS)	
Grade	Income Range ($ per hour)	Grade	Income Range ($ per hour)	Grade	Income Range ($ per hour)
1	$ 5.97 - $ 6.96	1	$ 6.56 - $ 7.66	1	$ 9.57 - $11.17
2	$ 6.61 - $ 7.73	2	$ 7.27 - $ 8.51	2	$10.09 - $11.80
3	$ 7.15 - $ 8.33	3	$ 7.85 - $ 9.18	3	$10.62 - $12.39
4	$ 7.79 - $ 9.07	4	$ 8.56 - $10.00	4	$11.26 - $13.13
5	$ 8.40 - $ 9.82	5	$ 9.25 - $10.79	5	$11.89 - $13.88
6	$ 9.04 - $10.57	6	$ 9.95 - $11.62	6	$12.52 - $14.61
7	$ 9.66 - $11.30	7	$10.64 - $12.43	7	$13.13 - $15.32
8	$10.28 - $11.97	8	$11.32 - $13.18	8	$13.70 - $15.98
9	$10.81 - $12.63	9	$11.91 - $13.89	9	$14.24 - $16.62
10	$11.38 - $13.29	10	$12.52 - $14.61	10	$14.81 - $17.27
11	$11.95 - $13.95	11	$13.14 - $15.35	11	$15.21 - $17.74
12	$12.52 - $14.61	12	$13.75 - $16.05	12	$15.73 - $18.36
13	$13.08 - $15.25	13	$14.39 - $16.78	13	$16.39 - $19.12
14	$13.63 - $15.93	14	$15.01 - $17.53	14	$17.17 - $20.03
15	$14.20 - $16.57	15	$15.65 - $18.26	15	$18.06 - $21.08
				16	$19.08 - $22.26
				17	$20.23 - $23.61
				18	$21.51 - $25.09
				19	$22.89 - $26.72

Appendix E
The Sign-in Sheet

APPENDIX E: SIGN-IN-SHEET

LIBRARY OF CONGRESS - FLEXI-TIME, COMPFLEX AND OVERTIME REGISTER

Office _____ Supervisor _____ Date _____ Certified by and Date _____

1. Sign in by order of arrival (do not sign in before 6:30 a.m.) USE PEN.
2. If you take sick or annual leave during the day, indicate the number of hours taken in the appropriate column.
3. Sign in and out to the nearest five minutes, e.g. 7:35 not 7:33. (For an 8-hour workday, leave 8½ hours after the time you arrive; for a 9-hour workday, leave 9½ hours after the time you arrive, e.g., if you arrive at 7:33 a.m., you leave at 4:03 or 5:03 p.m., respectively).

SIGNATURE	F / CF	TIME IN	MID DAY FLEX (Times recorded include a ½ hour lunch period)		TIME OUT	NUMBER OF LEAVE HOURS				OVERTIME			
			Leave	Return		From	To	Hours	Type	From	To	Hours	Type
1.													
2.													
3.													
4.													
5.													
6.													
7.													
8.													
9.													
10.													
11.													
12.													
13.													
14.													
15.													
16.													
17.													

REMARKS:

LW 5/76 (rev 7/83)

64

Appendix F
The Ten Standard Federal
Regions of the United States

Connecticut, Maine, Massachusetts,
New Hampshire, Rhode Island, & Vermont . . . . Region 1

New Jersey, New York, Puerto Rico, & Virgin Islands . . . . Region 2

Delaware, District of Columbia, Maryland,
Pennsylvania, Virginia, & West Virginia . . . . Region 3

Alabama, Florida, Georgia, Kentucky, Mississippi,
North Carolina, South Carolina, & Tennessee . . . . Region 4

Illinois, Indiana, Michigan, Minnesota,
Ohio, & Wisconsin . . . . Region 5

Arkansas, Louisiana, New Mexico, Oklahoma, & Texas . . . . Region 6

Iowa, Kansas, Missouri, & Nebraska . . . . Region 7

Colorado, Montana, North Dakota,
South Dakota, Utah, & Wyoming . . . . Region 8

Arizona, California, Guam, Hawaii, Nevada, &
Trust Territory of the Pacific Islands* . . . . Region 9

Alaska, Idaho, Oregon, & Washington . . . . Region 10

*Caroline Islands, Mariana Islands, Marshall Islands

Appendix G
Federal Job Information Centers

Following is a list of Federal Job Information Centers. These centers are operated by the Office of Personnel Management for the purpose of providing general information on federal employment. They assist people by providing information on applying for federal jobs, supplying appropriate forms—such as the Standard Form 171—and conducting certain tests that are required for some jobs.

ALABAMA
Southerland Building
806 Governors Dr., S.W.
Huntsville 35801
205/453-5070

ALASKA
Federal Building
701 C St., Box 22
Anchorage 99513
907/271-5821

ARIZONA
522 N. Central Ave.
Phoenix 85004
602/261-4736

ARKANSAS
700 W. Capitol Ave.
Little Rock 72201
501/378-5842

CALIFORNIA
845 S. Figueroa
Los Angeles 90017
213/688-3360

1029 J. St., Room 202
Sacramento 95814
916/440-3441

880 Front St.
San Diego 92188
714/293-6165

211 Main St., Second Floor
San Francisco 94105
415/974-9725

COLORADO
1845 Sherman St.
Denver 80203
303/837-3509

CONNECTICUT
450 Main St., Room 613
Hartford 06103
203/722-3096

DISTRICT OF COLUMBIA
1900 E. Street, N.W.
Washington 20415
202/737-9616

FLORIDA
80 N. Hughey Ave.
Orlando 32801
305/420-6148

GEORGIA
75 Spring St., S.W.
Atlanta 30303
404/221-4315

GUAM
238 O'Hara St.
Room 308
Agana 96910
344-5242

HAWAII
300 Ala Moana Blvd.
Honolulu 96850
808/546-8600

ILLINOIS
55 E. Jackson
Room 1401
Chicago 60604
312/353-5136

INDIANA
46 E. Ohio St.
Room 124
Indianapolis 46204
317/269-7161

IOWA
210 Walnut St.
Room 191
Des Moines 50309
515/284-4545

KANSAS
120 S. Market St.
Room 101
Wichita 67202
316/269-6106
(Pottawattamie and Scott Counties:
402/221-3815)

LOUISIANA
610 South St.
Room 849
New Orleans 70130
504/589-2764

MARYLAND
101 W. Lombard St.
Baltimore 21201
301/962-3822

MASSACHUSETTS
3 Center Plaza
Boston 02108
617/223-2571

MICHIGAN
477 Michigan Ave.
Room 565
Detroit 48226
313/226-6950

MINNESOTA
Federal Building
Ft. Snelling, Twin Cities 55111
612/725-4430

MISSISSIPPI
100 W. Capitol St.
Suite 335
Jackson 39260
603/965-4585

MISSOURI
601 E. 12th St.
Kansas City 64106
816/374-5702

815 Olive St.
St. Louis 63101
314/425-4285

NEBRASKA
215 N. 17th St.
Room 1010
Omaha 68102
402/221-3815

NEW HAMPSHIRE
80 Daniel St.
Room 104
Portsmouth 03801
603/436-7720

NEW JERSEY
970 Broad St.
Newark 07102
201/645-3673
(Camden: 215/597-7440)

NEW MEXICO
421 Gold Ave., S.W.
Albuquerque 87102
505/766-5583

NEW YORK
26 Federal Plaza
New York City 10278
212/264-0422

1000 S. Clinton St.
Syracuse 13260
315/423-5660

NORTH CAROLINA
310 New Bern Ave.
Box 25069
Raleigh 27611
919/755-4361

OHIO
200 W. 2nd St.
Dayton 45402
513/225-2720

OKLAHOMA
200 N.W. Fifth St.
Room 205
Oklahoma City 73102
405/231-4948

OREGON
1220 S.W. Third St.
Portland 97204
503/221-3141

PENNSYLVANIA
Federal Building
Room 168
Harrisburg 17108
717/782-4494

600 Arch St.
Philadelphia 19106
215/597-7440

1000 Liberty Ave.
Pittsburgh 00918
809/753-4209

PUERTO RICO
Federico Degetau Federal Building
Carlos E. Chardon St.
Hato Rey, P.R. 00918
809/753-4343

RHODE ISLAND
John O. Pastori Federal Building
Room 310
Providence 02903
401/528-5251

SOUTH CAROLINA
334 Meeting St.
Charleston 29403
803/724-4328

TENNESSEE
100 N. Main St.
Suite 1312
Memphis 38103
901/521-3956

TEXAS
1100 Commerce St.
Room 6B4
Dallas 75242
214/767-8035

701 San Jacinto St.
4th Floor
Houston 77002
713/226-2375

643 E. Durango Blvd.
San Antonio 78206
512/229-6611

VIRGINIA
200 Granby Mall
Room 220
Norfolk 23510
804/441-3355

WASHINGTON
915 Second Ave.
Seattle 98174
206/442-4365

WEST VIRGINIA
500 Quarrier St.
Charleston 25301
304/343-6181

Appendix H
State Employment
Security Offices

Listed below are the headquarters for Employment Security agencies in the United States and its possessions. These offices can be of tremendous assistance in helping you find work with federal agencies and with state, county, and municipal governments. Also, one shouldn't forget that they can direct you to some excellent jobs in the private sector. For information regarding the Employment Security Office nearest you, call the office in your state listed below.

Alabama
649 Monroe St.
Montgomery, AL 36130
205/832-3626

Alaska
416 Harris St.
P.O. Box 3-7000
Juneau, AK 99811
907/465-2714

Arizona
1300 W. Washington St.
P.O. Box 6123
Phoenix, AZ 85005
602/255-4333

Arkansas
P.O. Box 2981
Little Rock, AR 72203
501/371-2121

California
800 Capitol Mall
Sacramento, CA 95814
916/445-9212

Colorado
251 E. 12th Ave.
Denver, CO 80203
303/866-6233

Connecticut
200 Folly Brook Blvd.
Wethersfield, CT 06109
203/566-4280

Delaware
Stockton Building
Rte. 273 and Chapman Road
Newark, DE 19711
302/368-6810

District of Columbia
500 C St., N.W.
Washington, D.C. 20001
202/724-3932

Florida
201 Caldwell Building
107 E. Madison St.
Tallahassee, FL 32301
904/488-7228

Georgia
290 State Labor Building
254 Washington St., S.W.
Atlanta, GA 30334
404/656-3014

Hawaii
1347 Kapiolani Blvd.
P.O. Box 3680
Honolulu, HI 96814
808/548-6468

Idaho
317 Main St.
P.O. Box 35
Boise, ID 83735
208/334-2731

Illinois
910 S. Michigan Ave.
Chicago, IL 60605
312/793-5700

Indiana
10 N. Senate Ave.
Indianapolis, IN 46204
317/232-7671

Iowa
1000 E. Grand Ave.
Des Moines, IA 50319
515/281-5361

Kansas
401 Topeka Ave.
Topeka, KS 66603
913/296-5076

Kentucky
275 E. Main St.
Frankfort, KY 40621
502/564-5331

Louisiana
1001 N. 23rd St.
P.O. Box 44094
Baton Rouge, LA 70804
504/342-3012

Maine
20 Union St.
P.O. Box 309
Augusta, ME 04330
207/289-2411

Maryland
1100 N. Eutaw St.
Room 616
Baltimore, MD 21201
301/383-5070

Massachusetts
Charles F. Hurley Building
Government Center
Stanford and Cambridge Sts.
Boston, MA 02114
617/727-6600

Michigan
7310 Woodward Ave.
Detroit, MI 48202
313/876-5000

Minnesota
390 N. Robert St.
St. Paul, MN 55101
612/296-3711

Mississippi
1520 W. Capitol St.
P.O. Box 1699
Jackson, MS 39205
601/961-7400

Missouri
421 E. Dunklin St.
P.O. Box 59
Jefferson City, MO 65104
314/751-3215

Montana
Employment Security Building
Lockey and Roberts Sts.
P.O. Box 1728
Helena, MT 59620
406/449-2723

Nebraska
550 S. 16th St.
P.O. Box 94600
State House Station
Lincoln, NE 68509
402/475-8451

Nevada
500 E. 3rd St.
Carson City, NV 89713
702/885-4635

New Hampshire
32 S. Main St.
Concord, NH 03301
603/224-3311

New Jersey
602 Labor and Industry Building
John Fitch Plaza
Trenton, NJ 08625
609/292-7275

New Mexico
TIWA Building
401 Broadway N.E.
P.O. Box 1928
Albuquerque, NM 87103
505/842-3239

New York State Campus
Building 12
Albany, NY 12240
518/457-2612

North Carolina
100 Shore Building
214 W. Jones St.
Raleigh, NC 27611
919/733-7546

North Dakota
1000 E. Divide Ave.
P.O. Box 1537
Bismarck, ND 58502
701/224-2836

Ohio
145 S. Front St.
Columbus, OH 43215
614/466-6078

Oklahoma
200 Will Rogers Memorial
   Office Building
2401 N. Lincoln Blvd.
Oklahoma City, OK 73105
405/521-3794

Oregon
305 Employment Building
875 Union St., N.E.
Salem, OR 97311
503/378-3211

Pennsylvania
1720 Labor and
   Industry Building
7th and Forster Sts.
Harrisburg, PA 17121
717/787-6223

Rhode Island
24 Mason St.
Providence, RI 02903
401/277-3600

South Carolina
1550 Gadsden St.
P.O. Box 995
Columbia, SC 29202
803/758-2686

South Dakota
700 N. Illinois St.
Pierre, SD 57501
605/773-3101

Tennessee
536 Cordell Hull Building
436 6th Ave. N.
Nashville, TN 37219
615/741-2131

Texas
638 TEC Building
101 E. 15th St.
Austin, TX 78778
512/397-4500

Utah
174 Social Hall Ave.
P.O. Box 11249
Salt Lake City, UT 84147
801/533-2400

Vermont
5 Green Mountain Dr.
P.O. Box 488
Montpelier, VT 05602
802/229-0311

Virginia
703 E. Main St.
P.O. Box 1358
Richmond, VA 23211
804/786-3001

Washington
212 Maple Park
Olympia, WA 98504
206/753-5114

West Virginia
610 State Office Building 4
112 California Ave.
Charleston, WV 25305
304/348-2630

Wisconsin
200 General Executive
   Facility I
201 E. Washington Ave.
Madison, WI 53707
608/266-7074

Wyoming
100 Midwest St.
Casper, WY 82602
307/235-3200

American Samoa
Dept. of Manpower Resources
Pago Pago, AS 96799
633-4485

Guam
P.O. Box 23458
Agana, GU 96921
477-9283

Puerto Rico
Metro Center Building
Seventh Floor
G.P.O Box 4452
San Juan, PR 00936
809/767-1515

Virgin Islands
P.O. Box 1090
Charlotte Amalie
St. Thomas, VI 00801
809/774-4504

Appendix I
State Government General
Information Telephone Numbers

Following are the general information telephone numbers for state governments throughout the country. For information regarding jobs with state governments, you should contact someone at one of these numbers. They can either provide you with what you need or direct you to the office nearest you that can.

Alabama
(205) 832-6011

Alaska
(907) 456-2111

Arizona
(602) 255-4900

Arkansas
(501) 371-3000

California
(916) 322-9900

Colorado
(303) 866-5000

Connecticut
(203) 566-2211

Delaware
(302) 736-4000

District of Columbia
(202) 727-1000

Florida
(904) 488-1234

Georgia
(404) 656-2000

Hawaii
(808) 548-2211

Idaho
(208) 334-2411

Illinois
(217)782-2000

Indiana
(317) 232-3140

Iowa
(515) 281-5011

Kansas
(913) 296-0111

Kentucky
(502) 564-2500

Louisiana
(504) 342-6600

Maine
(207) 289-1110

Maryland
(301) 269-6200

Massachusetts
(617) 727-2121

Michigan
(517) 373-1837

Minnesota
(612) 296-6013

Mississippi
(601) 354-7011

Missouri
(314) 751-2151

Montana
(406) 449-2511

Nebraska
(402) 471-2311

Nevada
(702) 885-5000

New Hampshire
(603) 271-1110

New Jersey
(609) 292-6000

New Mexico
(505) 827-4011

New York
(518) 474-2121

North Carolina
(919) 733-1110

North Dakota
(701) 224-2000

Ohio
(614) 466-2000

Oklahoma
(405) 521-2011

Oregon
(503) 378-3131

Pennsylvania
(717) 787-2121

Rhode Island
(401) 277-2000

South Carolina
(803) 758-0221

South Dakota
(605) 773-3011

Tennessee
(615) 741-3011

Texas
(512) 475-2323

Utah
(801) 533-4000

Vermont
(802) 828-1110

Virginia
(804) 786-0000

Washington
(206) 753-5000

West Virginia
(304) 348-3456

Wisconsin
(608) 266-2211

Wyoming
(307) 777-7011

Appendix J
Regional Offices for Agencies of the United States Government

Following are listings of regional offices for most agencies and departments of the federal government. In cases where departments follow the ten standard regions of the federal government, the number appearing to the left of an entry refers to the federal region that office serves. In cases where an agency does not follow the ten standard federal regions, the states served by each office listed are given.

ACTION
Regional Headquarters

1. 441 Stuart Street, 4th Floor
   Boston, MA 02116
   617/223-4501

2. 1161 J.K. Javits Federal Building
   New York, NY 10278
   212/264-4747

3. 108 U.S. Customhouse
   Philadelphia, PA 19106
   215/597-9972

4. 101 Marietta Tower, Room 2524
   Atlanta, GA 30323
   404/221-2859

5. 10 West Jackson Blvd., 3rd Floor
   Chicago, IL 60604
   312/353-5107

6. 301 Old Post Office Building
   Box 370
   Dallas, TX 75221
   214/767-9494

7. The office in Region 7 no longer exists.

8. Columbine Building, Room 201
   Denver, CO 80203
   303/837-2671

9. 211 Main Street, Room 533
   San Francisco, CA 94105
   415/974-0673

10. 1111 Third Avenue
    Seattle, WA 98101
    206/442-1558

CIVIL AERONAUTICS BOARD
Office of Congressional, Community and Consumer Affairs (Regional Directors)

EASTERN REGION: Alabama, Connecticut, Delaware, District of Columbia, Florida, Georgia, Illinois, Indiana, Kentucky, Maine, Maryland, Massachusetts, Michigan, Mississippi, New Hampshire, New Jersey, New York, North Carolina, Ohio, Pennsylvania, Puerto Rico, Rhode Island, South Carolina, Tennessee, Virgin Islands, Virginia, West Virginia, Wisconsin

1825 Connecticut Avenue, NW, Room 504
Washington, DC 20428
202/673-5930

WESTERN REGION: Arkansas, Colorado, Iowa, Kansas, Louisiana, Minnesota, Missouri, Nebraska, New Mexico, North Dakota, Oklahoma, South Dakota, Texas

Parkway Plaza, Box 61646
Dallas/Fort Worth Airport
Irving, TX 75261
214/574-2936

PACIFIC REGION: Arizona, California, Hawaii, Idaho, Montana, Nevada, Oregon, Trust Territory of the Pacific Islands, Utah, Washington, Wyoming

Hillsdale Executive Center, Room 395
San Mateo, CA 94403
415/574-3153

ALASKA FIELD OFFICE: Alaska

Federal Building
701 C Street, Box 27
Anchorage, AK 99513
907/271-5146

COMMERCE DEPARTMENT
Bureau of the Census (Regional Directors)

ATLANTA REGION: Alabama, Florida, Georgia, Tennessee

1365 Peachtree Street, NE, Room 625
Atlanta, GA 30309
404/881-2271

BOSTON REGION: Connecticut, Maine, Massachusetts, New Hampshire, New York (northern), Rhode Island, Vermont

441 Stuart Street, 10th Floor
Boston, MA 02116
617/223-2327

CHARLOTTE REGION: North Carolina, South Carolina, Virginia, Washington, D.C.

230 South Tryon Street, Room 800
Charlotte, NC 28202
704/371-6142

CHICAGO REGION: Illinois, Indiana

55 East Jackson Boulevard, Room 1304
Chicago, IL 60604
312/353-6251

DALLAS REGION: Arkansas, Louisiana, Mississippi, New Mexico, Texas

111 Commerce Street, Room 3C-54
Dallas, TX 75242
214/767-0625

DENVER REGION: Arizona, Colorado, Kansas, Montana, Nebraska, North Dakota, Oklahoma, South Dakota, Utah, Wyoming

7655 West Mississippi Avenue, Box 26750
Denver, CO 80226
214/234-3924

DETROIT REGION: Michigan, Ohio

565 Federal Building, Courthouse
Detroit, MI 48226
313/226-7742

KANSAS CITY REGION: Iowa, Minnesota, Missouri, Wisconsin

I Gateway Center
Kansas City, KS 66101
913/236-3278

LOS ANGELES REGION: California (southern)

11777 San Vicente Boulevard, Room 810
Los Angeles, CA 90049
213/209-6616

NEW YORK REGION: New Jersey (northern), New York (southern and New York City)

37-130 J.K. Javits Federal Building
New York, NY 10278
212/264-3860

PHILADELPHIA REGION: Delaware, Maryland, New Jersey (southern), Pennsylvania, West Virginia

9244 W.J. Green, Jr. Federal Building
Philadelphia, PA 19106
215/597-4920

SEATTLE REGION: California (northern), Idaho, Nevada, Oregon, Washington

Lake Union Building
Seattle, WA 98109
206/442-7828

Economic Development Administration
(Regional Directors)

ATLANTA REGION: Alabama, Florida, Georgia,
Kentucky, Michigan, North Carolina, South
Carolina, Tennessee

1365 Peachtree Street, NE, Room 700
Atlanta, GA 30309
404/881-7401

AUSTIN REGION: Arkansas, Louisiana, New
Mexico, Oklahoma, Texas

American Bank Tower Building, Room 600
Austin, TX 78701
512/482-5461

CHICAGO REGION: Illinois, Indiana,
Michigan, Minnesota, Ohio, Wisconsin

Insurance Exchange Building, Room A1630
Chicago, IL 60604
312/353-7706

DENVER REGION: Colorado, Iowa, Kansas,
Missouri, Montana, Nebraska, North Dakota,
South Dakota, Utah, Wyoming
Tremont Center
Denver, CO 80206
303/837-4714

PHILADELPHIA REGION: Connecticut,
Delaware, District of Columbia, Maine,
Maryland, Massachusetts, New Hampshire,
New Jersey, New York, Pennsylvania, Puerto
Rico, Rhode Island, Vermont, Virginia, Virgin
Islands, West Virginia

600 Federal Reserve Bank Building
105 North 7th Street
Philadelphia, PA 19106
215/597-4603

SEATTLE REGION: Alaska, American Samoa,
Arizona, California, Guam, Hawaii, Idaho,
Nevada, Oregon, Washington

Lake Union Building, Room 500
Seattle, WA 98109
206/442-0596

Minority Business Development Agency
(Regional Directors)

Alabama, Florida, Georgia, Kentucky,
Mississippi, North Carolina, South Carolina,
Tennessee

1371 Peachtree Street, NE, Room 505
Atlanta, GA 30309
404/881-3094

Illinois, Indiana, Iowa, Kansas, Minnesota,
Missouri, Nebraska, Ohio, Wisconsin

55 East Monroe Street, Room 1440
Chicago, IL 60603
312/353-0182

Arkansas, Colorado, Louisiana, Montana,
New Mexico, North Dakota, Oklahoma, South
Dakota, Texas, Utah, Wyoming

7819 East Cabell Federal Building
Dallas, TX 75242
214/767-8001

Connecticut, Maine, Massachusetts, New
Hampshire, New Jersey, New York, Puerto Rico,
Rhode Island, Vermont, Virgin Islands

37-118 J.K. Javits Federal Building
New York, NY 10278
212/264-3262

Alaska, Arizona, California, Hawaii, Idaho,
Nevada, Oregon, Washington

1504 P. Burton Federal Building
U.S. Courthouse, Box 36114
San Francisco, CA 94102
415/556-7234

Delaware, District of Columbia, Maryland,
Pennsylvania, Virginia, West Virginia

1730 K Street, NW, Room 420
Washington, DC 20006
202/634-7897

National Oceanic and Atmospheric Administration, National Marine Fisheries Service (Regional Directors)

ALASKA REGION: Alaska
Federal Building
709 9th Street
Route 543
Juneau, AK 99801
907/586-7221

NORTHEAST REGION: Connecticut, Delaware, District of Columbia, Illinois, Indiana, Maine, Maryland, Massachusetts, Michigan, Minnesota, New Hampshire, New Jersey, New York, Ohio, Pennsylvania, Rhode Island, Vermont, Virginia, West Virginia, Wisconsin

Federal Building
Gloucester, MA 01930
617/281-3600

NORTHWEST REGION: Colorado, Idaho, Montana, North Dakota, Oregon, South Dakota, Utah, Washington, Wyoming

7600 Sand Point Way NE, C15700
Seattle, WA 98115
206/527-6150

SOUTHEAST REGION: Alabama, Arkansas, Florida, Georgia, Iowa, Kansas, Kentucky, Louisiana, Mississippi, Missouri, Nebraska, New Mexico, North Carolina, Oklahoma, Puerto Rico, South Carolina, Tennessee, Texas, Virgin Islands

9450 Koger Boulevard
St. Petersburg, FL 33702
813/893-3141

SOUTHWEST REGION: American Samoa, Arizona, California, Guam, Hawaii, Nevada, Trust Territory of the Pacific Islands

300 South Ferry Street
Terminal Island, CA 90731
213/548-2575

National Oceanic and Atmospheric Administration, National Weather Service (Regional Directors)

ALASKA REGION: Alaska

Federal Building
701 C Street, Box 23
Anchorage, AK 99513
907/271-5136

CENTRAL REGION: Colorado, Illinois, Indiana, Iowa, Kansas, Kentucky, Michigan, Minnesota, Missouri, Nebraska, North Dakota, South Dakota, Wisconsin, Wyoming

1736 Federal Office Building
601 East 12th Street
Kansas City, MO 64106
816/374-5463

EASTERN REGION: Connecticut, Delaware, District of Columbia, Maine, Maryland, Massachusetts, New Jersey, New York, North Carolina, Ohio, Pennsylvania, Rhode Island, South Carolina, Vermont, Virginia, West Virginia

585 Stewart Avenue
Garden City, NY 11530
516/228-5400

PACIFIC REGION: American Samoa, Guam, Hawaii, Trust Territory of the Pacific Islands, Wake Island

4110 Prince Kuhio Federal Building, Box 50027
Honolulu, HI 96850
808/546-5680

SOUTHERN REGION: Alabama, Alaska, Florida, Georgia, Louisiana, Mississippi, New Mexico, Oklahoma, Puerto Rico, Tennessee, Texas, Virgin Islands

Federal Building, Box 11188
Salt Lake City, UT 84147
801/524-5122

COMMISSION ON CIVIL RIGHTS
Regional Directors

1. Connecticut, Maine, Massachusetts, New Hampshire, Rhode Island, Vermont

55 Summer Street, 8th Floor
Boston, MA 02110
617/223-4671

2. New Jersey, New York

1639 J.K. Javits Federal Building
New York, NY 10278
212/264-0543

3. Delaware, District of Columbia, Maryland, Pennsylvania, Virginia, West Virginia

2120 L Street, NW, Room 510
Washington, DC 20037
202/254-6670

4. Alabama, Florida, Georgia, Kentucky, Mississippi, North Carolina, South Carolina, Tennessee

Citizens Trust Bank Building, Room 362
Atlanta, GA 30303

5. Illinois, Indiana, Michigan, Minnesota, Ohio, Wisconsin

3280 J.C. Kluczynski Federal Building
Chicago, IL 50504
312/353-7479

6. Arkansas, Louisiana, New Mexico, Oklahoma, Texas

Heritage Plaza, Ist Floor
San Antonio, TX 78204
512/229-5570

7. Iowa, Kansas, Missouri

3103 Old Federal Office Building
911 Walnut Street
Kansas City, MO 64106
816/374-2454

8. Colorado, Montana, North Dakota, South Dakota, Utah, Wyoming

1020 15th Street, Room 2235
Denver, CO 80202
303/837-2211

9. Arizona, California, Hawaii, Nevada

3660 Wilshire Boulevard, Room 810
Los Angeles, CA 90010
213/688-3437

10. Alaska, Idaho, Oregon, Washington

2852 H.M. Jackson Federal Building
Seattle, WA 98174
206/442-1246

COMMODITY FUTURES TRADING COMMISSION
Regional Directors

CENTRAL REGION: Illinois, Indiana, Michigan, Minnesota, North Dakota, Ohio, South Dakota, Wisconsin

Sears Tower, Room 4600
Chicago, IL 60606
312/353-6642

EASTERN REGION: Alabama, Connecticut, Delaware, District of Columbia, Florida, Georgia, Kentucky, Maine, Maryland, Massachusetts, Mississippi, New Hampshire, New Jersey, New York, North Carolina, Pennsylvania, Puerto Rico, Rhode Island, South Carolina, Tennessee, Vermont, Virgin Islands, West Virginia

1 World Trade Center, Room 4747
New York, NY 10048
212/466-2071

SOUTHWESTERN REGION: Arkansas, Colorado, Iowa, Kansas, Louisiana, Missouri, Nevada, New Mexico, Oklahoma, Texas

4901 Main Street, Room 400
Kansas City, MO 64112
816/374-2994

WESTERN REGION: Alaska, Arizona, California, Hawaii, Idaho, Montana, Nevada, Oregon, Utah, Washington, Wyoming

10850 Wilshire Boulevard, Room 510
Los Angeles, CA 90024
213/209-6783

CONSUMER PRODUCT SAFETY COMMISSION
Regional Directors

MIDWESTERN REGION: Illinois, Indiana, Iowa, Michigan, Minnesota, Nebraska, North Dakota, Ohio, South Dakota, Wisconsin

2945 J.C. Klyczynski Federal Building
Chicago, IL 60604
312/353-8260

NORTHEASTERN REGION: Connecticut, District of Columbia, Delaware, Maine, Maryland, Massachusetts, New Hampshire, New Jersey, New York, Pennsylvania, Puerto Rico, Rhode Island, Vermont, Virgin Islands

6 World Trade Center, 6th Floor
New York, NY 10048
212/264-1125

SOUTHEASTERN REGION: Alabama, Florida, Georgia, Kentucky, Mississippi, North Carolina, South Carolina, Tennessee, Virginia, West Virginia

800 West Peachtree Street, NW, Room 210
Atlanta, GA 30308
404/881-2231

SOUTHWESTERN REGION: Arkansas, Colorado, Kansas, Louisiana, Missouri, New Mexico, Oklahoma, Texas

1C10 East Cabell Federal Building
Dallas, TX 75242
214/767-0841

WESTERN REGION: Alaska, Arizona, California, Hawaii, Idaho, Montana, Nevada, Oregon, Utah, Washington, Wyoming

555 Battery Street, Room 416
San Francisco, CA 94111
415/556-1816

EDUCATION DEPARTMENT
Secretarial Representatives
(Refer to Appendix F for boundaries)

1. 526 J.W. McCormack Post Office and U.S. Courthouse
   Boston, MA 02109
   617/223-7500

2. J.K. Javits Federal Building
   New York, NY 10278
   212/264-7005

3. Gateway Building, Room 16350
   Philadelphia, PA 19104
   215/596-1001

4. 101 Marietta Tower, Room 2221
   Atlanta, GA 30323
   404/221-2502

5. 300 South Wacker Drive, 16th Floor
   Chicago, IL 60606
   312/353-5215

6. 1200 Main Tower Building, Room 1460
   Dallas, TX 75202
   214/767-3626

7. 11 Oak Building, 9th Floor
   Kansas City, MO 64106
   816/374-2276

8. 380 Federal Office Building
   Denver, CO 80294
   303/837-3544

9. 50 United Nations Plaza, Room 205
   San Francisco, CA 94102
   415/556-4920

10. 3rd Broad Building, 1st Floor
    2901 3rd Avenue
    Seattle, WA, 98121
    206/399-0460

EDUCATION DEPARTMENT, REHABILITATION SERVICES ADMINISTRATION
Regional Commissioners
(Refer to Appendix F for boundaries)

1. E-400 J.F. Kennedy Federal Building
   Boston, MA 02203
   617/223-6820

2. 4106 J.K. Javits Federal Building
    New York, NY 10278
    212/264-4016

3. Gateway Building, Room 821
    Philadelphia, PA 19101
    215/596-0317

4. 101 Marietta Tower, Room 821
    Atlanta, GA 30323
    404/221-2352

5. 300 South Wacker Drive, 15th Floor
    Chicago, IL 60606
    312/886-5372

6. 1200 Main Tower Building, 1400
    Dallas, TX 75202
    214/767-2961

7. Il Oak Building, 10th Floor West
    Kansas City, MO 64106
    816/374-2381

8. 7415 Federal Building
    Denver, CO 80202
    303/837-2135

9. 50 United Nations Plaza, Room 480
    San Francisco, CA 94102
    415/556-7333

10. 3rd & Broad Building, Room 120
    2901 3rd Avenue
    Seattle, WA 98121
    206/442-5331

ENERGY DEPARTMENT, Operations Offices
Operations Managers

ALBUQUERQUE OPERATIONS OFFICE: Arizona, Arkansas, Kansas, Louisiana, Missouri, New Mexico, Oklahoma, Texas

Box 5400
Albuquerque, NM 87115
504/844-6917

CHICAGO OPERATIONS OFFICE: Connecticut, Delaware, Illinois, Indiana, Iowa, Maine, Massachusetts, Michigan, Minnesota, New Hampshire, New Jersey, New York, Ohio, Pennsylvania, Rhode Island, Virginia, Vermont, Wisconsin

9800 South Cass Avenue
Argonne, IL 60439
312/972-2000

IDAHO OPERATIONS OFFICE: Colorado, Idaho, Montana, Nebraska, North Dakota, South Dakota, Utah, Washington

550 2nd Street
Idaho Falls, ID 83401
208/526-0lll

NEVADA OPERATIONS OFFICE: Nevada

Box 14100
Las Vegas, NV 89114
702/734-3211

OAK RIDGE OPERATIONS OFFICE: Arkansas, Oregon, Washington

825 Jadwin Avenue, Box 550
Richland, WA 99532
509/376-7395

SAN FRANCISCO OPERATIONS OFFICE: American Samoa, California, Guam, Hawaii, Trust Territory of the Pacific Islands

1333 Broadway
Oakland, CA 94612
415/273-7111

SAVANNAH RIVER OPERATIONS OFFICE: Alabama, Florida, Georgia, Mississippi, Puerto Rico, South Carolina, Virgin Islands

Box A
Aiken, SC 29801
803/725-2277

Federal Energy Regulatory Commission (Regional Engineers)

ATLANTA REGION: Alabama, Florida, Georgia, Kentucky, Mississippi (eastern), North Carolina,

South Carolina, Tennessee, Virginia (southern)

730 Peachtree Street, NE, Room 500
Atlanta, GA 30308
404/881-4134

CHICAGO REGION: Illinois, Indiana, Iowa, Michigan, Minnesota, Missouri (eastern), Montana (eastern), Nebraska (eastern), North Dakota, Ohio (western), South Dakota, Wisconsin

3130 J.C. Kluczynski Federal Building
Chicago, IL 60604
312/353-6173

FORT WORTH REGION: Arkansas, Colorado, Kansas, Louisiana, Mississippi (western), Missouri (eastern), Nebraska (western), New Mexico, Oklahoma, Texas, Wyoming

F.G. Lanham Federal Building
Fort Worth, TX 76102
817/334-2631

NEW YORK REGION: Connecticut, Delaware, Maine, Maryland, Massachusetts, New Hampshire, New Jersey, New York, Ohio (eastern), Pennsylvania, Rhode Island, Vermont, Virginia (northern), Washington, D.C., West Virginia

2207 J.K. Javits Federal Building
New York, NY 10278
212/264-3687

SAN FRANCISCO REGION: Arizona, California, Idaho, Montana (western), Nevada, Oregon, Utah, Washington

333 Market Street, 6th Floor
San Francisco, CA 94105
415/974-7150

Power Administrations
(Administrators)

ALASKA POWER ADMINISTRATION: Alaska

Box 50
Juneau, AK 99802
907/586-7405

BONNEVILLE POWER ADMINISTRATION: California (northern), Idaho, Montana (western), Nevada (northern), Oregon, Utah (northern), Washington, Wyoming (northern)

Box 3621
Portland, OR 97208
503/230-5101

SOUTHEASTERN POWER ADMINISTRATION: Alabama, Florida, Georgia, Kentucky, Mississippi, North Carolina, South Carolina, Tennessee, Virginia, West Virginia

Samuel Elbert Building
Elbert, GA 30635
404/283-3261

SOUTHWESTERN POWER ADMINISTRATION: Arkansas, Kansas, Louisiana, Missouri, Oklahoma, Texas (eastern)

Box 1619
Tulsa, OK 74101
918/496-9329

WESTERN POWER ADMINISTRATION: Arizona, California (southern), Colorado, Iowa (eastern), Minnesota (southern), Montana (eastern), Nebraska, Nevada (western), New Mexico, North Dakota, South Dakota, Texas (western), Utah, Wyoming

Box 3402
Golden, CO 80401
303/231-1511

ENVIRONMENTAL PROTECTION AGENCY
Regional Administrators
(Refer to Appendix F for boundaries)

1. 2203 J.F. Kennedy Federal Building
    Boston, MA 02203
    617/223-7210

2. 900 J.K. Javits Federal Building
    New York, NY 10278
    212/264-2525

3. Furtis Building
    Philadelphia, PA 19106
    215/597-9815

4. 345 Courtland Street, NE
   Atlanta, GA 30365
   404/881-4727

5. J.C. Kluczynski Federal Building
   Chicago, IL 60604
   312/353-2000

6. 1st International Building
   Dallas, TX 60604
   214/767-2600

7. 11 Oak Building, 16th Floor
   Kansas City, MO 64106
   816/374-5493

8. 1860 Lincoln Street
   Denver, CO 80295
   303/837-3895

9. 215 Fremont Street
   San Francisco, CA 94105
   415/975-8153

10. 1200 6th Avenue
    Seattle, WA 98101
    206/442-1200

EQUAL EMPLOYMENT OPPORTUNITY COMMISSION
District Directors

ATLANTA DISTRICT: Georgia, South Carolina

Citizens Trust Building, 10th Floor
Atlanta, GA 30335
404/221-6091

BALTIMORE DISTRICT: District of Columbia, Maryland, Virginia

109 Market Place, Room 4000
Baltimore, MD 21202
301/962-3932

BIRMINGHAM DISTRICT: Alabama, Mississippi

2121 8th Avenue, North 8th
Birmingham, AL 35203
205/254-1166

CHARLOTTE DISTRICT: North Carolina

1301 East Morehead Street
Charlotte, NC 28204
704/371-6437

CHICAGO DISTRICT: Illinois (northern)

930 Federal Building
Chicago, IL 60605
312/353-8550

CLEVELAND DISTRICT: Ohio

75 Euclid Avenue
Cleveland, OH 44114
216/522-7425

DALLAS DISTRICT: Oklahoma, Texas (northern)

1900 Pacific Building, 13th Floor
Dallas, TX 75201
214/767-4589

DENVER DISTRICT: Colorado, Montana, Nebraska, North Dakota, South Dakota, Wyoming

1531 Stout Street, 6th Floor
Denver, CO 80202
303/837-2771

DETROIT DISTRICT: Michigan

660 Woodward Avenue, Room 600
Detroit, MI 48226
313/226-7639

HOUSTON DISTRICT: Texas (southern)

405 Main Street, 6th Floor
Houston, TX 77002
713/226-2601

INDIANAPOLIS DISTRICT: Indiana

456 Federal Building, U.S. Courthouse
Indianapolis, IN 46204
317/269-7210

LOS ANGELES DISTRICT: California (southern), Nevada

3255 Wilshire Boulevard, 9th Floor
Los Angeles, CA 90010
213/688-3413

MEMPHIS DISTRICT: Kentucky, Tennessee

Mid-Memphis Tower, Room 502
Memphis, TN 38104
901/521-2540

MIAMI DISTRICT: Panama Canal, Florida

Dupont Plaza Center, Room 414
Miami, FL 33131
305/350-5381

MILWAUKEE DISTRICT: Iowa, Minnesota, Wisconsin

800 H.S. Reuss Federal Building
Milwaukee, WI 53203
414/291-1111

NEW ORLEANS DISTRICT: Arkansas, Louisiana

503 F.E. Hebert Federal Building
New Orleans, LA 70130
504/589-3842

NEW YORK DISTRICT: Connecticut, Maine, Massachusetts, New Hampshire, New York, Puerto Rico, Rhode Island, Vermont, Virgin Islands

90 Church Street, Room 1501
New York, NY 10007
212/264-3332

PHILADELPHIA DISTRICT: Delaware, New Jersey, Pennsylvania, West Virginia

127 North 4th Street, Room 300
Philadelphia, PA 19106
215/597-7784

PHOENIX DISTRICT: Arizona, New Mexico, Utah

135 North 2nd Street, 4th Floor
Phoenix, AZ 85003
602/261-3882

ST. LOUIS DISTRICT: Illinois (southern), Kansas, Missouri, Nebraska

625 North Euclid
St Louis, MO 63108
314/279-6585

SAN FRANCISCO DISTRICT: American Samoa, California (northern), Guam, Hawaii, North Mariana Islands, Wake Islands

10 United Nations Plaza, 4th Floor
San Francisco, CA 94102
415/556-0260

SEATTLE DISTRICT: Alaska, Idaho, Oregon, Washington

Dexter Horton Building, 7th Floor
Seattle, WA 98104
206/442-0968

FARM CREDIT ADMINISTRATION
Office of Examination
(Regional Directors)

CENTRAL REGION: Arkansas, Colorado, Illinois, Indiana, Kansas, Kentucky, Missouri, New Mexico, Ohio, Oklahoma, Tennessee, Texas

12101 Woodcrest Exec Drive, Room 315
St Louis, MO 63141
314/263-7101

EASTERN REGION: Alabama, Connecticut, Delaware, District of Columbia, Florida, Georgia, Louisiana, Maine, Maryland, Massachusetts, Mississippi, New Hampshire, New Jersey, New York, North Carolina, Pennsylvania, Puerto Rico, Rhode Island, South Carolina, Vermont, Virginia, Virgin Islands, West Virginia

3710 Landmark Drive, Room 208
Columbia, SC 29204
803/765-5603

WESTERN REGION: Alaska, Arizona, California, Hawaii, Idaho, Iowa, Michigan, Minnesota, Montana, Nebraska, Nevada, North Dakota, Oregon, South Dakota, Utah, Washington, Wisconsin, Wyoming

2850 Metro Drive, Room 729
Bloomington, MN 55420
612/854-3703

Sub-Office

Washington Trust Financial Center, Room 1107
Spokane, WA 99204
509/456-6840

FEDERAL COMMUNICATIONS COMMISSION
Regional Directors

ATLANTA REGION: Alabama, Florida, Georgia, North Carolina, Puerto Rico, South Carolina, Tennessee, Virginia, Virgin Islands

101 Marietta Tower, Room 2111
Atlanta, GA 30303
(Mailing: Box 1775, ZIP 30301)
404/221-6500

BOSTON REGION: Connecticut, Delaware, District of Columbia, Maine, Maryland, Massachusetts, New Hampshire, New Jersey, New York, Pennsylvania, Rhode Island, Vermont, West Virginia

1500 U.S. Customhouse
Boston, MA 02109
617/223-7226

CHICAGO REGION: Illinois, Indiana, Kentucky, Michigan, Minnesota, Ohio, Wisconsin

1550 Northwest Highway, Room 306
Park Ridge, IL 60068
312/353-0368

KANSAS CITY REGION: Arkansas, Colorado, Iowa, Kansas, Louisiana, Mississippi, Missouri, Nebraska, New Mexico, North Dakota, Oklahoma, South Dakota, Texas, Wyoming

Brywood Office Tower, Room 320
Kansas City, MO 64133
816/926-5179

SAN FRANCISCO REGION: Arizona, California, Nevada, Utah

211 Main Street, Room 537
San Francisco, CA 94105
415/974-0702

SEATTLE REGION: Alaska, American Samoa, Guam, Hawaii, Idaho, Midway Islands, Montana, Oregon, Swains Island, Trust Territory of the Pacific Islands, Wake Island, Washington

3244 HM Jackson Federal Building
Seattle, WA 98174
206/442-5544

FEDERAL DEPOSIT INSURANCE CORPORATION
Regional Directors

Alabama, Florida, Georgia, North Carolina, South Carolina

233 Peachtree Street, NE, Room 2400
Atlanta, GA 30043
404/221-6631

Connecticut, Maine, Massachusetts, New Hampshire, Rhode Island, Vermont

60 State Street, 17th Floor
Boston, MA 02109
617/223-6420

Illinois, Indiana

Sears Tower, Room 6116
Chicago, IL 60606
312/353-2600

Kentucky, Ohio, West Virginia

I Nationwide Plaza, Room 2600
Columbus, OH 43215
614/469-7301

Colorado, New Mexico, Oklahoma, Texas

350 North St. Paul Street, Room 2000
Dallas, TX 75201
214/767-5501

Kansas, Missouri

2345 Grand Avenue, Room 1500
Kansas City, MO 64108
816/374-2851

Minnesota, Wisconsin

1 South Pickney Street, Room 813
Madison, WI 53703
608/264-5226

Arkansas, Louisiana, Mississippi, Tennessee

1 Commerce Square, Room 1800
Memphis, TN 53703
901/521-3872

Minnesota, Montana, North Dakota, South
Dakota, Wyoming

730 2nd Avenue South, Room 266
Minneapolis, MN 55402
612/725-6241

New Jersey, New York, Puerto Rico, Virgin
Islands

345 Park Avenue, 21st Floor
New York, NY 10154
212/826-4762

Iowa, Nebraska

1700 Farnam Street, Room 1200
Omaha, NE 68102
402/221-3311

Delaware, District of Columbia, Maryland,
Pennsylvania, Virginia

1900 Market Street, Room 616
Philadelphia, PA 19103
215/597-2295

Alaska, Arizona, California, Guam, Hawaii,
Idaho, Nevada, Oregon, Utah, Washington

44 Montgomery Street, Room 3600
San Francisco, CA 94104
415/556-2736

FEDERAL EMERGENCY MANAGEMENT AGENCY
Regional Directors
(Refer to Appendix F for boundaries)

1. 442 J.W. McCormack Post Office,
   U.S. Courthouse
   Boston, MA 02109
   617/223-4741

2. 1349 J.K. Javits Federal Building
   New York, NY 10278
   212/264-8980

3. Curtis Building, 7th Floor
   Philadelphia, PA 19106
   215/597-9416

4. 1375 Peachtree Street, NE, Room 664
   Atlanta, GA 30309
   404/881-2400

5. 300 South Wacker Drive, 24th Floor
   Chicago, IL 60606
   312/886-3671

6. 206 Federal Reg. Center
   Denton, TX 76201
   817/387-5811

7. 300 Old Federal Office Building
   911 Walnut Street
   Kansas City, MO 64106
   816/374-5912

8. Federal Reg. Center, Building 710
   Denver, CO 80225
   303/234-2553

9. Presidio, Building 105
   San Francisco, CA 94129
   415/556-8795

10. Federal Reg. Center
    Bothell, WA 98011
    206/481-8800

FEDERAL HOME LOAN BANK BOARD
District Directors

Connecticut, Maine, Massachusetts, New Hampshire, Rhode Island, Vermont

1 Federal Street, 30th Floor
Boston, MA 02110
617/223-3206

New Jersey, New York, Puerto Rico, Virgin Islands

1 World Trade Center, Room 8830
New York, NY 10048
212/466-4669

Delaware, Pennsylvania, West Virginia

Gateway Center, Room 300
Pittsburgh, PA 15222
412/644-2666

Alabama, District of Columbia, Florida, Georgia, Maryland, North Carolina, South Carolina, Virginia

260 Peachtree Street, NW, 10th Floor
Atlanta, GA 30303
404/525-5778

Kentucky, Ohio, Tennessee

DuBois Tower, Room 2700
Cincinnati, OH 45202
513/684-2855

Indiana, Michigan

Indiana Tower, Room 1290
Indianapolis, IN 45204
317/269-6559

Illinois, Wisconsin

111 East Wacker Drive, Room 700
Chicago, IL 60601
312/353-8045

Iowa, Minnesota, Missouri, North Dakota, South Dakota

907 Walnut Street, Room 501
Des Moines, IA 50309
515/284-4310

Arkansas, Louisiana, Mississippi, New Mexico, Texas

Tower Building, Room 350
Little Rock, AR 72201
501/378-5374

Colorado, Kansas, Nebraska, Oklahoma

3 Townsite Plaza, Box 828
Topeka, KS 66601
913/295-2615

Arizona, California, Nevada

600 California Street, Room 310
San Francisco, CA 94108
415/556-1910

Alaska, Guam, Hawaii, Idaho, Montana, Oregon, Utah, Washington, Wyoming

600 Stewart Street, Room 610
Seattle, WA 98101
206/442-7584

FEDERAL INSPECTOR FOR THE ALASKA NATURAL GAS TRANSPORTATION SYSTEM
Field Director

ALASKA FIELD OFFICE

605 West 4th Avenue, Room 107
Anchorage, AK 99501
907/271-3668

FEDERAL LABOR RELATIONS AUTHORITY
Regional Directors

Connecticut, Maine, Massachusetts, New Hampshire, New York (exc. metro New York City area), Pennsylvania, Rhode Island, Vermont

441 Stuart Street, 9th Floor
Boston, MA 01226
617/223-0920

New Jersey, New York (metro New York City area only), Puerto Rico, Virgin Islands

24-102 J.K. Javits Federal Building
New York, NY 10278
212/264-4934

Delaware, District of Columbia, Maryland, Virginia, West Virginia

1111 18th Street, NW, Room 700
Washington, DC 10036
202/653-8507

Alabama, Florida, Georgia, Kentucky, Mississippi, North Carolina, South Carolina, Tennessee

1776 Peachtree Street, NW, Room 501N
Atlanta, GA 30309
404/881-2324

Illinois, Indiana, Michigan, Minnesota, Ohio, Wisconsin

175 West Jackson Boulevard, Room 1359-A
Chicago, IL 60604
312/353-6306

Arkansas, Louisiana, New Mexico, Oklahoma, Texas

450 Old Post Office Building, Box 2640
Dallas, TX 75221
214/767-4996

Colorado, Iowa, Kansas, Missouri, Montana, Nebraska, North Dakota, South Dakota, Utah, Wyoming

Rio Grande Building, Room 301
Denver, CO 80202
303/837-5224

American Samoa, Arizona, California (southern), Guam, Hawaii

World Trade Center, 10th Floor
Los Angeles, CA 90071
213/688-3805

Alaska, California (northern), Idaho, Nevada, Oregon, Washington

530 Bush Street, Room 542
San Francisco, CA 94108
415/556-8105

FEDERAL MARITIME COMMISSION
Officer Directors

ATLANTIC OFFICE: Connecticut, Maine, Massachusetts, New Hampshire, New Jersey, New York, Rhode Island, Vermont

6 World Trade Center, Room 614
New York, NY 10048
212/264-1430

GREAT LAKES OFFICE: Illinois, Indiana, Iowa, Kentucky, Michigan, Minnesota, Nebraska, North Dakota, Ohio, South Dakota, Wisconsin

Investigator-in-Charge
U.S. Customhouse
Chicago, IL 60607
312/353-0282

GULF OFFICE: Alabama, Arkansas, Florida, Georgia, Kansas, Louisiana, Mississippi, Missouri, North Carolina, Oklahoma, South Carolina, Tennessee, Texas

1035 F.E. Hebert Federal Building, Box 30550
New Orleans, LA 70190
504/589-6662

MID-ATLANTIC OFFICE: Delaware, District of Columbia, Maryland, Pennsylvania, Virginia, West Virginia

1100 L Street, NW, Room 11213
Washington, DC 20573
202/523-5860

PACIFIC OFFICE: Alaska, Arizona, California, Colorado, Hawaii, Idaho, Montana, Nevada, New Mexico, Oregon, Utah, Washington, Wyoming

525 Market Street, Room 2520
San Francisco, CA 94105
415/974-9756

PUERTO RICO OFFICE: Puerto Rico, Virgin Islands

726 Federal Building, Courthouse
Hato Rey, PR 00918
809/753-4198

FEDERAL MEDIATION AND CONCILIATION SERVICE
Regional Directors

CENTRAL REGION: Illinois (northern), Indiana, Michigan, Minnesota, North Dakota, Ohio (northern), South Dakota, Wisconsin

Insurance Exchange Building, Room 1659
Chicago, IL 60604
312/353-7350

EASTERN REGION: Connecticut, Delaware, District of Columbia, Maine, Massachusetts, New Hampshire, New Jersey, New York, Pennsylvania, Rhode Island, Vermont

2937 J.K. Javits Federal Building
New York, NY 10278
212/264-1000

SOUTHERN REGION: Alabama, Arkansas, Florida, Georgia, Illinois (southern), Kentucky, Louisiana, Maryland, Missouri (southeastern), Mississippi, North Carolina, Ohio (southern), Oklahoma, South Carolina, Tennessee, Texas (exc. western tip), Virginia, West Virginia

1422 West Peachtree Street, NW, Room 400
Atlanta, GA 30309
404/881-2473

WESTERN REGION: Alaska, Arizona, California, Colorado, Hawaii, Idaho, Iowa, Kansas, Missouri (northwestern), Montana, Nebraska, Nevada, New Mexico, Oregon, Texas (western tip), Virginia, West Virginia

525 Market Street, 29th Floor
San Francisco, CA 94105
415/974-9850

FEDERAL MINE SAFETY AND HEALTH REVIEW COMMISSION
(Administrative Law Judges)

Note: The Federal Mine Safety and Health Review Commission has only one regional office, in Denver, Colorado. Questions regarding other parts of the country should be directed to the Commission's Office of Public Information, 1730 K Street, NW, Washington, DC 20006, 202/653-5633.

Tremont Veterans Building, Room 400
Denver, CO 80204
303/837-3993

FEDERAL RESERVE SYSTEM
Federal Reserve Districts
(District Presidents)

Alabama, Florida, Georgia, Louisiana (southern), Mississippi (southern), Tennessee (eastern)

104 Marietta Street, NW, Box 1731
Atlanta, GA 30301
404/586-8500

Connecticut, Maine, Massachusetts, New Hampshire, Rhode Island, Vermont

600 Atlantic Avenue
Boston, MA 02106
617/973-3000

Illinois (northern), Indiana (northern), Iowa, Michigan, Wisconsin (southern)

J.H. Kluczynski Federal Building, Box 834
Chicago, IL 60609
312/322-5322

Kentucky (eastern), Ohio, Pennsylvania (western)

1455 East 6th Street, Box 6387
Cleveland, OH 44101
216/579-2000

Louisiana (northern), New Mexico (southern), Oklahoma (southeastern corner), Texas

400 South Akard Street, Station K
Dallas, TX 75222
214/651-6111

Colorado, Kansas, Missouri (western),
Nebraska, New Mexico (northern), Oklahoma
(exc. southeast corner), Wyoming

925 Grand Avenue
Kansas City, MO 64198
816/881-2000

Minnesota, Montana, North Dakota, South
Dakota, Wisconsin (northern)

250 Marquette Avenue
Minneapolis, MN 55480
612/340-2345

New Jersey (northern), New York

33 Liberty Street
New York, NY 10045
212/791-5000

Delaware, New Jersey (southern),
Pennsylvania (eastern)

Federal Reserve Bank Building, 3rd Floor
100 North 6th Street, Box 66
Philadelphia, PA 19105
215/574-6000

District of Columbia, Maryland, North
Carolina, South Carolina, Virginia, West
Virginia

701 East Byrd Street, Box 27622
Richmond, VA 23219
804/643-1250

Arkansas, Illinois (southern), Indiana
(southern), Kentucky (western), Mississippi
(northern), Missouri (eastern), Tennessee
(western)

411 Locust Street, Box 442
St Louis, MO 63166
314/444-8444

Arkansas, Arizona, California, Hawaii, Idaho,
Nevada, Oregon, Utah, Washington

101 Market Street
San Francisco, CA 94105
415/974-2000

FEDERAL TRADE COMMISSION
Regional Directors

Alabama, Florida, Georgia, North Carolina,
South Carolina, Tennessee, Virginia (exc.
metro Washington, DC area)

1718 Peachtree Street, NW, Room 1000
Atlanta, GA 30367
404/881-4836

Washington, DC area inquiries:

Public Reference Branch,
6th Street and Pennsylvania Avenue NW,
Washington, DC 20580
202/523-3598

Connecticut, Maine, Massachusetts, New
Hampshire, Rhode Island, Vermont

55 East Monroe Street, Room 1437
Chicago, IL 60603
617/353-4423

Delaware, Maryland (exc. metro Washington,
DC area), Michigan, New York (west of
Rochester), Ohio, Pennsylvania, West Virginia

Mail Building, Room 500
Cleveland, OH 44114
216/522-4207

Arkansas, Louisiana, New Mexico, Oklahoma,
Texas

8303 Elmbrook Drive
Dallas, TX 75247
214/767-7050

Colorado, Kansas, Montana, Nebraska, North
Dakota, South Dakota, Utah, Wyoming

Executive Tower Building, Room 2900
Denver, CO 80202
303/837-2271

Arizona, California (southern)

13209 Federal Building
11000 Wilshire Boulevard
Los Angeles, CA 90024
213/209-7575

New Jersey, New York (east of Rochester)

2243-EB J.K. Javits Federal Building
New York, NY 10278
212/264-1207

California (northern), Hawaii, Nevada

Federal Building U.S. Courthouse
Box 36005
San Francisco, CA 94102
415/556-1270

Honolulu Field Station

6324 Prince Kuhio Federal Building
Honolulu, HI 96850
808/546-5685

GENERAL SERVICES ADMINISTRATION
Regional Administrators
(Refer to Appendix F for boundaries)

NATIONAL CAPITAL REGION

7th and D Streets, NW, Room 7022
Washington, DC 20407
202/472-1100

1. 640 J.W. McCormack Post Office
    U.S. Courthouse
    Boston, MA 02109
    617/223-2601

2. 23-102 J.K. Javits Federal Building
    New York, NY 10278
    202/264-2600

3. 5128 Post Office
    U.S. Courthouse
    Philadelphia, PA 19107
    215/597-1237

4. 346 R.B. Russell Federal Building
    Atlanta, GA 30303
    404/221-3200

5. 3700 J.C. Kluczynski Federal Building
    Chicago, IL 60604
    312/353-5395

6. 1500 East Bannister Road
    Kansas City, MO 64131
    816/926-7201

7. 5827 F.G. Lanham Federal Building
    Fort Worth, TX 76102
    817/334-2321

8. Denver Federal Center, Building 41
    Denver, CO 80225
    303/234-4171

9. 525 Market Street, 28th Floor
    San Francisco, CA 94105
    415/974-9147

10. Federal Services Administration Center
    Auburn, WA 98002
    206/931-7000

Business Service Centers (Regional Directors)

NATIONAL CAPITAL REGION

7th & D Streets, SW, Room 1050
Washington, DC 20407
202/472-1804

1. L-I J.W. McCormack Post Office
    U.S. Courthouse
    Boston, MA 02109
    617/223-2868

2. 112 J.K. Javits Federal Building
    New York, NY 10278
    212/264-1234

3. 1300 Post Office
    U.S. Courthouse
    Philadelphia, PA 19107
    215/597-9613

4. 318 R.B. Russell Federal Building
    Atlanta, GA 30303
    404/221-5103

5. 3670 J.C. Kluczynski Federal Building
    Chicago, Il 60604
    312/353-5383

6. 1500 East Bannister Road, Room 1168
    Kansas City, MO 64131
    816/926-7203

7. 1A03 F.G. Lanham Federal Building
    Fort Worth, TX 76102
    817/334-3284

8. Denver Federal Center, Building 41
    Denver, CO 80225
    303/234-2216

9. 525 Market Street
    San Francisco, CA 94105
    415/974-9000

    Sub-office: Arizona, California (southern),
    Nevada (Clark
    County only)

    3259 Federal Building
    300 North Los Angeles Street
    Los Angeles, CA 90012
    213/688-3210

10. 440 H.M. Jackson Federal Building
    Seattle, WA 98174
    206/442-5556

HEALTH AND HUMAN SERVICES DEPARTMENT
Regional Directors
(Refer to Appendix F for boundaries)

1. 2411 J.F. Kennedy Federal Building
    Boston, MA 02203
    617/223-6831

2. 3835 J.K. Javits Federal Building
    New York, NY 10278
    212/264-4600

3. Gateway Building, Box 13716
    Philadelphia, PA 19101
    215/596-6492

4. 101 Marietta Tower, Room 1403
    Atlanta, GA 30323
    404/221-2442

5. 300 South Wacker Drive, 35th Floor
    Chicago, IL 60606
    312/353-5160

6. 1200 Main Tower Building, Room 1100
    Dallas, TX 75202
    214/767-3301

7. 210 Federal Office Building
    601 East 12th Street
    Kansas City, MO 64106
    816/374-2821

8. 1076 Federal Building
    Denver, CO 80294
    303/837-3373

9. 50 United Nations Plaza, Room 431
    San Francisco, CA 94102
    415/556-6746

10. 3rd & Broad Building
    2901 3rd Avenue
    Seattle, WA 98121
    206/442-0420

Health Care Financing Administration
(Regional Administrators)
(Refer to Appendix F for boundaries)

1. 1309 J.F. Kennedy Federal Building
    Boston, MA 02203
    617/223-6871

2. 3811 J.K. Javits Federal Building
    New York, NY 10278
    212/264-4488

3. Gateway Building, Box 7760
    Philadelphia, PA 19104
    215/596-1351

4. 101 Marietta Tower, Room 701
    Atlanta, GA 30323
    404/221-2329

5. Insurance Exchange Building, 8th Floor
    Chicago, IL 60604
    312/353-8057

6. Main Tower Building, Room 2400
    Dallas, TX 75202
    214/767-6427

7. 235 Federal Office Building
    601 East 12th Street
    Kansas City, MO 64106
    816/374-5233

8. 628 Federal Building
    Denver, CO 80294
    303/837-2111

9. 100 Van Ness Avenue, 14th Floor
    San Francisco, CA 94102
    415/556-0254

10. 3rd & Broad Building
    2901 3rd Avenue
    Seattle, WA 98121
    206/442-0425

Office of Human Development Services
(Regional Administrators)
(Refer to Appendix F for boundaries)

1. 2000 J.F. Kennedy Federal Building
    Boston, MA 02203
    617/223-3236

2. 4149 J.K. Javits Federal Building
    New York, NY 10278
    212/264-1487

3. Gateway Building, Box 13716
    Philadelphia, PA 19101
    215/596-6818

4. 101 Marietta Tower, Room 903
    Atlanta, GA 30323
    404/221-2398

5. 300 South Wacker Drive, 13th Floor
    Chicago, IL 60606
    312/353-8322

6. Main Tower Building, Room 2025
    Dallas, TX 75202
    214/767-4540

7. 384 Federal Office Building
    601 East 12th Street
    Kansas City, MO 64106
    816/374-3981

8. 1194 Federal Building
    Denver, CO 80294
    303/837-2622

9. 50 United Nations Plaza, Room 455
    San Francisco, CA 94102
    415/556-4027

10. 3rd & Broad Avenue
    Seattle, WA 98121
    206/442-2430

Public Health Service (Regional
Administrators)
(Refer to Appendix F for boundaries)

1. 1400 J.F. Kennedy Federal Building
    Boston, MA 02203
    617/223-6827

2. 3337 J.K. Javits Federal Building
    New York, NY 10278
    212/264-2560

3. Gateway Building, Box 13716
    Philadelphia, PA 19101
    215/596-2316

4. 101 Marietta Tower, Room 1002
    Atlanta, GA 30323
    404/221-2316

5. 300 South Wacker Drive, 34th Floor
    Chicago, IL 60606
    312-353-1385

6. Main Tower Building, Room 1800
   Dallas, TX 75202
   214/767-3879

7. Federal Office Building, 5th Floor
   601 East 12th Street
   Kansas City, MO 64106
   816/374-3291

8. 472 Federal Building
   Denver, CO 80294
   303/837-4461

9. 50 United Nations Plaza, Room 327
   San Francisco, CA 94102
   415/556-5810

10. 3rd & Broad Building
    2901 3rd Avenue
    Seattle, WA 98121
    206/442-0430

Social Security Administration (Regional Commissioners)
(Refer to Appendix F for boundaries)

1. 1100 J.F. Kennedy Federal Building
   Boston, MA 02203
   617/223-6810

2. 4033 J.K. Javits Federal Building
   New York, NY 10278
   212/264-3915

3. Gateway Building, Box 8788
   Philadelphia, PA 19101
   215/596-6941

4. 101 Marietta Tower, Room 2001
   Atlanta, GA 30301
   404/221-2475

5. 500 South Wacker Drive, Room 2719
   Chicago, IL 60606
   312/353-4247

6. Main Tower Building, Room 2535
   Dallas, TX 75202
   214/767-4210

7. 436 Federal Office Building
   601 East 12th Street
   Kansas City, MO 64106
   816/374-3701

8. 876 Federal Building
   Denver, CO 80294
   303/837-2388

9. 100 Van Ness Avenue, 28th Floor
   San Francisco, CA 94102
   415/556-4910

10. 3rd & Broad Building, Room 301
    2901 3rd Avenue
    Seattle, WA 98121
    206/442-0417

HOUSING AND URBAN DEVELOPMENT DEPARTMENT
Regional Administrators
(Refer to Appendix F for boundaries)

1. 800 J.F. Kennedy Federal Building
   Boston, MA 02203
   617/223-4066

2. 3451 J.K. Javits Federal Building
   New York NY 10278
   212/264-8068

3. Curtis Building, Room 900
   Philadelphia, PA 19106
   215/597-2560

4. 600 R.B. Russell Federal Building
   Atlanta, GA 30303
   404/221-5138

5. 300 South Wacker Drive, Room 2312
   Chicago, IL 60606
   312/353-5680

6. 221 West Lancaster Avenue, 9th Floor
   Fort Worth, TX 76113
   817/870-5401

7. 1103 Grand Avenue, Room 1200
   Kansas City, MO 64106
   816/374-2661

8. Executive Tower Building, 28th Floor
   Denver, CO 80202
   303/837-4513

9. 450 P. Burton Federal Building
   U.S. Courthouse
   Box 36003
   San Francisco, CA 94102
   415/556-4752

10. Arcade Plaza Building, Room 3003
    Seattle, WA 98101
    206/442-5414

INTERIOR DEPARTMENT
Special Assistants to the Secretary

Box 120
Anchorage, AK 99510
907/272-3422

Fort Mason, Building 201
San Francisco, CA 94123
415/556-1380

Bureau of Indian Affairs (Area Directors)

ABERDEEN AREA: Nebraska, North Dakota, South Dakota

Federal Building
Aberdeen, SD 57401
605/225-0250

ALBUQUERQUE AREA: Colorado, New Mexico (except northwest corner)

5301 Central Avenue, NE, Box 8327
Albuquerque, NM 87108
505/766-3710

ANADARKO AREA: Kansas, Oklahoma (western)

Federal Building, Box 368
Anadarko, OK 73005
405/247-6673

BILLINGS AREA: Montana, Wyoming

Federal Building, U.S. Courthouse
Billings, MT 59101
406/657-6315

EASTERN AREA: Alabama, Arkansas, Connecticut, Delaware, District of Columbia, Florida, Georgia, Illinois, Indiana, Kentucky, Iowa, Maine, Maryland, Massachusetts, Mississippi, Missouri, New Hampshire, New Jersey, New York, North Carolina, Ohio, Pennsylvania, Rhode Island, South Carolina, Tennessee, Texas, Virginia, West Virginia

1000 North Glebe Road
Arlington, VA 22202
703/235-2571

JUNEAU AREA: Alaska

Box 3-8000
Juneau, AK 99801
907/586-7177

MINNEAPOLIS AREA: Iowa, Michigan, Minnesota, Wisconsin

15 South 5th Street, 6th Floor
Minneapolis, MN 55402
612/349-3631

MUSKOGEE AREA: Oklahoma (eastern)

Federal Building
Muskogee, OK 74401
918/687-2295

WINDOW ROCK AREA: Arizona (northeast), New Mexico (northwest), Utah (southeast)

Navajo Area Office
Window Rock, AZ 86515
602/871-5151

PHOENIX AREA: Arizona (southern and central), Nevada, Utah (except southeast corner)

3030 North Central Avenue, Box 7007
Phoenix, AZ 85011
602/261-2305

PORTLAND AREA: Idaho, Oregon, Washington

1425 Irving Street, NE, Box 3785
Portland, OR 97208
503/231-6702

SACRAMENTO AREA: California

Federal Office Building
2800 Cottage Way
Sacramento, CA 95825
916/484-4682

Bureau of Land Management (State Directors)

Alabama, Arkansas, Connecticut, Delaware, District of Columbia, Florida, Georgia, Illinois, Indiana, Iowa, Kentucky, Louisiana, Maine, Maryland, Massachusetts, Michigan, Minnesota, Mississippi, Missouri, New Hampshire, New Jersey, North Carolina, Ohio, Pennsylvania, Rhode Island, South Carolina, Tennessee, Vermont, Virginia, West Virginia, Wisconsin

350 South Pickett Street
Alexandria, VA 22304
703/235-2833

Alaska

Federal Building, Box 13
Anchorage, AK 99513
907/271-5076

Montana, North Dakota, South Carolina

Granite Tower Building, Box 30157
Billings, MT 59107
406/657-6461

Idaho

3380 Americana Terrace
Boise, ID 83706
208/334-1401

Kansas, Nebraska, Wyoming

2515 Warren Avenue, Box 1828
Cheyenne, WY 82001
307/772-2326

Colorado

1037 20th Street
Denver, CO 80202
303/837-4325

Arizona

2400 Valley Bank Center
Phoenix, AZ 85073
602/261-3873

Oregon, Washington

825 NE Multnomah Street, Box 2965
Portland, OR 97208
503/231-6251

Nevada

3008 Federal Building, U.S. Courthouse
Box 12000
Reno, NV 89520
702/784-5451

California

E2841 Federal Building
2800 Cottage Way
Sacramento, CA 95825
916/484-4676

Utah

University Club Building
136 East South Temple
Salt Lake City, UT 84111
901/524-5311

New Mexico, Oklahoma, Texas

J.M. Montoya Federal Building, U.S. Courthouse
Santa Fe, NM 87501
505/988-6030

Bureau of Reclamation (Regional Directors)

LOWER COLORADO REGION: Arizona (except northeast corner), California (southern), Nevada (southern), Utah (southwest)

Nevada Highway & Park Street, Box 417
Boulder City, NV 89005
702/293-2161

LOWER MISSOURI REGION: Colorado (eastern), Kansas (northern), Nebraska, Wyoming (southeastern)

Denver Federal Center, Building 20
Box 25247
Denver, CO 80225
303/234-3131

MID-PACIFIC REGION: California (northern), Nevada (western)

W1105 Federal Building
2800 Cottage Way
Sacramento, CA 95825
916/484-4571

PACIFIC NORTHWEST REGION: Idaho, Montana (western), Nevada (northern), Oregon, Washington, Wyoming (western)

Federal Building, U.S. Courthouse, Box 043
550 West Fort Street
Boise, ID 83724
208/334-1908

SOUTHWEST REGION: New Mexico (eastern), Oklahoma, Texas

Commerce Building, Room 207
Amarillo, TX 79101
806/378-5400

UPPER COLORADO REGION: Colorado (western), New Mexico (northwestern), Utah (except southwestern corner), Wyoming (southwestern)

125 South State Street, Box 11568
Salt Lake City, UT 84147
801/524-5566

UPPER MISSOURI REGION: Montana (eastern), North Dakota, South Dakota, Wyoming (northern)

Federal Building, U.S. Courthouse
Box 2553
Billings, MT 59103
406/657-6214

U.S. Fish and Wildlife Service (Regional Directors)

California, Hawaii, Idaho, Nevada, Oregon, Washington

Lloyd 500 Building, Room 1692
Portland, OR 97232
503/429-6118

Arizona, New Mexico, Oklahoma, Texas

D. Chavez Federal Building, U.S. Courthouse
Box 1306
Albuquerque, NM 87103
505/766-2321

Illinois, Indiana, Iowa, Michigan, Minnesota, Missouri, Ohio, Wisconsin

Federal Building, Fort Snelling
Twin Cities, MN 55111
612/725-3563

Alabama, Arkansas, Florida, Georgia, Kentucky, Louisiana, Mississippi, North Carolina, Puerto Rico, South Carolina, Tennessee, Virginia

1200 R.B. Russell Federal Building
Atlanta, GA 30303
404/331-6891

Connecticut, Delaware, Maine, Maryland, Massachusetts, New Hampshire, New Jersey, New York, Pennsylvania, Rhode Island, Vermont, Virginia, West Virginia

I Gateway Center, Room 700
Newton Corner, MA 02158
617/965-5100, ext. 200

Colorado, Kansas, Montana, Nebraska, North Dakota, South Dakota, Utah, Wyoming

134 Union Boulevard, 3rd Floor
Lakewood, CO 80228
303/234-2209

Alaska

1101 East Tudor Road
Anchorage, AK 99503
907/276-3800

Washington, DC

U.S. Fish and Wildlife Service
Room 3256
C Street between 18th & 19th Streets, NW
Washington, DC 20240
202/343-4717

Geological Survey (Director's
Representatives)

CENTRAL REGION: Arkansas, Colorado, Iowa, Kansas, Louisiana, Missouri, Montana, Nebraska, New Mexico, North Dakota, Oklahoma, South Dakota, Texas, Utah, Wyoming

Denver Federal Center, Box 25046
Denver, CO 80225
303/234-2351

EASTERN REGION: Alabama, Connecticut, Delaware, District of Columbia, Florida, Georgia, Illinois, Indiana, Kentucky, Maine, Maryland, Massachusetts, Michigan, Minnesota, Mississippi, New Hampshire, New Jersey, New York, North Carolina, Ohio, Pennsylvania, Puerto Rico, Rhode Island, South Carolina, Tennessee, Vermont, Virginia, Virgin Islands, West Virginia, Wisconsin

12201 Sunrise Valley Drive, Room 7A100
Reston, VA 22092
703/860-7414

WESTERN REGION: Alaska, Arizona, California, Hawaii, Idaho, Nevada, Oregon, Washington

345 Middlefield Road
Menlo Park, CA 94015
415/323-8111, ext. 2711

Minerals Management Service, Offshore Minerals Management

ALASKA OCS REGION: Alaska

800 A Street, Room 201
Box 101159
Anchorage, AK 99510
907/271-4304

ATLANTIC OCS REGION: Connecticut, Delaware, Florida (eastern), Georgia, Maine, Maryland, Massachusetts, New Hampshire, New Jersey, New York, North Carolina, Pennsylvania, South Carolina, Virginia

1591 Kidwell Drive, Room 601
Vienna, VA 22180
703/285-2165

GULF OF MEXICO OCS REGION: Alabama, Florida (western), Louisiana, Mississippi, Texas

3301 Causeway Boulevard, Box 7944
Metairie, LA 70010
504/838-0589

PACIFIC OCS REGION: California, Oregon, Washington

1340 West 6th Street, Room 240
Los Angeles, CA 90017
213/688-2048

National Park Service (Regional Directors)

ALASKA REGION: Alaska

2525 Gambell Street
Anchorage, AK 99503
907/271-4226

MID-ATLANTIC REGION: Delaware, District of Columbia, Maryland, Pennsylvania, Virginia, West Virginia

143 South 3rd Street
Philadelphia, PA 19106
215/597-7013

MIDWEST REGION: Illinois, Indiana, Iowa, Kansas, Michigan, Minnesota, Missouri, Nebraska, Ohio, Wisconsin

1709 Jackson Street
Omaha, NE 68102
402/221-3431

NATIONAL CAPITAL REGION: Washington, DC
Metro Area

1100 Ohio Drive, SW
Washington, DC 20242
202/426-6612

NORTH ATLANTIC REGION: Connecticut,
Maine, Massachusetts, New Hampshire, New
Jersey, New York, Rhode Island, Vermont

15 State Street
Boston, MA 02109
617/223-3769

PACIFIC NORTHWEST REGION: Idaho,
Oregon, Washington

2001 6th Avenue
Seattle, WA 98121
206/442-5565

ROCKY MOUNTAIN REGION: Colorado,
Montana, North Dakota, South Dakota, Utah,
Wyoming

655 Parfet Street, Box 25287
Denver, CO 80225
303/234-2500

SOUTHEAST REGION: Alabama, Florida,
Georgia, Kentucky, Mississippi, North Caro-
lina, Puerto Rico, South Carolina, Tennessee,
Virgin Islands

1094 R.B. Russell Federal Building
Atlanta, GA 30303
404/221-5185

SOUTHWEST REGION: Arizona (eastern),
Arkansas, Louisiana, New Mexico, Oklahoma,
Texas

Box 728
Santa Fe, NM 87501
505/988-6388

WESTERN REGION: Arizona (western),
California, Hawaii, Nevada

P. Burton Federal Building, U.S. Courthouse
Box 36063
San Francisco, CA 94102
415/556-4196

INTERSTATE COMMERCE COMMISSION
Regional Managers

Connecticut, Maine, Massachusetts, New
Hampshire, New Jersey, New York, Rhode
Island, Vermont

Analex Building, Room 501
Boston, MA 02114
617/223-2372

Delaware, District of Columbia, Maryland,
Ohio, Pennsylvania, Virginia, West Virginia

620 Federal Reserve Bank Building
101 North 7th Street
Philadelphia, PA 19106
215/597-4449

Alabama, Florida, Georgia, Kentucky,
Mississippi, North Carolina, South Carolina,
Tennessee

1776 Peachtree Street, NW, Room 300
Atlanta, GA 30309
404/881-4371

Illinois, Indiana, Michigan, Minnesota, North
Dakota, South Dakota, Wisconsin

1304 E.M. Dirksen Federal Building
Chicago, IL 60604
312/353-6204

Arkansas, Iowa, Kansas, Louisiana, Missouri,
Nebraska, Oklahoma, Texas

411 West 7th Street, Room 600
Fort Worth, TX 76102
817/334-3101

Alaska, Arizona, California, Colorado, Hawaii, Idaho, Montana, Nevada, New Mexico, Oregon, Utah, Washington, Wyoming

211 Main Street, Room 500
San Francisco, CA 94105
415/974-7011

JUSTICE DEPARTMENT
Antitrust Division (Regional Chiefs)

Alabama, Florida, Georgia, Mississippi, North Carolina, South Carolina, Tennessee

1776 Peachtree Street, NW, Room 420
Atlanta, GA 30309
404/881-3828

Colorado (eastern), Illinois, Indiana, Iowa, Kansas, Michigan (western), Minnesota, Missouri, Nebraska, North Dakota, South Dakota, Wisconsin

2634 E.M. Dirksen Federal Building
Chicago, IL 60604
312/353-7530

Kentucky, Michigan (eastern), Ohio, West Virginia

995 A.J. Celebrezze Federal Building
Cleveland, OH 44199
216/522-4070

Arkansas, Louisiana, Oklahoma, Texas

8C6 East Cabell Federal Building
Dallas, TX 75242
214/767-8051

Arizona, New Mexico: This office was dissolved in 1982.

Connecticut, Maine, Massachusetts, New Hampshire, New Jersey (northern), New York, Rhode Island, Vermont

3630 J.K. Javits Federal Building
New York, NY 10278
212/264-0390

Delaware, District of Columbia, Maryland, New Jersey (southern), Virginia

11400 U.S. Courthouse
Philadelphia, PA 19106
215/597-7405

Alaska, California, Colorado (western), Hawaii, Idaho, Montana, Nevada, Oregon, Utah, Washington, Wyoming

P. Burton Federal Building, U.S. Courthouse
Box 36046
San Francisco, CA 94102
415/556-6300

Bureau of Prisons (Regional Directors)

NORTH CENTRAL REGION: Illinois, Indiana, Iowa, Kansas, Michigan, Minnesota, Missouri, Nebraska, Ohio, Wisconsin

10920 Ambassador Drive
Kansas City, MO 64153
816/891-7007

NORTHEAST REGION: Connecticut, Delaware, District of Columbia, Maine, Maryland, Massachusetts, New Hampshire, New Jersey, New York, Pennsylvania, Puerto Rico, Rhode Island, Vermont, Virginia, Virgin Islands, West Virginia

Scott Plaza II, Industrial Highway
Philadelphia, PA 19113
215/596-1871

SOUTH CENTRAL REGION: Arkansas, Louisiana, New Mexico, Oklahoma, Texas

1607 Main Street, Room 700
Dallas, TX 75201
214/767-0012

SOUTHEAST REGION: Alabama, Florida, Georgia, Kentucky, Mississippi, North Carolina, South Carolina, Tennessee

523 McDonnough Boulevard, SE
Atlanta, GA 30315
404/221-3531

WESTERN REGION: Alaska, Arizona, California, Colorado, Hawaii, Idaho, Montana, Nevada, North Dakota, Oregon, South Dakota, Utah, Washington, Wyoming

Crocker Financial Center, 5th Floor
Burlingame, CA 94010
415/347-0721

Community Relations Service (Regional Directors)
(Refer to Appendix F for boundaries)

1. 100 Summer Street, Room 1920
   Boston, MA 02110
   617/223-5170

2. 3402 J.K. Javits Federal Building
   New York, NY 10278
   212/264-0700

3. 309 U.S. Courthouse
   Philadelphia, PA 19106
   215/597-2344

4. Citizens Trust Bank Building, Room 900
   Atlanta, GA 30303
   404/242-6174

5. Insurance Exchange Building, Room 1113
   Chicago, IL 60604
   312/353-4391

6. 138-35 East Cabell Federal Building
   Dallas, TX 75242
   214/767-0824

7. 2411 Old Federal Office Building
   911 Walnut Street
   Kansas City, MO 64106
   816/374-2022

8. 1531 Stout Street, 4th Floor
   Denver, CO 80202
   303/837-2973

9. 1275 Market Street, Room 1050
   San Francisco, CA 94103
   415/556-2485

10. 1898 H.M. Jackson Federal Building
    Seattle, WA 98174
    206/442-4465

Drug Enforcement Administration
Divisional Offices (Special Agents in Charge)

ATLANTA DIVISION: Georgia, North Carolina, South Carolina, Tennessee

230 Houstone Street, NE
Atlanta, GA 30303
404/221-4401

BOSTON DIVISION: Connecticut, Maine, Massachusetts, New Hampshire, Rhode Island, Vermont

G-64 J.F. Kennedy Federal Building
Boston, MA 02203
617/223-2170

CHICAGO DIVISION: Illinois, Indiana, Minnesota, North Dakota, Wisconsin

1800 E.M. Dirksen Federal Building
Chicago, IL 60604
312/353-7875

DALLAS DIVISION: Oklahoma, Texas (northern)

1800 Regal Row
Dallas, TX 75235
214/767-7151

DENVER DIVISION: Colorado, New Mexico, Utah, Wyoming

316 U.S. Customs House
Denver, CO 80202
303/837-3951

DETROIT DIVISION: Kentucky, Michigan, Ohio

357 Federal Building
Detroit, MI 48226
313/226-7290

HOUSTON DIVISION: Texas (southern)

4299 San Felipe Street, Room 200
Houston, TX 77027
713/526-4950

LOS ANGELES DIVISION: California
(southern), Guam, Hawaii, Nevada

World Trade Center, Room 800
Los Angeles, CA 90071
213/688-2650

MIAMI DIVISION: Caribbean, Florida

8400 Northwest 53rd Street
Miami, FL 33166
305/591-4870

NEWARK DIVISION: New Jersey

806 P.W. Rodino Jr. Federal Building
Newark, NJ 07102
201/645-6060

NEW ORLEANS DIVISION: Alabama,
Arkansas, Louisiana, Mississippi

1661 Canal Street, Room 2200
New Orleans, LA 70112
504/682-3894

NEW YORK DIVISION: New York

555 West 57th Street, Room 1900
New York, NY 10019
212/399-5151

PHILADELPHIA DIVISION: Delaware,
Pennsylvania

10224 W.J. Green Jr. Federal Building
Philadelphia, PA 19106
215/597-9530

PHOENIX DIVISION: Arizona

Valley Bank Center, Room 1980
201 North Central Avenue
Phoenix, AZ 85073
602/261-4866

ST. LOUIS DIVISION: Iowa, Kansas, Missouri,
Nebraska, South Dakota

Chromalloy Plaza, Room 200
120 South Central Avenue
St Louis, MO 63105
314/425-3241

SAN DIEGO DIVISION: California (southern)

402 West 35th Street
National City, CA 92050
714/293-5654

SAN FRANCISCO DIVISION: California
(northern)

12212 P. Burton Federal Building, U.S.
Courthouse
San Francisco, CA 94102
415/556-6771

SEATTLE DIVISION: Alaska, Idaho, Montana,
Oregon, Washington

220 West Mercer, Room 301
Seattle, WA 98119
206/442-5443

WASHINGTON, D.C. DIVISION: District of
Columbia, Maryland, Virginia, West Virginia

400 6th Street, SW, Room 2558
Washington, DC 20024
202/724-7834

Immigration and Naturalization Service
(Regional Commissioners)

EASTERN REGION: Connecticut, Delaware,
District of Columbia, Maine, Maryland,
Massachusetts, New Hampshire, New Jersey,
New York, Pennsylvania, Puerto Rico, Rhode
Island, Vermont, Virginia, Virgin Islands, West
Virginia

Federal Building
Burlington, VT 05401
802/951-6223

NORTHERN REGION: Alaska, Colorado,
Idaho, Illinois, Indiana, Iowa, Kansas,

Michigan, Minnesota, Missouri, Montana, Nebraska, North Dakota, Ohio, Oregon, South Dakota, Utah, Washington, Wisconsin, Wyoming

Federal Building, Fort Snelling
Twin Cities, MN 55111
612/725-4451

SOUTHERN REGION: Alabama, Arkansas, Florida, Georgia, Kentucky, Louisiana, Mississippi, New Mexico, North Carolina, Oklahoma, South Carolina, Tennessee, Texas

Skyline Center Building
311 North Stemmons Freeway
Dallas, TX 75207
214/767-6000

WESTERN REGION: Arizona, California, Hawaii, Nevada

Terminal Island
San Pedro, CA 90731
213/548-2371

Justice Management Division (Regional Audit Office Directors)

Alabama, Florida, Georgia, Kentucky, Mississippi, North Carolina, Puerto Rico, South Carolina, Tennessee, Virgin Islands

101 Marietta Tower, Room 2322
Atlanta, GA 30323
404/221-5928

Connecticut, Delaware, District of Columbia, Maine, Maryland, Massachusetts, New Hampshire, New Jersey, New York, Pennsylvania, Rhode Island, Vermont, Virginia, West Virginia

5205 Leesburg Pike, Room 1600
Falls Church, VA 22041
703/756-6277

Illinois, Indiana, Iowa, Kansas, Michigan, Minnesota, Missouri, Nebraska, Ohio, Wisconsin

Insurance Exchange Building, Room A-1335
Chicago, IL 60604
312/353-1203

Arkansas, Colorado, Louisiana, Montana, New Mexico, North Dakota, Oklahoma, South Dakota, Texas, Utah, Wyoming

333 West Colfax, Room 320
Denver, CO 80203
303/837-3638

Dallas Area Office

7A20 East Cabell Federal Building, U.S. Courthouse
Dallas, TX 75242
214/767-2103

Alaska, American Samoa, Arizona, California, Guam, Hawaii, Idaho, Nevada, Oregon, Washington

1818 Gilbreth Road, Room 153
Burlingame, CA 94010
415/692-5783

JUSTICE DEPARTMENT
United States Parole Commission
(Regional Commissioners)

NORTH CENTRAL REGION: Illinois, Indiana, Iowa, Kansas, Michigan, Minnesota, Missouri, Nebraska, Ohio, Wisconsin

10920 Ambassador Drive, Room 220
Kansas City, MO 64153
816/891-1395

NORTHEAST REGION: Connecticut, Delaware, District of Columbia, Maine, Maryland, Massachusetts, New Hampshire, New Jersey, New York, Pennsylvania, Puerto Rico, Rhode Island, Vermont, Virginia, Virgin Islands, West Virginia

Scott Plaza II, 6th Floor, Industrial Highway
Philadelphia, PA 19113
215/596-1868

SOUTH CENTRAL REGION: Alaska, Louisiana, New Mexico, Oklahoma, Texas

555 Griffin Square Building, Room 820
Dallas, TX 75202
214/767-0024

SOUTHEAST REGION: Alabama, Florida, Georgia, Kentucky, Mississippi, North Carolina, South Carolina, Tennessee

715 McDonnough Blvd, SE
Atlanta, GA 30315
404/221-3515

WESTERN REGION: Alaska, Arizona, California, Colorado, Hawaii, Idaho, Montana, North Dakota, Nevada, Oregon, South Dakota, Utah, Washington, Wyoming

Crocker Financial Center Building, 5th Floor
Burlingame, CA 94010
415/347-4737

LABOR DEPARTMENT
Regional Representatives
(Refer to Appendix F for boundaries)

1. 1608 J.F. Kennedy Federal Building
    Boston, MA 02203
    617/223-4220

2. 1515 Broadway, Room 3585
    New York, NY 10036
    212/944-3442

3. Gateway Building, Room 14100
    Philadelphia, PA 19104
    215/596-1116

4. 1375 Peachtree Street, NE, Room 624
    Atlanta, GA 30309
    404/881-4366

5. J.C. Kluczynski Federal Building, 39th Floor
    Chicago, IL 60604
    312/353-4703

6. 555 Griffin Square Building, Room 741
    Dallas, TX 75202
    214/767-6807

7. 2508 Old Federal Office Building
    911 Walnut Street
    Kansas City, MO 64106
    816/374-6371

8. 1452 Federal Building
    Denver, CO 80294
    303/837-5619

9. 10001 P. Burton Federal Building, U.S. Courthouse
    San Francisco, CA 94102
    415/556-4025

10. 6049 Federal Office Building
    909 1st Avenue
    Seattle, WA 98174
    206/442-7060

Bureau of Labor Statistics (Regional Commissioners)

Alabama, Florida, Georgia, Kentucky, Mississippi, North Carolina, South Carolina, Tennessee

1372 Peachtree Street, NE, Room 540
Atlanta, GA 30367
404/881-2161

Connecticut, Maine, Massachusetts, New Hampshire, Rhode Island, Vermont

1603 J.F. Kennedy Federal Building
Boston, MA 02203
617/223-6727

Illinois, Indiana, Michigan, Minnesota, Ohio, Wisconsin

J.C. Kluczynski Federal Building, 9th Floor
Chicago, IL 60604
312/353-7226

Arkansas, Louisiana, New Mexico, Oklahoma, Texas

555 Griffin Square Building, 2nd Floor
Dallas, TX 75202
214/767-6953

Colorado, Iowa, Kansas, Missouri, Montana, Nebraska, North Dakota, South Dakota, Utah, Wyoming

1500 Old Federal Office Building
911 Walnut Street
Kansas City, MO 64106
816/374-2378

New Jersey, New York, Canal Zone, Puerto Rico, Virgin Islands

1515 Broadway, Room 3456
New York, NY 10036
212/944-3117

Delaware, District of Columbia, Maryland, Pennsylvania, Virginia, West Virginia

Gateway Building (Box 13309)
Philadelphia, PA 19101
215/596-1151

Alaska, American Samoa, Arizona, California, Hawaii, Idaho, Nevada, Oregon, Trust Territory of the Pacific Islands, Washington

P. Burton Federal Building, U.S. Courthouse
San Francisco, CA 94102
415/556-3178

Employment Standards Administration
(Regional Administrators)
(Refer to Appendix F for boundaries)

1. 1612-C J.F. Kennedy Federal Building
   Boston, MA 02203
   617/223-4305

2. 1515 Broadway, Room 3300
   New York, NY 10036
   212/944-3351

3. 2 Gateway Building, Room 15320
   Philadelphia, PA 19104
   15/596-1185

4. 1371 Peachtree Street, NE, Room 105
   Atlanta, GA 30367
   404/881-2818

5. J.C. Kluczynski Federal Building, 9th Floor
   Chicago, IL 60604
   312/353-7280

6. 555 Griffin Square Building, Room 800
   Dallas, TX 75202
   214/767-6894

7. 2000 Old Federal Office Building
   911 Walnut Street
   Kansas City, MO 64106
   816/374-5381

8. 1442 Federal Building
   Denver, CO 80294
   303/837-5903

9. 10353 P. Burton Federal Building, U.S.
       Courthouse
   San Francisco, CA 94102
   415/556-1318

10. 4141 Federal Office Building
    909 1st Avenue
    Seattle, WA 98174
    206/442-1536

Employment and Training Administration
(Regional Administrators)
(Refer to Appendix F for boundaries)

1. 1707 J.F. Kennedy Federal Building
   Boston, MA 02203
   617/223-6440

2. 1515 Broadway, Room 3713
   New York, NY 10036
   212/944-3210

3. Gateway Building, Box 8796
   Philadelphia, PA 19101
   215/596-6336

4. 1371 Peachtree Street, NE, Room 405
   Atlanta, GA 30309
   404/881-4411

5. J.C. Kluczynski Federal Building, 6th Floor
   Chicago, IL 60604
   312/353-0313

6. 555 Griffin Square Building, Room 316
    Dallas, TX 75202
    214/767-6877

7. 800 Old Federal Office Building
    911 Walnut Street
    Kansas City, MO 64106
    816/374-3796

8. 1676 Federal Building
    Denver, CO 80294
    303/837-4477

9. P. Burton Federal Building, U.S. Courthouse
    Box 36084
    San Francisco, CA 94102
    415/556-7414

10. Federal Office Building
    909 1st Avenue
    Seattle, WA 98174
    206/442-7700

Labor-Management Services Administration
(Regional Administrators)

Alabama, Florida, Georgia, Kentucky,
Mississippi, North Carolina, South Carolina,
Tennessee

1371 Peachtree Street, NE, Room 300
Atlanta, GA 30367
404/881-4237

Illinois (part), Indiana, Michigan, Minnesota,
Ohio, Wisconsin

1060 J.C. Kluczynski Federal Building
Chicago, IL 60604
312/353-0133

Arkansas, Colorado, Iowa, Illinois (part),
Kansas, Louisiana, Missouri, Montana,
Nebraska, New Mexico, North Dakota,
Oklahoma, South Dakota, Texas, Utah,
Wyoming

2200 Old Federal Office Building
911 Walnut Street
Kansas City, MO 64106
816/374-5131

Connecticut, Maine, Massachusetts, New
Hampshire, New Jersey, New York, Puerto Rico,
Rhode Island, Vermont, Virgin Islands

1515 Broadway, Room 3515
New York, NY 10036
212/944-3408

Delaware, District of Columbia, Maryland,
Pennsylvania, Virginia, West Virginia

Gateway Building, Room 14120
Philadelphia, PA 19104
215/596-1134

Alaska, Arizona, California, Hawaii, Idaho,
Nevada, Oregon, Washington

9061 P. Burton Federal Building, U.S.
    Courthouse
San Francisco, CA 94102
415/556-5915

Mine Safety and Health Administration,
Office of Coal Mine Safety and Health (District
Managers)

EASTERN PENNSYLVANIA ANTHRACITE AREA

Penn Place
20 North Penn Avenue
Wilkes-Barre, PA 18701
717/826-6321

CENTRAL AND WESTERN PENNSYLVANIA
BITUMINOUS AREA

4800 Forbes Avenue
Pittsburgh, PA 15213
412/621-4500

NORTHERN WEST VIRGINIA BITUMINOUS
AREA

5012 Mountaineer Mall
Morgantown, WV 26505
304/291-4277

SOUTHERN WEST VIRGINIA BITUMINOUS
AREA

Box 112
Mount Hope, WV 25880
304/877-6405

VIRGINIA BITUMINOUS AREA

Box 560
Norton, VA 24273
703/679-0230

EASTERN KENTUCKY BITUMINOUS AREA

218 High Street
Pikeville, KY 41501
606/437-9616

CENTRAL KENTUCKY, ALABAMA, GEORGIA
AND TENNESSEE BITUMINOUS AREA

Box 572
Barbourville, KY 40906
606/546-5123

ILLINOIS, INDIANA, AND OHIO
BITUMINOUS AREA

Box 418
Vincennes, IN 47591
812/882-7616

ALASKA, COLORADO, UTAH, WASHINGTON
AND WYOMING BITUMINOUS AREA

Box 25367
Denver, CO 80225
303/234-2293

WESTERN KENTUCKY, OKLAHOMA AND TEXAS
BITUMINOUS AREA

Box 473
Madisonville, KY 42431
502/821-4180

Occupational Safety and Health
Administration (Regional Administrators)
(Refer to Appendix F for boundaries)

1. 1 Dock Square Building, 4th Floor
Boston, MA 02109
617/223-6710

2. 1515 Broadway, Room 3445
New York, NY 10036
212/944-3432

3. Gateway Building, Room 2100
Philadelphia, PA 19104
215/596-1201

4. 1375 Peachtree Street, NE, Room 587
Atlanta, GA 30367
404/881-3573

5. 3244 J.C. Kluczynski Federal Building
Chicago, IL 60604
312/353-2220

6. 555 Griffin Square Building, Room 602
Dallas, TX 75202
214/767-4731

7. 406 Old Federal Office Building
911 Walnut Street
Kansas City, MO 64106
816/374-5861

8. 1554 Federal Building
Denver, CO 80294
303/837-3601

9. P. Burton Federal Building, U.S. Courthouse
Box 36017
San Francisco, CA 94102
415/556-7260

10. 6003 Federal Office Building
909 1st Avenue
Seattle, WA 98174
206/442-5930

Women's Bureau (Regional Administrators)

1. 1600-C J.F. Kennedy Federal Building
Boston, MA 02203
617/223-4036

2. 1515 Broadway, Room 3575
New York, NY 10036
212/944-3445

3. Gateway Building, Room 13280
    Philadelphia, PA 19104
    215/596-1183

4. 1371 Peachtree Street, NE, Room 323
    Atlanta, GA 30367
    404/881-4461

5. J.C. Kluczynski Federal Building, 10th Floor
    Chicago, IL 60604
    312/353-6985

6. 555 Griffin Square Building, Room 863
    Dallas, TX 75202
    214/767-6985

7. 2511 Old Federal Office Building
    911 Walnut Street
    Kansas City, MO 64106
    816/374-6108

8. 1456 Federal Building
    Denver, CO 80294
    303/837-4138

9. 11411 P. Burton Federal Building, U.S.
    Courthouse
    San Francisco, CA 94102
    415/556-2377

10. 1029 Federal Office Building
    Seattle, WA 98174
    206/442-1534

MERIT SYSTEMS PROTECTION BOARD
Regional Directors

Alabama, Florida, Georgia, Kentucky,
Mississippi, North Carolina, South Carolina,
Tennessee

1776 Peachtree Street, NE, 3rd Floor
Atlanta, GA 30309
404/881-3631

Connecticut, Maine, Massachusetts, New
Hampshire, Rhode Island, Vermont

100 Summer Street, Room 1736
Boston, MA 02110
617/223-2556

Illinois, Indiana, Michigan, Minnesota, Ohio,
Wisconsin

J.C. Kluczynski Federal Building, 31st Floor
Chicago, IL 60604
312/353-2923

Arkansas, Louisiana, New Mexico, Oklahoma,
Texas

6F20 East Cabell Federal Building
Dallas, TX 75242
214/767-0555

Colorado, Montana, North Dakota, South
Dakota, Utah, Wyoming

Denver Federal Center, Building 46
Box 25025
Denver, CO 80225
303/234-3725

District of Columbia, Maryland, Virginia
(Greater Washington, DC Area)

5203 Leesburg Pike, Room 1109
Falls Church, VA 22041
703/756-6250

New Jersey, New York, Puerto Rico, Virgin
Islands

2339 J.K. Javits Federal Building
New York, NY 10278
212/264-9372

Delaware, Maryland (exc. metro Washington,
DC area), Pennsylvania, Virginia (exc. metro
Washington, DC area), West Virginia

501 U.S. Customhouse
Philadelphia, PA 19106
215/597-4446

Iowa, Kansas, Missouri, Nebraska

1740 Federal Building
St. Louis, MO 63101
314/425-4295

Arizona, California, Hawaii, Nevada

525 Market Street, Room 2400
San Francisco, CA 94105
415/974-9703

Alaska, Idaho, Oregon, Washington

1840 H.M. Jackson Federal Building
Seattle, WA 98174
206/442-0395

Office of the Special Counsels

HEADQUARTERS: Canal Zone, Connecticut,
Delaware, District of Columbia, Maine,
Maryland, Massachusetts, New Hampshire,
New Jersey, New York, North Carolina,
Pennsylvania, Puerto Rico, Rhode Island,
South Carolina, Vermont, Virginia, Virgin
Islands, West Virginia

1120 Vermont Avenue, NW
Washington, DC 20419
202/653-7188

CHICAGO FIELD OFFICE: Illinois, Indiana,
Iowa, Kansas, Michigan, Minnesota, Missouri,
Nebraska, North Dakota, Ohio, South Dakota,
Wisconsin

300 South Wacker Drive
Chicago, IL 60606
312/886-0441

DALLAS FIELD OFFICE: Alabama, Arkansas,
Florida, Georgia, Kentucky, Louisiana,
Mississippi, New Mexico, Oklahoma,
Tennessee, Texas

2A5 East Cabell Federal Building
Dallas, TX 75242
214/767-8871

SAN FRANCISCO FIELD OFFICE: Alaska,
Arizona, California, Colorado, Hawaii, Idaho,
Montana, Nevada, Oregon, Utah,
Washington, Wyoming

11454 P. Burton Federal Building, U.S.
   Courthouse
Box 36007
San Francisco, CA 94102
415/556-9450

NATIONAL CREDIT UNION ADMINISTRATION
Regional Directors

Connecticut, Maine, Massachusetts, New
Hampshire, New Jersey, New York, Puerto Rico,
Rhode Island, Vermont, Virgin Islands

441 Stuart Street
Boston, MA 01226
617/223-6807

Delaware, District of Columbia, Maryland,
Pennsylvania, Virginia, West Virginia

1776 G Street, NW, 7th Floor
Washington, DC 20006
202/682-1900

Alabama, Arkansas, Florida, Georgia,
Kentucky, Louisiana, Mississippi, North
Carolina, South Carolina, Tennessee

1365 Peachtree Street, NE, Room 500
Atlanta, GA 30367
404/881-3127

Illinois, Indiana, Iowa, Michigan, Minnesota,
Missouri, North Dakota, Ohio, South Dakota,
Wisconsin

3346 J.C. Kluczynski Federal Building
Chicago, IL 60604
312/886-9697

Arizona, Colorado, Idaho, Kansas, Montana,
Nebraska, Nevada, New Mexico, Oklahoma,
Texas, Utah, Wyoming

Grant Building, Room 407
611 East 6th Street
Austin, TX 78701
512/482-5131

Denver Sub-Office

Lea Complex
10455 East 25th Avenue
Aurora, CO 80010
303/837-3795

Alaska, American Samoa, California, Guam,
Hawaii, Oregon, Washington

77 Geary Street, 2nd Floor
San Francisco, CA 94108
415/556-6277

NATIONAL LABOR RELATIONS BOARD
Regional Directors

Walker Building, 3rd Floor
Boston, MA 02116
617/223-3330

3614 J.K. Javits Federal Building
New York, NY 10278
212/264-0330

901 Federal Building
Buffalo, NY 14202
716/846-4934

1 Independence Mall, 7th Floor
Philadelphia, PA 19106
215/597-7608

Chandler Building, 4th Floor
Baltimore, MD 21202
301/962-2737

1501 W.S. Moorhead Federal Building
Pittsburgh, PA 15222
412/644-2944

300 P.V. McNamara Federal Building
Detroit, MI 48226
313/226-3210

1695 A.J. Celebrezze Federal Building
Cleveland, OH 44199
216/522-3725

3003 Federal Building
Cincinnati, OH 45202
513/684-3621

101 Marietta Tower, Room 2400
Atlanta, GA 30323
404/221-2861

447 U.S. Courthouse, Federal Building
Winston-Salem, NC 27101
919/761-3240

700 Twiggs Street, Room 511
Box 3322
Tampa, FL 33602
813/228-2646

E.M. Dirksen Federal Building
Chicago, IL 60604
312/353-7574

Tucker Boulevard, North, Room 448
St. Louis, MO 63101
314/425-4142

600 F.E. Herbert Federal Building
New Orleans, LA 70130
504/589-6396

8A24 F.G. Lanham Federal Building
Fort Worth, TX 76102
817/334-2938

1 Gateway Center, Room 616
Kansas City, KS 66101
913/374-4434

316 Federal Building, U.S. Courthouse
Minneapolis, MN 55401
612/725-2601

2948 H.M. Jackson Federal Building
Seattle, WA 98174
206/442-7542

13018 P. Burton Federal Building, U.S.
   Courthouse
San Francisco, CA 94102
415/556-6721

City National Bank Building, 24th Floor
Los Angeles, CA 90014
213/688-5204

1600 P.D. Rodino Jr. Federal Building
Newark, NJ 07102
201/645-3240

1 Allen Center, Room 920
Houston, TX 77002
713/229-7726

591 F. Degatau Federal Building
Hato Rey, PR 00918
809/753-4225

238 Minton-Capehard Federal Building
Indianapolis, IN 46204
317/269-7401

Mid-Memphis Tower, Room 800
Memphis, TN 38104
901/521-2707

260 U.S. Custom House
Denver, CO 80202
303/837-5551

3030 North Central Avenue, 2nd Floor
Phoenix, AZ 85012
602/241-2373

16 Court Street, 4th Floor
Brooklyn, NY 11241
212/330-7700

1240 H.S. Reuss Federal Building
Milwaukee, WI 53203
414/291-3870

12100 Federal Building, U.S. Post Office
Los Angeles, CA 90024
213/209-7371

Breuner Building, 2nd Floor, Box 12983
Oakland, CA 94604
415/273-4285

Savings Center Tower, 16th Floor
Peoria, IL 61602
309/671-7083

NATIONAL TRANSPORTATION SAFETY BOARD
Field Office Chiefs

AVIATION: Alaska

701 C Street, Room C-145
Box 11
Anchorage, AK 99513
907/271-5001

AVIATION: Alabama, District of Columbia,
Georgia, Kentucky, Maryland, Mississippi,
North Carolina, South Carolina, Tennessee,
Virginia, West Virginia
HIGHWAY: Alabama, Florida, Georgia,
Louisiana, Mississippi, North Carolina, Puerto
Rico, South Carolina, Tennessee
RAILROAD: Alabama, Florida, Georgia,
Mississippi, Puerto Rico, South Carolina

1720 Peachtree Street, NW
Atlanta, GA 30309
404/881-7385

AVIATION: Colorado, Montana, North
Dakota, South Dakota, Utah, Wyoming

RAILROAD: Colorado, Montana, North Dakota, South Dakota, Utah, Wyoming

10255 East 25th Avenue, Room 14
Aurora, CO 80010
303/837-4491

AVIATION: Illinois, Indiana, Michigan, Minnesota, Ohio, Wisconsin
RAILROAD: Illinois, Indiana, Michigan, Minnesota, Ohio, Wisconsin

O'Hare Lake Office Plaza, Room 140
Des Plaines, IL 60018
312/827-8858

AVIATION: Arkansas, Louisiana, New Mexico, Oklahoma, Texas
PIPELINE: Alabama, Arizona, Arkansas, California, Colorado, Kansas, Louisiana, Mississippi, Missouri, Nevada, New Mexico, Oklahoma, Texas, Utah
RAILROAD: Arkansas, Louisiana, New Mexico, Oklahoma, Texas

7A07 F.G. Lanham Building
Fort Worth, TX 76102
817/334-2616

AVIATION: Connecticut, Delaware, Maine, Massachusetts, New Hampshire, New Jersey, New York, Pennsylvania, Rhode Island, Vermont
HIGHWAY: Connecticut, Delaware, District of Columbia, Maine, Massachusetts, Maryland, Michigan, New Hampshire, New Jersey, New York, Ohio, Pennsylvania, Rhode Island, Vermont, Virginia, West Virginia
RAILROAD: Connecticut, Delaware, Maine, Massachusetts, New Hampshire, New Jersey, New York, Pennsylvania, Rhode Island, Vermont

102 Federal Building
J.F. Kennedy Int'l Airport
Jamaica, NY 11430
212/917-1266

AVIATION: Iowa, Kansas, Missouri, Nebraska
HIGHWAY: Arkansas, Illinois, Indiana, Iowa, Kansas, Kentucky, Minnesota, Missouri,

Nebraska, North Dakota, Oklahoma, South Dakota, Texas, Wisconsin
RAILROAD: Iowa, Kansas, Missouri, Nebraska

1748 Federal Office Building
601 East 12th Street
Kansas City, MO 64106
816/374-3576

AVIATION: Arizona, California, Hawaii, Nevada
HIGHWAY: Alaska, Arizona, California, Colorado, Hawaii, Idaho, Montana, Nevada, New Mexico, Oregon, Utah, Washington, Wyoming
RAILROAD: Arizona, California, Hawaii, Nevada

15000 Aviation Boulevard
Box 6117
Lawndale, CA 90261
213/536-6041

AVIATION: Florida, Puerto Rico

4471 NW 36th Street, Room 230
Miami Springs, FL 33166
305/526-2940

AVIATION: Idaho, Oregon, Washington
RAILROAD: Idaho, Oregon, Washington

Airport Plaza Building, Room 303
Seattle, WA 98188
206/764-3782

HAZARDOUS MATERIALS AND PIPELINE:
Alaska, Connecticut, Delaware, District of Columbia, Florida, Georgia, Hawaii, Idaho, Illinois, Indiana, Iowa, Kentucky, Maine, Maryland, Massachusetts, Minnesota, Montana, Nebraska, New Hampshire, New Jersey, New York, North Carolina, North Dakota, Ohio, Oregon, Pennsylvania, Puerto Rico, Rhode Island, South Carolina, South Dakota, Tennessee, Vermont, Virginia, Washington, West Virginia, Wisconsin, Wyoming

800 Independence Avenue, SW
Washington, DC 20594
202/382-0670

RAILROAD: District of Columbia, Kentucky, Maryland, North Carolina, Tennessee, Virginia, West Virginia

800 Independence Avenue, SW
Washington, DC 20594
202/382-6840

Administrative Law Judges

CIRCUIT I: California, Hawaii

Federal Building, Box 6117
Lawndale, CA 90261
213/536-6045

CIRCUIT II: Alaska, Arizona, Colorado, Idaho, Montana, Nevada, New Mexico, Oregon, Utah, Washington, Wyoming

10255 East 25th Avenue, Room 8
Aurora, CO 80010
303/837-4685

CIRCUIT III: Arkansas, Illinois, Indiana, Iowa, Kansas, Kentucky, Michigan, Minnesota, Missouri, Nebraska, North Dakota, Ohio, Oklahoma, South Dakota, Texas, Wisconsin

800 Independence Avenue, SW, Room 822
Washington, DC 20594
202/382-6760

CIRCUIT IV: Connecticut, Delaware, District of Columbia, Maine, Maryland, Massachusetts, New Hampshire, New Jersey, New York, Pennsylvania, Rhode Island, Vermont, Virginia, West Virginia

800 Independence Avenue, SW, Room 822B
Washington, DC 20594
202/382-6760

CIRCUIT V: Alabama, Florida, Georgia, Louisiana, Mississippi, North Carolina, Puerto Rico, South Carolina, Tennessee

800 Independence Avenue, SW, Room 822
Washington, DC 20594
202/382-6760

NUCLEAR REGULATORY COMMISSION
Regional Administrators

Connecticut, Delaware, District of Columbia, Maine, Maryland, Massachusetts, New Hampshire, New Jersey, New York, Pennsylvania, Rhode Island, Vermont

631 Park Avenue
King of Prussia, PA 19406
215/337-1299

Alabama, Canal Zone, Florida, Georgia, Kentucky, Mississippi, North Carolina, Puerto Rico, South Carolina, Tennessee, Virginia, Virgin Islands, West Virginia

101 Marietta Tower, Room 3100
Atlanta, GA 30303
404/221-5500

Illinois, Indiana, Iowa, Michigan, Minnesota, Missouri, Ohio, Wisconsin

799 Roosevelt Road
Glen Ellyn, IL 60137
312/932-5677

Arkansas, Colorado, Idaho, Kansas, Louisiana, Montana, Nebraska, New Mexico, North Dakota, Oklahoma, South Dakota, Texas, Utah, Wyoming

611 Ryan Plaza Drive, Room 1000
Arlington, TX 76011
817/860-8225

Alaska, Arizona, California, Hawaii, Nevada, Oregon, Trust Territory of the Pacific Islands, Washington

1450 Maria Lane, Room 210
Walnut Creek, CA 94596
415/943-3707

OCCUPATIONAL SAFETY AND HEALTH REVIEW COMMISSION
First Judges

Note: There are no specific regions assigned to the offices listed below.

1365 Peachtree Street, NE, Room 240
Atlanta, GA 30309
404/881-4197

420 J.W. McCormack Post Office
U.S. Courthouse
Boston, MA 02109
617/223-3757

55 East Monroe Street, Room 1530
Chicago, IL 60603
312/353-2564

7811 East Cabell Federal Building
Dallas, TX 75242
214/767-5271

Prudential Plaza, Room 1718
Denver, CO 80265
303/327-2281

1515 Broadway, Room 3800
New York, NY 10036
212/944-3455

608 U.S. Courthouse, Customhouse
1114 Market Street
St. Louis, MO 63101
314/425-5071

OFFICE OF PERSONNEL MANAGEMENT
Regional Directors
(Refer to Appendix F for boundaries)

1. J.W. McCormack Post Office, U.S.
   Courthouse
   10th Floor
   Boston, MA 02109
   617/223-2539

2. 3014 J.K. Javits Federal Building
   New York, NY 10278
   212/264-0440

3. 3400 W.J. Green Jr. Federal Building
   Philadelphia, PA 19106
   215/597-4543

4. 904A R.B. Russell Federal Building
   Atlanta, GA 30303
   404/221-3459

5. J.C. Kluczynski Federal Building, 30th Floor
   Chicago, IL 60604
   312/353-2901

6. 4D22 East Cabell Federal Building
   Dallas, TX 75242
   214/767-8227

7. 1256 Federal Office Building
   St. Louis, MO 63103
   314/425-4262

8. Denver Federal Center, Room 20
   Denver, CO 80225
   303/234-2023

9. 525 Market Street, 23rd Floor
   San Francisco, CA 94105
   415/454-9662

10. 2552 H.M. Jackson Federal Building
    Seattle, WA 98174
    206/442-7536

UNITED STATES POSTAL SERVICE
Regional Postmasters General

CENTRAL REGION: Illinois, Indiana, Iowa, Kansas, Kentucky, Michigan, Minnesota, Missouri, Nebraska, North Dakota, Ohio, South Dakota, Wisconsin

Main Post Office Building
Chicago, IL 60699
312/886-2000

EASTERN REGION: Delaware, District of Columbia, Maryland, New Jersey (southern), New York (southern), Pennsylvania, Virginia, West Virginia

Box 8601
Philadelphia, PA 19197
215/496-6001

NORTHEAST REGION: Connecticut, Maine, Massachusetts, New Hampshire, New Jersey (northern), New York (northern), Puerto Rico, Rhode Island, Vermont, Virgin Islands

1633 Broadway
New York, NY 10098
212/974-8200

SOUTHERN REGION: Alabama, Arkansas, Florida, Georgia, Louisiana, Mississippi, North Carolina, Oklahoma, South Carolina, Tennessee, Texas

Mid-Memphis Tower
Memphis, TN 38166
901/722-7532

WESTERN REGION: Alaska, Arizona, California, Colorado, Hawaii, Idaho, Montana, Nevada, New Mexico, Oregon, Trust Territory of the Pacific Islands, Utah, Washington, Wyoming

850 Cherry Avenue
San Bruno, CA 94099
415/876-9200

RAILROAD RETIREMENT BOARD
Regional Directors

ATLANTA REGION: Alabama, Arkansas, Florida, Georgia, Kentucky (southern), Louisiana, Mississippi, North Carolina, South Carolina, Tennessee, Virginia, West Virginia

101 Marietta Tower, Room 2304
Atlanta, GA 30323
404/221-2690

NEW YORK REGION: Connecticut, Delaware, District of Columbia, Maine, Maryland, Massachusetts, New Hampshire, New Jersey, New York, Pennsylvania, Rhode Island, Vermont, Virginia (Washington, DC metro area)

3415 J.K. Javits Federal Building
New York, NY 10278
212/264-8495

CLEVELAND REGION: Illinois (central), Indiana, Michigan, Ohio, Pennsylvania (western)

493 A.J. Celebrezze Federal Building
Cleveland, OH 44199
216/522-4043

KANSAS CITY REGION: Colorado (eastern), Illinois (northern and southwestern), Iowa, Kansas, Minnesota, Missouri, Nebraska, North Dakota, South Dakota, Texas (eastern), Wisconsin, Wyoming (eastern)

257 Federal Office Building
601 East 12th Street
Kansas City, MO 64106
816/374-3278

SAN FRANCISCO REGION: Alaska, Arizona, California, Colorado (western), Hawaii, Idaho, Montana, Nevada, New Mexico, Oregon, Texas (western), Utah, Washington, Wyoming (western)

211 Main Street, Room 370
San Francisco, CA 94105
415/556-2584

SECURITIES AND EXCHANGE COMMISSION
Regional Administrators

New Jersey, New York

1102 J.K. Javits Federal Building
New York, NY 10278
212/264-1636

Connecticut, Maine, Massachusetts, New Hampshire, Rhode Island, Vermont

Analex Building
Boston, MA 02114
617/223-2721

Alabama, Florida, Georgia, Louisiana (eastern), Mississippi, North Carolina, Puerto Rico, South Carolina, Tennessee, Virgin Islands

1375 Peachtree Street, NE, Room 788
Atlanta, GA 30367
404/881-4768

Illinois, Indiana, Iowa, Kansas (Kansas City only), Kentucky, Michigan, Minnesota, Missouri, Ohio, Wisconsin

1204 E.M. Dirksen Federal Building
Chicago, IL 60604
312/353-7390

Arkansas, Kansas (exc. Kansas City), Louisiana (western), Oklahoma, Texas

411 West 7th Street, 8th Floor
Fort Worth, TX 76102
817/334-3821

Colorado, Nebraska, New Mexico, North Dakota, South Dakota, Utah, Wyoming

410 17th Street, Room 700
Denver, CO 80202
303/837-2071

Arizona, California, Guam, Hawaii, Nevada

5757 Wilshire Boulevard, Room 500E
Los Angeles, CA 90036
213/468-3107

Alaska, Idaho, Montana, Oregon, Washington

3040 H.M. Jackson Federal Building
Seattle, WA 98174
206/442-7990

Delaware, District of Columbia, Maryland, Pennsylvania, Virginia, West Virginia

Ballston Center Tower No. 3
Arlington, VA 22203
703/235-3701

SELECTIVE SERVICE SYSTEM
Regional Directors

Connecticut, Delaware, District of Columbia, Maine, Maryland, Massachusetts, New Hampshire, New Jersey, New York, Pennsylvania, Rhode Island, Vermont

Selective Service System, Region 1
Philadelphia, PA 19185
215/755-4332

Alabama, Florida, Georgia, Kentucky, Mississippi, North Carolina, Puerto Rico, South Carolina, Tennessee, Virginia, Virgin Islands, West Virginia

Selective Service System, Region 2
Marietta, GA 30060
404/429-6602

Illinois, Indiana, Michigan, Minnesota, Ohio, Wisconsin

Selective Service System, Region 3
Great Lakes, IL 60088
312/688-4540

Arkansas, Louisiana, New Mexico, Oklahoma, Texas

Selective Service System, Region 4
Dallas, TX 75387
214/767-7296

Alaska, Arizona, California, Guam, Hawaii, Idaho, Nevada, Oregon, Washington

Selective Service System, Region 5
San Francisco, CA 94136
415/556-3411

Colorado, Iowa, Kansas, Missouri, Montana, Nebraska, North Dakota, South Dakota, Utah, Wyoming

Selective Service System, Region 6
Denver, CO 80250
303/361-8155

SMALL BUSINESS ADMINISTRATION
Regional Administrators
(Refer to Appendix F for boundaries)

1. 60 Batterymarch, 10th Floor
   Boston, MA 02110
   617/223-3204

2. 29-118 J.K. Javits Federal Building
   New York, NY 10278
   212/264-7772

3. 231 St. Asaphs Road, Room 646
   Bala Cynwyd, PA 19004
   215/596-5889

4. 1375 Peachtree Street, NE, 5th Floor
   Atlanta, GA 30309
   404/881-4994

5. 838 E.M. Dirksen Federal Building
   Chicago, IL 60604
   312/353-0359

6. 1720 Regal Row, Room 230
   Dallas, TX 75235
   214/767-7643

7. Old Federal Office Building, 23rd Floor
   911 Walnut Street
   Kansas City, MO 64106
   816/374-5288

8. Executive Tower Building, 22nd Floor
   Denver, CO 80202
   303/837-5441

9. P. Burton Federal Building, U.S. Courthouse
   Box 36044
   San Francisco, CA 94102
   415/556-7487

10. Dexter Horton Building, 5th Floor
    Seattle, WA 98104
    206/442-5676

TRANSPORTATION DEPARTMENT
Regional Representatives of the Secretary
(Refer to Appendix F for boundaries)

Regions 1, 2, 3
Independence Building, Room 1000
Philadelphia, PA 19106
215/597-9430

4. 1720 Peachtree Road, NW, Room 515
   Atlanta, GA 30309
   404/881-3738

5. 300 South Wacker Drive, Room 700
   Chicago, IL 60606
   312/353-4000

6. 7A29 F.G. Lanham Federal Building
   Fort Worth, TX 76102
   817/334-2725

Regions 7, 8
601 East 12th Street
Kansas City, MO 64106
816/374-5801

Regions 9, 10
211 Main Street
San Francisco, CA 94105
415/974-8464

United States Coast Guard (Area
Commanders)

ATLANTIC AREA: Alabama, Arkansas, Canal
Zone, Colorado, Connecticut, Delaware,
District of Columbia, Florida, Georgia, Illinois,
Indiana, Iowa, Kansas, Kentucky, Louisiana,
Maine, Maryland, Massachusetts, Michigan,
Minnesota, Mississippi, Missouri, Nebraska,
New Hampshire, New Jersey, New Mexico,
New York, North Carolina, North Dakota, Ohio,
Oklahoma, Pennsylvania, Puerto Rico, Rhode
Island, South Carolina, South Dakota,
Tennessee, Texas, Vermont, Virginia, Virgin
Islands, West Virginia, Wisconsin, Wyoming

Governors Island
New York, NY 10004
212/668-7133

PACIFIC AREA: Alaska, Arizona, California,
Guam, Hawaii, Idaho, Montana, Nevada,
Oregon, Utah, Washington

Government Island
Alameda, CA 94501
415/536-6193

Federal Aviation Administration (Regional Directors)

ALASKA REGION: Alaska

701 C Street, Box 14
Anchorage, AK 99513
907/271-5645

CENTRAL REGION: Iowa, Kansas, Missouri, Nebraska

1501 Federal Office Building
601 East 12th Street
Kansas City, MO 64106
816/374-5626

EASTERN REGION: Delaware, District of Columbia, Maryland, New Jersey, New York, Pennsylvania, Virginia, West Virginia

Federal Building
J.F. Kennedy Int'l Airport
Jamaica, NY 11430
212/917-1005

GREAT LAKES REGION: Illinois, Indiana, Michigan, Minnesota, North Dakota, Ohio, South Dakota, Wisconsin

2300 East Devon Avenue
Des Plaines, IL 60018
312/694-7294

NEW ENGLAND REGION: Connecticut, Maine, Massachusetts, New Hampshire, Rhode Island, Vermont

12 New England Executive Park
Box 510
Burlington, MA 01803
617/273-7244

NORTHWEST MOUNTAIN REGION: Colorado, Idaho, Montana, Oregon, Utah, Washington, Wyoming

17900 Pacific Highway South
Seattle, WA 98168
206/431-2001

SOUTHERN REGION: Alabama, Florida, Georgia, Kentucky, Mississippi, North Carolina, Puerto Rico, Rep. of Panama, South Carolina, Tennessee, Virgin Islands

Box 20636
Atlanta, GA 30320
404/763-7222

SOUTHWEST REGION: Arkansas, Louisiana, New Mexico, Oklahoma, Texas

4400 Blue Mound Road, Box 1689
Fort Worth, TX 76101
817/877-2100

WESTERN-PACIFIC REGION: Arizona, California, Hawaii, Nevada

Worldway Postal Center, Box 92007
Los Angeles, CA 90009
213/536-6427

Federal Highway Administration (Regional Administrators)
(Refer to Appendix F for boundaries)

Regions 1, 2
729 L.W. O'Brien Federal Building
Albany, NY 12207
518/472-6476

3. 1633 G.H. Fallon Federal Building
    Baltimore, MD 2101
    301/962-2773

4. 1720 Peachtree Road, NW, Room 200
    Atlanta, GA 30367
    404/881-4078

5. 18209 Dixie Highway
    Homewood, IL 60430
    312/799-6300

6. 8A00 F.G. Lanham Federal Building
    Fort Worth, TX 76102
    817/334-3232

7. 6301 Rockhill Road
    Kansas City, MO 64141
    816/926-7563

8. 555 Zang Street, Box 25246
    Denver, CO 80225
    303/234-4051

9. 2 Embarcadero Center, Room 530
    San Francisco, CA 94111
    415/556-3850

10. Mohawk Building, Room 412
    Portland, OR 97204
    503/221-2053

Federal Railroad Administration (Regional Directors)

CENTRAL REGION: Illinois, Indiana, Michigan, Minnesota, Wisconsin

165 North Canal Street, 14th Floor
Chicago, IL 60606
312/353-6203

EASTERN REGION: Delaware, District of Columbia, Maryland, Ohio, Pennsylvania, Virginia, West Virginia

Independence Building, Room 1020
Philadelphia, PA 19106
215/597-0750

MIDWEST REGION: Iowa, Kansas, Missouri, Nebraska

1807 Old Federal Office Building
911 Walnut Street
Kansas City, MO 64106
816/374-2497

NORTHEAST REGION: Connecticut, Maine, Massachusetts, New Hampshire, New Jersey, New York, Rhode Island, Vermont

Analex Building, Room 1307
Boston, MA 02114
617/223-2775

NORTHWEST REGION: Idaho, Montana, North Dakota, Oregon, South Dakota, Washington, Wyoming

Mead Building, Room 302
421 SW 5th Avenue
Portland, OR 97204
503/221-3011

SOUTHERN REGION: Alabama, Florida, Georgia, Kentucky, Mississippi, North Carolina, South Carolina, Tennessee

1720 Peachtree Road, NW, Room 440A
North Tower Building
Atlanta, GA 30309
404/881-2751

SOUTHWEST REGION: Arkansas, Louisiana, New Mexico, Oklahoma, Texas

11A23 F.G. Lanham Federal Building
Fort Worth, TX 76102
817/334-3601

WESTERN REGION: Alaska, Arizona, California, Colorado, Hawaii, Nevada, Utah

2 Embarcadero Center, Room 630
San Francisco, CA 94111
415/556-6411

Maritime Administration (Regional Directors)

CENTRAL REGION: Alabama, Arkansas, Florida (western), Iowa, Kansas, Kentucky, Louisiana, Mississippi, Missouri, Nebraska, Oklahoma, Tennessee, Texas

International Trade Mart Building, Room 2830
New Orleans, LA 70130
504/589-6556

EASTERN REGION: Connecticut, Delaware, District of Columbia, Florida (eastern), Georgia, Maine, Maryland, Massachusetts, New Hampshire, New Jersey, New York (eastern), North Carolina, Puerto Rico, Rhode Island, South Carolina, Vermont, Virginia, West Virginia

3737 J.K. Javits Federal Building
New York, NY 10278
212/264-1300

GREAT LAKES REGION: Illinois, Indiana, Michigan, Minnesota, New York (western), Ohio, Pennsylvania (western)

2300 East Devon Avenue, Building 5, Room 254
Box 508
Des Plaines, IL 60018
312/298-4535

WESTERN REGION: Alaska, Arizona, California, Colorado, Hawaii, Idaho, Montana, Nevada, New Mexico, North Dakota, Oregon, South Dakota, Utah, Washington, Wyoming

P. Burton Federal Building, U.S. Courthouse
Box 36073
San Francisco, CA 94102
415/556-3816

National Highway Traffic Safety Administration
(Regional Administrators)
(Refer to Appendix F for boundaries)

1. 55 Broadway
   Cambridge, MA 02142
   617/494-2680

2. 222 Mamaroneck Avenue, Room 204
   White Plains, NY 10605
   914/683-9690

3. 793 Elkridge Landing Road, Room D-203
   Linthicum, MD 21090
   301/962-7693

4. 1720 Peachtree Road, NW, Room 501
   Atlanta, GA 30309
   404/881-4537

5. Executive Plaza, Room 214
   Chicago Heights, IL 60411
   312/756-1950

6. A26 F.G. Lanham Federal Building
   Fort Worth, TX 76102
   817/334-3653

7. Box 19515
   Kansas City, MO 64141
   816/926-7887

8. 555 Zang Street, 1st Floor
   Lakewood, CO 80228
   303/234-3253

9. 2 Embarcadero Center, Room 610
   San Francisco, CA 94111
   415/556-6415

10. 3140 H.M. Jackson Federal Building
    Seattle, WA 98174
    206/442-5934

Research and Special Programs Administration, Materials Transportation Bureau
(Regional Chiefs)

CENTRAL REGION: Illinois, Indiana, Iowa, Kansas, Michigan, Minnesota, Missouri, Nebraska, Ohio, Wisconsin

1802 Old Federal Office Building
911 Walnut Street
Kansas City, MO 64106
816/374-2654

EASTERN REGION: Connecticut, Delaware, District of Columbia, Maine, Maryland, Massachusetts, New Hampshire, New Jersey, New York, Pennsylvania, Puerto Rico, Rhode Island, Vermont, Virginia, West Virginia

Nassif Building, Room 8321
Washington, DC 20590
202/755-9435

SOUTHERN REGION: Alabama, Florida, Georgia, Kentucky, Mississippi, North Carolina, South Carolina, Tennessee

1776 Peachtree Road, NW, Room 505N
Atlanta, GA 30309
404/881-2632

SOUTHWEST REGION: Arkansas, Louisiana, New Mexico, Oklahoma, Texas

2116 Federal Building
Houston, TX 77004
713/750-1746

WESTERN REGION: Alaska, Arizona, California, Colorado, Hawaii, Idaho, Montana, Nevada, North Dakota, Oregon, South Dakota, Utah, Washington, Wyoming

555 Zang Street
Lakewood, CO 80228
303/234-2313

Urban Mass Transportation Administration
(Regional Administrators)
(Refer to Appendix F for boundaries)

1. 55 Broadway
    Cambridge, MA 02142
    617/494-2055

2. 14-110 J.K. Javits Federal Building
    New York, NY 10278
    212/264-8162

3. Independence Building, Room 1010
    Philadelphia, PA 19106
    215/597-8098

4. 1720 Peachtree Road, NW, Room 400
    Atlanta, GA 30309
    404/881-3948

5. 300 South Wacker Drive, Room 1720
    Chicago, IL 60606
    312/353-2789

6. 9A32 F.G. Lanham Federal Building
    Fort Worth, TX 76102
    817/334-3787

7. 6301 Rockhill Road, Room 100
    Kansas City, MO 64131
    816/926-5053

8. Prudential Plaza, Room 1822
    Denver, CO 80265
    303/837-3242

9. 2 Embarcadero Center, Room 620
    San Francisco, CA 94111
    415/556-2884

10. 3142 H.M. Jackson Federal Building
    Seattle, WA 98174
    206/442-4210

TREASURY DEPARTMENT
Bureau of Alcohol, Tobacco and Firearms
(Regional Regulatory Administrators)

MIDWEST REGION: Illinois, Indiana, Iowa, Kansas, Kentucky, Michigan, Minnesota, Missouri, Nebraska, North Dakota, Ohio, South Dakota, West Virginia, Wisconsin

J.C. Kluczynski Federal Building, 15th Floor
Chicago, IL 60604
312/353-3778

NORTH ATLANTIC REGION: Connecticut, Delaware, District of Columbia, Maine, Maryland, Massachusetts, New Hampshire, New Jersey, New York, Pennsylvania, Puerto Rico, Rhode Island, Vermont, Virginia

6 World Trade Center, 6th Floor
New York, NY 10048
212/264-2328

SOUTHEAST REGION: Alabama, Florida, Georgia, Mississippi, North Carolina, South Carolina, Tennessee

3835 Northeast Expressway
Atlanta, GA 30340
404/455-2631

SOUTHWEST REGION: Arkansas, Colorado, Louisiana, New Mexico, Oklahoma, Texas, Wyoming

Old Santa Fe Federal Building, Room 701
Dallas, TX 75242
214/767-2260

WESTERN REGION: Alaska, Arizona, California, Hawaii, Idaho, Montana, Nevada, Oregon, Utah, Washington

525 Market Street, 34th Floor
San Francisco, CA 94105
415/474-9616

Comptroller of the Currency (Deputy Comptrollers)

CENTRAL DISTRICT: Illinois, Indiana, Kentucky, Michigan, Ohio, Wisconsin

Sears Tower, Room 5750
Chicago, IL 60606
312/353-0300

MIDWESTERN DISTRICT: Iowa, Kansas, Minnesota, Missouri, Nebraska, North Dakota, South Dakota

911 Main Street, Room 2616
Kansas City, MO 64105
816/374-6431

NORTHEASTERN DISTRICT: Connecticut, Delaware, District of Columbia, Maine, Maryland, Massachusetts, New Hampshire, New Jersey, New York, Pennsylvania, Puerto Rico, Rhode Island, Vermont, Virgin Islands

1211 Avenue of the Americas, Room 44250
New York, NY 10036
212/944-3495

SOUTHEASTERN DISTRICT: Alabama, Florida, Georgia, Mississippi, North Carolina, South Carolina, Tennessee, Virginia, West Virginia

Peachtree Cain Tower, Room 2700
Atlanta, GA 30303
404/221-4926

SOUTHWESTERN DISTRICT: Arkansas, Louisiana, New Mexico, Oklahoma, Texas

1201 Elm Street, Room 3800
Dallas, TX 75270
214/767-4400

WESTERN DISTRICT: Alaska, Arizona, California, Colorado, Guam, Hawaii, Idaho, Montana, Nevada, Oregon, Utah, Washington, Wyoming

44 Montgomery Street, Room 3600
San Francisco, CA 94104
415/974-8561

United States Customs Service (Regional Commissioners)

NEW YORK REGION: New Jersey (northern), New York (southeastern)

6 World Trade Center, Room 716
New York, NY 10048
212/466-4444

NORTH CENTRAL REGION: Illinois, Indiana, Iowa, Kansas, Kentucky, Michigan, Minnesota, Missouri, Nebraska, North Dakota, Ohio, Pennsylvania (city of Erie), South Dakota, Wisconsin

55 East Monroe Street, Room 1501
Chicago, IL 60603
312/353-4733

NORTHEAST REGION: Connecticut, Delaware, District of Columbia, Maine, Maryland, Massachusetts, New Hampshire, New Jersey (southern), New York (northern and western), Pennsylvania (exc. Erie), Rhode Island, Vermont

100 Summer Street
Boston, MA 02110
617/223-7506

PACIFIC REGION: Alaska, Arizona, California, Hawaii, Idaho, Montana, Nevada, Oregon, Utah, Washington, Wyoming

7401 Federal Building
300 North Los Angeles Street, Box 2071
Los Angeles, CA 90053
213/688-5900

SOUTH CENTRAL REGION: Alabama, Arkansas, Louisiana, Mississippi, Tennessee

423 Canal Street, Room 337
New Orleans, LA 70130
504/589-6324

SOUTHEAST REGION: Florida, Georgia, North Carolina, Puerto Rico, South Carolina, Virginia, Virgin Islands, West Virginia

99 SE 5th Street
Miami, FL 33131
305/350-5952

SOUTHWEST REGION: Colorado, New Mexico,
Oklahoma, Texas

5850 San Felipe Street, Room 500
Houston, TX 77057
713/953-6843

Internal Revenue Service (Regional
Commissioners)

CENTRAL REGION: Indiana, Kentucky,
Michigan, Ohio, West Virginia

7110 Federal Building
Cincinnati, OH 45202
513/684-3613

MID-ATLANTIC REGION: Delaware, District
of Columbia, Maryland, New Jersey,
Pennsylvania, Virginia

841 Chestnut Street
Philadelphia, PA 19107
215/597-2040

MIDWEST REGION: Illinois, Iowa, Minnesota,
Missouri, Nebraska, North Dakota, South
Dakota, Wisconsin

1 North Wacker Drive, 10th Floor
Chicago, IL 60606
312/886-5600

NORTH ATLANTIC REGION: Connecticut, Maine,
Massachusetts, New Hampshire, New York,
Rhode Island, Vermont

90 Church Street, Room 1108
New York, NY 10007
212/264-7061

SOUTHEAST REGION: Alabama, Florida,
Georgia, Mississippi, North Carolina, South
Carolina, Tennessee

600 Federal Building
Atlanta, GA 30043
404/221-6048

SOUTHWEST REGION: Arkansas, Colorado,
Kansas, Louisiana, New Mexico, Oklahoma,
Texas, Wyoming

7839 Churchill Way
Dallas, TX 75251
214/767-5855

WESTERN REGION: Alaska, Arizona, California,
Hawaii, Idaho, Montana, Nevada, Oregon,
Utah, Washington

525 Market Street
San Francisco, CA 84105
415/974-949

Appendix K
Key Vacancy Announcement

THE LIBRARY OF CONGRESS
Washington, D.C. 20540

VACANCY
ANNOUNCEMENT

(1) Vac. Ann. No.: _____ 50233

(2) Opening Date: _____ May 6, 1985

(3) Closing Date: _____ May 20, 1985

(Vacancy Announcements may be extended beyond the closing date. To determine if this vacancy announcement has been extended, contact the Employment Office.)

(4) POSITION: Supply Clerk (Data Transcribing)
GS-2005-05 (3203) $14,390 - $18,710

(5) POSITION LOCATION: Associate Librarian for Management, Procurement & Supply Division, Materiel Section; Landover Center Annex, Landover, Maryland

TYPE OF APPOINTMENT: Permanent
Non-Supervisory, bargaining unit position

(6) NUMBER OF VACANCIES: One

(8) BRIEF DESCRIPTION OF DUTIES: Under the general supervision of the Head, Materiel Section, the incumbent performs a wide range of clerical and technical support work necessary for the effective operation of the Materiel Section. Responsible for technical inventory management work involved in the maintenance and adjustment of inventory accounts and the records of all property and supply transactions, the establishment of stock levels, and the issuance of furniture, equipment, supplies, publications, service items and other essential materials. Performs all functions related to the hardware operations of the CRT terminal, for input, edit, and retrieval of information used in the management of inventory. Periodically examines data bank files, removing obsolete material to maintain its usefulness. Processes and controls Library wide stock issue requests for furniture and equipment. Assures proper authorization, budget approval, and fund authorization. Reviews stock records to determine availability noting possible item substitution.

(9) MINIMUM QUALIFICATIONS:
EXPERIENCE: One year of general clerical experience and six months of specialized experience at the GS-4 level in the Federal service or at a comparable level of difficulty outside the Federal service. Specialized experience is experience in supply work or closely related activities which have required the applicant to acquire and apply a knowledge of the rules, regulations and procedures, and program requirements of one or more areas of a supply system or in functions related to supply such as procurement, property disposal or quality control where the applicant was required to know, apply, or use special regulations, procedures, and forms.

(10) EDUCATIONAL REQUIREMENT: Graduation from high school

continued on reverse

MINIMUM REQUIREMENTS MUST BE MET BY _____ May 20, 1985

HOW TO APPLY:
1. Library of Congress employees must submit **Form LW 16/56, Employee Application.**
2. All other applicants must submit **Standard Form 171, Personal Qualifications Statement.**
3. Submit applications to: **The Library of Congress, Employment Office**
James Madison Memorial Building, LM 107
101 Independence Avenue, S. E.
Washington, D. C. 20540

NOTE:
a. All applications must be received by the final closing date to receive consideration for this vacancy announcement.
b. Civil Service status is not required.
c. United States citizenship is required for most positions.
d. All applications and attachments become the property of the Library of Congress.

LW 2/84 (rev 4/84)   The Library of Congress is an Equal Opportunity Employer

Because the Library of Congress is in the Legislative Branch of the Federal Government, there is no number 7: *AREA OF CONSIDERATION* which is found solely on vacancy announcements from agencies of the Executive Branch.

VACANCY ANNOUNCEMENT 50233

⑩ SUBSTITUTIONS:

CONT'D
A) Two full years of undergraduate education (60 semester hours or 90 quarter hours or the equivalent) may be substituted for the required general experience.

B) A bachelor's degree may be substituted for both the general and specialized experience requirements stated above.

⑫ TEST REQUIREMENTS: Passing of the Library's clerical test and the typing test with a net speed of 25 wpm. LC employees who are not currently in a position requiring typing at 25 wpm and all other applicants who have not been certified for the required typing speed within the past year must pass an accepted typing test. When the posted closing date has been extended, the final date for meeting test requirements will also be extended until the date the vacancy is announcement is actually closed.

⑪ QUALITY RANKING FACTORS: Evidence of the knowledges, skills and abilities cited in the quality ranking factors below may be demonstrated by experience, education, training, self-development, outside activities, awards and commendations. To receive appropriate credit, such evidence must be stated on the application form or supplemental forms.

1. Knowledge of Supply Management practices (50%)

2. Knowledge of data entry by CRT, particularly as it relates to Supply Management (25%)

3. Ability to work and deal effectively with others (25%)

NOTE: To receive credit for factor #1, knowledge of supply management practices, applicants should describe any experience operating an automated, mechanical or manual supply/inventory system, and should list any courses or training received in inventory management or supply. To receive credit for factor #2, applicants should describe all data entry or computer-related experience and list any related coursework.

***The Library reserves the right to fill any number of the above-described positions that are or become vacant during the life of this vacancy announcement.

Appendix L
Sample Vacancy Announcements from Various Federal Agencies

Issue Date: October 15, 1985

Closing Date: November 5, 1985

Merit Program

Announcement Number: OS/I-85-136

VACANCY ANNOUNCEMENT

U.S. DEPARTMENT OF COMMERCE

Title, Series & Grade:
Librarian (Law)
GM-1410-13

Vacancy Location:
Office of the Secretary
Office of the General
  Counsel
Immediate Office
Washington, D.C.

THIS POSITION IS COVERED BY MERIT PAY

WHO MAY APPLY: Status and non-status applicants.

Duties: The incumbent has supervisory and technical responsibility for developing and administering the Law Library for the Office of the General Counsel. Utilizing advanced library administration and management techniques incumbent formulates and implements policies and objectives of the Library, establishing internal procedures, determining nature and scope of the collection and services to be provided; plans, organizes, directs, and coordinates the selection, acquisition, and maintenance of the Law Library collection, determining policies for selection and retention of materials, both hard copy and microfilm, deciding the method of disposal for unwanted materials; maintains sound bibliographic control of the collection to ensure ready identification, access, and retrieval of materials; directs lending and reference services, providing background materials for specific work projects, performing searches on automated legal information systems; provides functional advice and guidance on all Professional library functions. Directs administrative management activities of the Law Library, including planning and justifying facilities, budget planning, personnel management, and public relations. Serves as Contracting Officer and Technical Representative for all Departmentwide contracts for automated legal information retrieval systems; provides extensive assistance to the Federal Library Committee's FEDLINK. Prepares analytical, evaluative reports requiring an understanding of basic research problems. Serves as liaison with key management officials.

QUALIFICATIONS: Applicant must meet qualifications requirements outlined in OPM's Qualification Standards (Handbook X-118).

EVALUATION OF QUALIFIED CANDIDATES will be on the basis of experience, training, self-development, outside activities and awards. Dates and hours of training and types and dates of awards should be included on the application. Performance appraisals will be given due weight prior to making a selection decision.

Vacancy announced under the competitive procedures of the O/S Office of Personnel Operations Merit Assignment Plan. This plan may be reviewed in the Personnel Office, Room 1069, Herbert C. Hoover Building. Employees in other buildings and field activity employees contact your Administrative Officer.

NOTE: The U.S. Department of Commerce is an equal opportunity employer. Vacancies are filled in accordance with non-discrimination policies of the U.S. Government.

FORM CD-260 (REV. 10-77)
PRESCRIBED BY D.A.O. 202-335

USCOMM-DC 1766-P78

THE LIBRARY OF CONGRESS
Washington, D.C. 20540

VACANCY
ANNOUNCEMENT

Vac. Ann. No.: __50285__

Opening Date: __May 6, 1985__

Closing Date: __May 20, 1985__

(Vacancy Announcements may be extended beyond the closing date. To determine if this vacancy announcement has been extended, contact the Employment Office.)

POSITION: Clerical Assistant
GS-301-4 (2897) $12,862 - $16,723

PROMOTION POTENTIAL: Promotion plan to GS-5

POSITION LOCATION: Library Environment Resources Office, Office of The Librarian; James Madison Memorial Building

TYPE OF APPOINTMENT: Indefinite
Non-supervisory, bargaining unit position

NUMBER OF VACANCIES: One

BRIEF DESCRIPTION OF DUTIES: Under the supervision of the Office Assistant, types (using typewriter and word processing equipment) and proofreads correspondence, reports and specifications of a technical nature; edits correspondence for grammatical correctness, accuracy of spelling, punctuation, and capitalization, for a professional staff of managers, interior designers, engineers, space management specialists and consultants. Maintains various files, greets visitors, schedules appointments and receives telephone calls.

MINIMUM QUALIFICATIONS:
EXPERIENCE: One year of general clerical experience including six months at the GS-3 level in the Federal service or at a comparable level of difficulty outside the Federal service. Good knowledge of English usage, ability to deal effectively with people, ability to work under pressure, and ability to perform clerical and editorial duties.

EDUCATIONAL REQUIREMENT: Graduation from high school.

SUBSTITUTIONS: Two years of college (60 semester hours or 90 quarter hours or equivalent) may be substituted for the experience requirement.

TEST REQUIREMENTS: Passing of the Library's clerical test and the typing test with a minimum speed of 40 wpm. LC employees who are not currently in a position requiring typing at 40 wpm and all other applicants who have not been certified for the required typing speed within the past year must pass an accepted typing test. When the posted closing date has been extended, the final date for meeting test requirements will also be extended until the date the vacancy announcement is actually closed.

***The Library reserves the right to fill any number of the above-described positions that are or become vacant during the life of this vacancy announcement.

MINIMUM REQUIREMENTS MUST BE MET BY _____ May 20, 1985 _____   MC/DC/N

HOW TO APPLY: 1. Library of Congress employees must submit **Form LW 16/56, Employee Application.**
2. All other applicants must submit **Standard Form 171, Personal Qualifications Statement.**
3. Submit applications to: **The Library of Congress, Employment Office**
James Madison Memorial Building, LM 107
101 Independence Avenue, S. E.
Washington, D. C. 20540

NOTE: a. All applications must be received by the final closing date to receive consideration for this vacancy announcement.
b. Civil Service status is not required.
c. United States citizenship is required for most positions.
d. All applications and attachments become the property of the Library of Congress.

LW 2/84 (rev 4/84)   **The Library of Congress is an Equal Opportunity Employer**

live, work and travel overseas

OPENING DATE: March 30, 1984   ANNOUNCEMENT NO: 84-07
    CLOSING DATE: April 30, 1984

DEPARTMENT OF DEFENSE
OFFICE OF DEPENDENTS SCHOOLS
===================================JOB OPPORTUNITY===================================

POSITION: Supply Management Officer   LOCATION: DoDDS-Pacific
           GM-2003-13   Regional Headquarters
                                                         Okinawa, Japan
TOUR OF DUTY: 2 years

AREA OF CONSIDERATION: Government-wide, Reinstatement Eligibles, Handicapped
                        Individuals and Disabled Veterans

==

HOW TO APPLY: Qualified applicants should submit a completed Standard Form 171,
Personal Qualifications Statement and attached Performance Element Appraisal,
plus a supplement which concisely addresses the knowledge, skills and/or abilities
described under ranking factors outlined below, to Central Civilian Personnel
Office, 18th Combat Support Group/DPCI, APO San Francisco 96239.

==

DUTIES AND RESPONSIBILITIES: Works under very general supervision. Supervisor
outlines functional assignments and provides overall policy guidance. Incumbent
manages the supply program with substantial independence. Supervisor reviews
and evaluates performance in terms of effectiveness and achievement of results.
Plans, organizes and directs the region supply program. Directs and conducts
specialized supply activities in the broad areas of requirements determination,
maintenance management, contract management, inventory management, storage
management, distribution, packaging, cataloging, procurement, property utiliza-
tion, disposal, transportation and fund control. Directs the procurement and
acquisition of material primarily from DSA, GSA and USAMMAE. Manages the supply
training program for educator and supply personnel to insure unity to thrust

and facilitate currency with technical supply
programs. Applies a working knowledge of
computer techniques to enhance functional
control of the computerized supply system.
Participates with subordinate and lateral
organizations in meetings/discussions to
coordinate supply activities and provide
guidance and assistance.

Supply Management Officer cont'd
==================================

QUALIFICATION REQUIREMENTS: General and specialized experience as outlined in the 2003 series in the Office of Personnel Management (OPM) Handbook X-118.

RANKING FACTORS: 1) Knowledge of supply management operations. 2) Ability to design and implement computer based automated supply systems. 3) Knowledge of transportation operations. 4) Knowledge of warehouse operations. 5) Ability to supervise. 6) Ability to forecast requisition needs and to manage distribution. 7) Ability to communicate well, both orally and in writing.

PHYSICAL REQUIREMENTS: In addition to possessing emotional and mental stability, applicants must be physically able to efficiently perform duties without being a hazard to themselves or to others.

SECURITY CLEARANCE: This position involves access to classified information.

MERIT PROMOTION PROCEDURES: Applicants who meet the minimum requirements will be rated as "Qualified" or "Best Qualified" based on the following factors: Amount and type of experience relating to the duties of the position to be filled, and recency of experience.

GENERAL: Only currently employed career and career conditional employees, reinstatement eligibles, handicapped individuals and disabled veterans need apply.

CONSIDERATION WILL BE GIVEN TO ALL QUALIFIED
APPLICANTS WITHOUT REGARD TO RACE, COLOR, CREED,
SEX, AGE, NATIONAL ORIGIN OR NON-DISQUALIFYING HANDICAP

Additional copies of this announcement may be obtained from DoD Office of Dependents Schools, Hoffman Building 1, 2461 Eisenhower Avenue, Alexandria, Virginia 22331, Telephone: (202) 325-0885.

Applications will not be returned; therefore DO NOT SUBMIT original documents. Submit Performance Element Appraisal.

In addition to return rights provided by DoD CPM, Chapter 301, and placement by the DoD Priority Placement Program, DoDDS has negotiated servicing agreements with the Military Departments which provide for continued consideration in appropriate career programs while serving overseas with DoDDS, provided the requirements of the applicable career program are met.

Subject to a two-year probationary period unless exempted after review of the official personnel file by the selecting official.

Appendix M
Blank Standard Application
Form (SF-171)

Application for Federal Employment—SF 171

Read the instructions before you complete this application. *Type or print clearly in dark ink.*

Form Approved:
OMB No. 3206-0012

GENERAL INFORMATION

1 What kind of job are you applying for? *Give title and announcement number (if any)*

2 If the announcement lists several job titles, which jobs are you applying for?

3 Social Security Number

4 Birth date *(Month, Day, Year)*

5 Name *(Last, First, Middle)*

Street address or RFD number *(include apartment number, if any)*

City | State | ZIP Code

6 Other names ever used

7 Sex *(for statistical use)*
☐ Male ☐ Female

8 Home Phone
Area Code | Number

9 Work Phone
Area Code | Number | Ext.

10 Were you ever employed as a civilian by the Federal Government? If "**NO**", go to **11**. If "**YES**", mark each type of job you held with an "**X**".
☐ Temporary ☐ Career-Conditional ☐ Career ☐ Excepted
What is your highest grade, classification series and job title?

Dates at highest grade: FROM   TO

11 Do you have any applications for Federal employment on file with the U.S. Office of Personnel Management? If "**NO**", mark here ☐ and go to **12**. If "**YES**", write below and continue in **47** the information for each application: (a) the name of the office that has your application; (b) the title of the job; (c) the date of your Notice of Results; and (d) your rating.

DO NOT WRITE IN THIS AREA

FOR USE OF EXAMINING OFFICE ONLY

Material
☐ Submitted
☐ Returned

Entered register:

Notations:

Form reviewed:
Form approved:

Option	Grade	Earned Rating	Preference	Aug. Rating
			☐ 5 Points (Tent.)	
			☐ 10 Pts. (30%) Or More Comp. Dis.	
			☐ 10 Pts. Less Than 30% Comp. Dis.	
			☐ Other 10 Points	
			☐ Disallowed	

Initials and Date

☐ Being Investigated

ANNOUNCEMENT NO.

APPLICATION NO.

FOR USE OF APPOINTING OFFICER ONLY

Preference has been verified through proof that the separation was under honorable conditions, and other proof as required.

☐ 5-Point   ☐ 10-Point—30% or More Compensable Disability   ☐ 10-Point—Less Than 30% Compensable Disability   ☐ 10-Point—Other

Signature and Title

Agency | Date

AVAILABILITY

12 When can you start work? *(Month and Year)*

13 What is the **lowest** pay you will accept?
Pay $_____ per _____ OR Grade _____

14 Are you willing to work: | YES | NO
A. In the Washington, D.C., metropolitan area? | |
B. Outside the 50 United States? | |
C. Any place in the United States? | |
D. Only in *(list the location[s])*

15 Are you willing to work:
A. 40 hours per week (full-time)? | |
B. 25-32 hours per week (part-time)? | |
C. 17-24 hours per week (part-time)? | |
D. 16 or fewer hours per week (part-time)? | |
E. In an intermittent job (on-call/seasonal)? | |
F. Weekends, shifts, or rotating shifts? | |

16 Are you willing to take a temporary job lasting:
A. 5 to 12 months (sometimes longer)? | |
B. 1 to 4 months? | |
C. Less than 1 month? | |

17 Are you willing to travel away from home for:
A. 1 to 5 nights each month? | |
B. 6 to 10 nights each month? | |
C. 11 or more nights each month? | |

MILITARY SERVICE AND VETERAN PREFERENCE

18 Have you served on active duty in the United States Military Service? *If your only active duty was training in the Reserves or National Guard, answer "NO". If "NO", go to 22.* | YES | NO

19 Were you honorably discharged from the military service? *If your discharge was changed to "honorable" or "general" by a Discharge Review Board, answer "YES". If you received a clemency discharge, answer "NO". If "NO", explain in 47.* | |

20 Did you or will you retire at or above the rank of major or lieutenant commander? | |

21 List the dates, branch, and serial number for all active duty service.

FROM	TO	BRANCH OF SERVICE	SERIAL NUMBER

22 Place an "**X**" in the box next to your Veteran Preference claim. Mark only **one** box. *See the instructions for eligibility information.*

1 NO PREFERENCE

2 5-POINT PREFERENCE—You must show proof when you are hired.

10-POINT PREFERENCE—**If you claim 10-point preference, you must complete a Standard Form 15, which is available at any Federal Job Information Center. ATTACH THE COMPLETED SF 15 TO THIS APPLICATION, TOGETHER WITH THE PROOF REQUESTED IN THE SF 15.**

3 Non-compensably disabled or Purple Heart recipient.

4 Compensably disabled (less than 30%).

5 Spouse, widow(er), or mother.

6 Compensably disabled (30% or more).

THE FEDERAL GOVERNMENT IS AN EQUAL OPPORTUNITY EMPLOYER

Page 1   PREVIOUS EDITION USABLE   NSN 7540-00-935-7150   171-108

Standard Form 171 (Rev. 2/84)
Office of Personnel Management
FPM Chapter 295

WORK EXPERIENCE *If you have no work experience, write "NONE" in A below and go to 25 on page 3*

23 May we ask your present employer about your character, qualifications and work record? A "NO" will not affect our review of your qualifications. If you answer "NO" and we need to contact your present employer before we can offer you a job, we will contact you first............... | YES | NO |

24 READ **WORK EXPERIENCE** ON THE INSTRUCTION PAGE BEFORE YOU BEGIN
- Describe your current or most recent job in Block **A** and work backwards, describing each job you held **during the past 10 years**.
- You may sum up in one block work that you did **more than 10 years ago**. But, if that work **is related** to the type of job you are applying for, describe each related job in a separate block.
- If you were **unemployed** for longer than **3 months**, list the dates and your address(es) at that time in **47**. Do **not** list unemployment that was more than 10 years ago.

- INCLUDE VOLUNTEER WORK *(non-paid work)*—**If the work** *(or a part of the work)* **is like the job you are applying for,** complete **all** parts of the experience block just as you would for a paying job. You may receive credit for work experience with religious, community, welfare, service, and other organizations.
- INCLUDE MILITARY SERVICE—You should complete **all** parts of the experience block just as you would for a non-military job, including all supervisory experience. Describe each major change of duties or responsibilities in a separate experience block.
- IF YOU NEED MORE EXPERIENCE BLOCKS OR MORE SPACE TO DESCRIBE A JOB— **For more blocks,** use the SF 171-A or sheets of paper the same size as this page (be sure to include **all** information we ask for in **A** or **B** below). On **each** sheet show your name, Social Security Number, and the announcement number or job title. **For more space** continue in **47** or on a sheet of paper as described above.
- IF YOU NEED TO UPDATE (ADD MORE RECENT JOBS), use the SF 172 or a sheet of paper as described above.

A | Name and address of employer's organization *(include ZIP Code, if known)* | Dates employed *(give month and year)* From: To: | Average number of hours per week |
Salary or earnings Starting $ per Ending $ per	Place of employment City State
Exact title of your job	Your immediate supervisor Name / Area Code Telephone Number	Number and job titles of any employees you supervise(d)
Kind of business or organization *(manufacturing, accounting, social service, etc.)*	If Federal employment *(civilian or military)*, list: series, grade or rank, and the date of your last promotion	Your reason for wanting to leave

Description of work: Describe your specific duties, responsibilities and accomplishments in this job. *If you describe more than one type of work (for example, carpentry and painting, or personnel and budget), write the approximate percentage of time you spent doing each.*

For Agency Use (skill codes, etc.)

B | Name and address of employer's organization *(include ZIP Code, if known)* | Dates employed *(give month and year)* From: To: | Average number of hours per week |
Salary or earnings Starting $ per Ending $ per	Place of employment City State
Exact title of your job	Your immediate supervisor Name / Area Code Telephone Number	Number and job titles of any employees you supervised
Kind of business or organization *(manufacturing, accounting, social service, etc.)*	If Federal employment *(civilian or military)*, list series, grade or rank, and the date of your last promotion	Your reason for leaving

Description of work: Describe your specific duties, responsibilities and accomplishments in this job. *If you describe more than one type of work (for example, carpentry and painting, or personnel and budget), write the approximate percentage of time you spent doing each.*

For Agency Use (skill codes, etc.)

Page 2   *FOR MORE EXPERIENCE BLOCKS SEE SF 171-A ON BACK OF INSTRUCTION PAGE*

APPENDIX M: BLANK APPLICATION (SF-171)

─────────◄──────── ATTACH ANY ADDITIONAL FORMS AND SHEETS HERE ────────►─────────

EDUCATION

25 Did you graduate from high school? *If you have a GED high school equivalency or will graduate within the next nine months, answer "YES".*

YES ❙ If "YES", give month and year of graduation: _____

NO ❙ If "NO", give the highest grade you completed: _____

26 Write the name and location *(city and state)* of the last high school you attended

27 Have you ever attended college or graduate school? YES ❙ If "YES", continue with **28**.   NO ❙ If "NO", go to **31**.

28 NAME AND LOCATION *(city, state and ZIP code)* OF COLLEGE OR UNIVERSITY. *If you expect to graduate within nine months, give the* **month** *and* **year** *you expect to receive your degree.*

	MONTH AND YEAR ATTENDED		NO. OF CREDITS COMPLETED	TYPE OF DEGREE *(e.g. BA, MA)*	YEAR OF DEGREE
	From	To	Semester Hours OR Quarter Hours		
1)					
2)					
3)					

29 CHIEF UNDERGRADUATE SUBJECTS *Show major on the first line*

	NO. OF CREDITS COMPLETED
	Semester Hours OR Quarter Hours
1)	
2)	
3)	

30 CHIEF GRADUATE SUBJECTS *Show major on the first line*

	NO. OF CREDITS COMPLETED
	Semester Hours OR Quarter Hours
1)	
2)	
3)	

31 Have you completed any other courses or training **related to the kind of jobs you are applying for** *(for example, trade, vocational, Armed Forces, or business)?* YES   NO   If "YES", give the information requested below *(More courses?—Use a sheet of paper)*   If "NO", go to **32**.

	MONTH AND YEAR TRAINING COMPLETED	TOTAL CLASSROOM HOURS	SUBJECT(S)	NAME AND LOCATION OF SCHOOL *(City, state, and ZIP code, if known)*	CERTIFICATE DIPLOMA etc. *(if any)*
1)					
2)					
3)					

SPECIAL SKILLS, ACCOMPLISHMENTS AND AWARDS

32 List your special qualifications, skills or accomplishments that may help you get a job. *Some examples are: skills with machines; most important publications (do not submit copies); public speaking and writing experience; membership in professional or scientific societies; patents or inventions; etc.*

33 How many words per minute can you:

TYPE?	TAKE DICTATION?

Agencies may test your skills before hiring you.

34 List **job-related** licenses or certificates that you have, such as: *registered nurse; lawyer; radio operator; driver's; pilot's; etc.*

	LICENSE OR CERTIFICATE	DATE OF LATEST LICENSE OR CERTIFICATE	STATE OR OTHER LICENSING AGENCY
1)			
2)			

35 Do you speak or read a language other than English *(include sign language)?* **Applicants for jobs that require a language other than English may be given an interview conducted solely in that language.** YES   NO   If "YES", list each language and place an "X" in each column that applies to you.   If "NO", go to **36**.

LANGUAGE(S)	CAN PREPARE AND GIVE LECTURES		CAN SPEAK AND UNDERSTAND		CAN TRANSLATE ARTICLES		CAN READ ARTICLES FOR OWN USE	
	Fluently	With Difficulty	Fluently	Passably	Into English	From English	Easily	With Difficulty
1)								
2)								

36 List any honors, awards, or fellowships you have received. For each, give the year it was received.

REFERENCES

37 List three people who are **not** related to you and who know your qualifications and fitness for the kind of job(s) for which you are applying. **Do not** list supervisors you listed under **24**.

	FULL NAME OF REFERENCE	PRESENT BUSINESS OR HOME ADDRESS *(Number, street, city, state, and ZIP code)*	TELEPHONE NUMBER(S) *(Include area code)*	BUSINESS OR OCCUPATION
1)				
2)				
3)				

Page **3**

0

BACKGROUND INFORMATION—*You must answer each question in this section before we can process your application*

Place an "X" in the proper column for each question below.

YES | NO

38 Are you a citizen of the United States? If "NO", write the country or countries you are a citizen of: _____

> **Important note about questions 39 through 44:** We will consider the date, facts, and circumstances of each event you list. In most cases you can still be considered for Federal jobs. However, if you fail to tell the truth or fail to list all relevant events, this failure may be grounds for not hiring you, for firing you after you begin work, or for criminal prosecution [18 USC 1001].

39 During the last **10 years**, were you **fired from any job** for any reason, did you **quit after being told that you would be fired**, or did you leave by mutual agreement because of specific problems? If "YES", use **47** to write for each job: a) the name of the employer; b) the approximate date you left the job, and c) the reason(s) why you left.....

> **When answering questions 40 through 44 you may omit:** 1) traffic fines of $100.00 or less; 2) any violation of law committed before your 18th birthday, if finally decided in juvenile court or under a youth offender law; 3) any conviction set aside under the Federal Youth Corrections Act or similar State law; 4) any conviction whose record was expunged under Federal or State law.

40 Have you **ever** been convicted of or forfeited collateral for **any felony**? ....
A felony is defined as any violation of law punishable by imprisonment of longer than one year, except for violations called misdemeanors under State law which are punishable by imprisonment of two years or less.

41 Have you **ever** been convicted of or forfeited collateral for any **firearms** or **explosives** violation? ....

42 During the last **10 years** have you forfeited collateral, been convicted, been imprisoned, been on probation, or been on parole? Do **not** include violations reported in **40** or **41** above. ....

43 Are you **now** under charges for **any** violation of law? ....

44 Have you **ever** been convicted by a **court-martial**? If no military service, answer "NO". ....

> **IF YOU ANSWERED "YES" TO 40, 41, 42, 43, or 44, GIVE DETAILS IN 47.** For each violation write the: 1) date; 2) charge; 3) place; 4) court; and 5) action taken.

45 Do any of your relatives work for the United States Government or the United States Armed Forces? Include: *father; mother; husband; wife; son; daughter; brother; sister; uncle; aunt; first cousin; nephew; niece; father-in-law; mother-in-law; son-in-law; daughter-in-law; brother-in-law; sister-in-law; stepfather; stepmother; stepson; stepdaughter; stepbrother; stepsister; half brother; and half sister.*
If "YES", use **47** to write for each of these relatives, their: a) name; b) relationship; c) department, agency, or branch of the Armed Forces.

46 Do you receive, or have you ever applied for retirement pay, pension, or other pay based on military, Federal civilian, or District of Columbia Government service? ....

ADDITIONAL SPACE FOR ANSWERS

47 Write the number to which each answer applies. **If you need more space**, use sheets of paper the same size as this page. On each sheet write your name, Social Security Number, and the announcement number or job title. Attach all additional sheets at the top of page 3.

SIGNATURE, CERTIFICATION, AND RELEASE OF INFORMATION

YOU MUST SIGN THIS APPLICATION. Read the following carefully before you sign.

A false statement on any part of your application may be grounds for not hiring you, or for firing you after you begin work. Also, you may be punished by fine or imprisonment (U.S. Code, Title 18, Section 1001).

> **I understand** that any information I give may be investigated as allowed by law or Presidential order;
> **I consent** to the release of information about my ability and fitness for Federal employment by *employers, schools, law enforcement agencies and other individuals and organizations,* to *investigators, personnel staffing specialists, and other authorized employees of the Federal Government.*
> **I certify** that, to the best of my knowledge and belief, **all** of my statements are true, correct, complete, and made in good faith.

48 SIGNATURE *(Sign each application in dark ink)*

49 DATE SIGNED *(Month, day, year)*

☆ GPO : 1984 O - 421-526 (136)

Standard Form 171-A—Continuation Sheet for SF 171

Form Approved:
OMB No. 3206-0012

• Attach all SF 171-A's to your application at the top of page 3.

1. Name *(Last, First, Middle)*	2. Social Security Number

3. Job Title or Announcement Number You Are Applying For	4. Date Completed

ADDITIONAL WORK EXPERIENCE BLOCKS IF NEEDED

☐ Name and address of employer's organization *(include ZIP Code, if known)*	Dates employed *(give month and year)* From: To:	Average number of hours per week
	Salary or earnings Starting $ per Ending $ per	Place of employment City State

Exact title of your job	Your immediate supervisor Name	Area Code Telephone Number	Number and job titles of any employees you supervised

Kind of business or organization *(manufacturing, account-ing, social service, etc.)*	If Federal employment *(civilian or military)*, list series, grade or rank, and the date of your last promotion	Your reason for leaving

Description of work: Describe your specific duties, responsibilities and accomplishments in this job. *If you describe more than one type of work (for example, carpentry and painting, or personnel and budget), write the approximate percentage of time you spent doing each.*

For Agency Use (skill codes, etc.)

☐ Name and address of employer's organization *(include ZIP Code, if known)*	Dates employed *(give month and year)* From: To:	Average number of hours per week
	Salary or earnings Starting $ per Ending $ per	Place of employment City State

Exact title of your job	Your immediate supervisor Name	Area Code Telephone Number	Number and job titles of any employees you supervised

Kind of business or organization *(manufacturing, account-ing, social service, etc.)*	If Federal employment *(civilian or military)*, list series, grade or rank, and the date of your last promotion	Your reason for leaving

Description of work: Describe your specific duties, responsibilities and accomplishments in this job. *If you describe more than one type of work (for example, carpentry and painting, or personnel and budget), write the approximate percentage of time you spent doing each.*

For Agency Use (skill codes, etc.)

THE FEDERAL GOVERNMENT IS AN EQUAL OPPORTUNITY EMPLOYER

PREVIOUS EDITION USABLE   NSN 7540-00-935-7157   171-205

Standard Form 171-A (Rev. 2/84)
Office of Personnel Management
FPM Chapter 295

Appendix N
Vacancy Announcement for
Writer-Editor Position

THE LIBRARY OF CONGRESS
Washington, D.C. 20540

VACANCY
ANNOUNCEMENT

Vac. Ann. No.: __20388__

Opening Date: __June 23, 1982__

Closing Date: __July 3, 1982__

(Vacancy Announcements may be extended beyond the closing date. To determine if this vacancy announcement has been extended, contact the Employment Office.)

THIS CANCELS VACANCY ANNOUNCEMENT NUMBER 20284. THOSE APPLICANTS WHO APPLIED AND QUALIFIED UNDER 20284 WILL BE CONSIDERED AND NEED NOT REAPPLY.

POSITION: Writer-Editor
GS-09 (1082-09-4455) $19,477 - $25,318

POSITION LOCATION: Associate Librarian for National Programs, National Library Service for the Blind and Physically Handicapped, Publication and Media Section; Taylor Street Annex, 1291 Taylor Street, NW Washington, D.C.

TYPE OF APPOINTMENT: Permanent

NUMBER OF VACANCIES: One

BRIEF DESCRIPTION OF DUTIES:
Plans, researches, writes, edits and proofreads publications and informational materials for blind and physically handicapped users of the Library of Congress free reading program. Assists with the mailing list for all readers. On a deadline basis applies established guidelines and procedures and maintains schedules. Works with contractors, typesetters, printers, graphic designers and subject specialists to produce publications. Assists in developing and producing audio-visual materials.

MINIMUM QUALIFICATIONS:
SPECIALIZED EXPERIENCE: Two years of experience demonstrating clear, concise writing and editing according to established editorial style; making production schedules and meeting deadlines under pressure; working on joint or group projects effectively; marking copy for typesetters, printers, and other technical personnel; layout, paste-up and design. One year of this experience must have been at the GS-7 level in the Federal service or at a comparable level of difficulty outside the Federal service.

EDUCATIONAL REQUIREMENT: Bachelor's degree in English, Journalism or a related field.

Continued on reverse

THE STAFFING SPECIALIST FOR THIS ANNOUNCEMENT IS __Susan Kames__

MINIMUM REQUIREMENTS MUST BE MET BY __July 3, 1982__

HOW TO APPLY: 1. Library of Congress employees must submit **Form LW 16/56, Employee Application.**
2. All other applicants must submit **Standard Form 171, Personal Qualifications Statement.**
3. Submit applications to: **The Library of Congress, Employment Office**
James Madison Memorial Building, LM 107
101 Independence Avenue, S. E.
Washington, D. C. 20540

NOTE: a. All applications must be received by the final closing date to receive consideration for this vacancy announcement.
b. Civil Service status is not required.
c. United States citizenship is required for most positions.
d. All applications and attachments become the property of the Library of Congress.

LW 2/84 (rev 4/84)   **The Library of Congress is an Equal Opportunity Employer**

VACANCY ANNOUNCEMENT 20388

SUBSTITUTIONS:

a) For this position, three years of general experience may be substituted for the Educational requirement stated above.

b) For this position, a master's degree in English, journalism, or a related field may be substituted for the required Specialized Experience.

TEST REQUIREMENTS: Passing the LC typing test with a net speed of 25 wpm. LC employees who are not currently in a position requiring typing at 25 wpm and all other applicants who have not been certified for the required typing speed within the past year must pass the LC or another certified typing test. When the posted closing date has been extended, the final day for meeting test requirements will also be extended until the date the vacancy announcement is actually closed.

QUALITY RANKING FACTORS:

1. Knowledge of publication practices and procedures
2. Ability to work and deal effectively with others.

NOTE: To receive full credit for Factor #1, above, please provide details on the application form concerning coursework in creative writing, related subjects, experience in writing, copy editing, photocomposition, layout and design; as well as any awards, commendations, etc., in a related area. For Factor #2, please provide details on your dealings with librarians, automation specialists, if any, or technicians or professionals in any other field.

QUALIFICATIONS EVALUATION: Evidence of minimum qualifications and quality ranking factors may be demonstrated by experience, education, training, self-development, outside activities, awards, and commendations. To receive appropriate credit, such evidence must be stated on the application form or supplemental forms.

***The Library reserves the right to fill fewer than the number of vacancies specified above.

Appendix O
Completed SF-171 for
Writer-Editor Position

APPENDIX O: SF-171 FOR WRITER-EDITOR POSITION

Application for Federal Employment—SF 171

Read the instructions before you complete this application. *Type or print clearly in dark ink.*

Form Approved:
OMB No. 3206-0012

GENERAL INFORMATION

1 What kind of job are you applying for? *Give title and announcement number (if any)*
Writer-Editor   #20388

2 If the announcement lists several job titles, which jobs are you applying for?
Open

3 Social Security Number
490 | 555 | 8560

4 Birth date *(Month, Day, Year)*
7/2/54

5 Name *(Last, First, Middle)*
Delich, Marcie D.
Street address or RFD number *(include apartment number, if any)*
1320 Martha Custis Drive
City
Alexandria
State
VA
ZIP Code
22302

6 Other names ever used
N/A

7 Sex *(for statistical use)*
☐ Male   ☒ Female

8 Home Phone
Area Code | Number
703 | 555-0020

9 Work Phone
Area Code | Number | Ext
202 | 555-3414

10 Were you ever employed as a civilian by the Federal Government? If "**NO**", go to **11**.
If "**YES**", mark each type of job you held with an "**X**".
☐ Temporary   ☐ Career-Conditional   ☐ Career   ☐ Excepted
What is your highest grade, classification series and job title?

Dates at highest grade: FROM _____ TO _____

11 Do you have any applications for Federal employment on file with the U.S. Office of Personnel Management? If "**NO**", mark here ☒ and go to **12**. If "**YES**", write below and continue in **47** the information for each application: (a) the name of the office that has your application; (b) the title of the job; (c) the date of your Notice of Results; and (d) your rating.

FOR USE OF EXAMINING OFFICE ONLY

Material
☐ Submitted
☐ Returned

Entered register:

Notations:

Form reviewed:
Form approved:

Option	Grade	Earned Rating	Preference	Aug. Rating
			☐ 5 Points (Tent.)	
			☐ 10 Pts. (30%) Or More Comp. Dis	
			☐ 10 Pts. Less Than 30% Comp. Dis	
			☐ Other 10 Points	
			☐ Disallowed	

Initials and Date

☐ Being Investigated

FOR USE OF APPOINTING OFFICER ONLY

Preference has been verified through proof that the separation was under honorable conditions, and other proof as required.

☐ 5-Point   ☐ 10-Point—30% or More Compensable Disability   ☐ 10-Point—Less Than 30% Compensable Disability   ☐ 10-Point—Other

Signature and Title

Agency   Date

AVAILABILITY

12 When can you start work? *(Month and Year)*
Immediately

13 What is the **lowest** pay you will accept?
Pay $_____ per _____ OR Grade 9

14 Are you willing to work:

	YES	NO
A. In the Washington, D.C., metropolitan area?	X	
B. Outside the 50 United States?		X
C. Any place in the United States?	X	
D. Only in *(list the location[s])*		

15 Are you willing to work:

	YES	NO
A. 40 hours per week (full-time)?	X	
B. 25-32 hours per week (part-time)?	X	
C. 17-24 hours per week (part-time)?	X	
D. 16 or fewer hours per week (part-time)?		X
E. In an intermittent job (on-call/seasonal)?		X
F. Weekends, shifts, or rotating shifts?	X	

16 Are you willing to take a temporary job lasting:

	YES	NO
A. 5 to 12 months (sometimes longer)?	X	
B. 1 to 4 months?	X	
C. Less than 1 month?		X

17 Are you willing to travel away from home for:

	YES	NO
A. 1 to 5 nights each month?	X	
B. 6 to 10 nights each month?		X
C. 11 or more nights each month?		X

MILITARY SERVICE AND VETERAN PREFERENCE

18 Have you served on active duty in the United States Military Service? *If your only active duty was training in the Reserves or National Guard, answer "NO". If "NO", go to 22.*
YES | NO → X

19 Were you honorably discharged from the military service? *If your discharge was changed to "honorable" or "general" by a Discharge Review Board, answer "YES". If you received a clemency discharge, answer "NO". If "NO", explain in 47.*

20 Did you or will you retire at or above the rank of major or lieutenant commander?

21 List the dates, branch, and serial number for all active duty service.

FROM	TO	BRANCH OF SERVICE	SERIAL NUMBER

22 Place an "**X**" in the box next to your Veteran Preference claim. Mark only **one** box. *See the instructions for eligibility information.*

☒ NO PREFERENCE

☐2 5-POINT PREFERENCE—You must show proof when you are hired.

10-POINT PREFERENCE—**If you claim 10-point preference, you must complete a Standard Form 15, which is available at any Federal Job Information Center. ATTACH THE COMPLETED SF 15 TO THIS APPLICATION, TOGETHER WITH THE PROOF REQUESTED IN THE SF 15.**

☐3 Non-compensably disabled or Purple Heart recipient.
☐4 Compensably disabled (less than 30%).
☐5 Spouse, widow(er), or mother.
☐6 Compensably disabled (30% or more).

THE FEDERAL GOVERNMENT IS AN EQUAL OPPORTUNITY EMPLOYER

Page 1   PREVIOUS EDITION USABLE   NSN 7540-00-935-7150   171-108

Standard Form 171 (Rev. 2/84)
Office of Personnel Management
FPM Chapter 295

152

WORK EXPERIENCE *If you have no work experience, write NONE in A below and go to 25 on page 3*

23 May we ask your present employer about your character, qualifications and work record? A "NO" will not affect our review of your qualifications. *If you answer "NO" and we need to contact your present employer before we can offer you a job, we will contact you first.* . . . .

	YES	NO
		X

• INCLUDE VOLUNTEER WORK *(non-paid work)*—**If the work** *(or a part of the work)* **is like the job you are applying for,** complete all parts of the experience block just as you would for a paying job. You may receive credit for work experience with religious, community, welfare, service, and other organizations.

24 READ **WORK EXPERIENCE** ON THE INSTRUCTION PAGE BEFORE YOU BEGIN
• Describe your current or most recent job in Block **A** and work backwards, describing each job you held **during the past 10 years.**
• You may sum up in one block work that you did **more than 10 years** ago. But, if that work **is related** to the type of job you are applying for, describe each related job in a separate block.
• If you were **unemployed** for longer than **3 months**, list the dates and your address(es) at that time in **47**. Do **not** list unemployment that was more than 10 years ago.

• INCLUDE MILITARY SERVICE—You should complete all parts of the experience block just as you would for a non-military job, including all supervisory experience. Describe each major change of duties or responsibilities in a separate experience block.
• IF YOU NEED MORE EXPERIENCE BLOCKS OR MORE SPACE TO DESCRIBE A JOB—
For more blocks, use the SF 171-A or sheets of paper the same size as this page (be sure to include all information we ask for in A or B below). On each sheet show your name, Social Security Number, and the announcement number or job title.
For more space continue in 47 or on a sheet of paper as described above.
• IF YOU NEED TO UPDATE (ADD MORE RECENT JOBS), use the SF 172 or a sheet of paper as described above.

A

Name and address of employer's organization *(include ZIP Code, if known)*	Dates employed *(give month and year)*		Average number of hours per week
Smithsonian Institution 1200 John Adams Drive Washington, D.C. 20524	From: 1/80	To: Present	40
	Salary or earnings Starting $15,450 per year Ending $17,980 per year		Place of employment City Washington, D.C. State

Exact title of your job	Your immediate supervisor			Number and job titles of any employees you supervise(d)
Editor	Name Joan Smith	Area Code 202	Telephone Number 555-6660	None

Kind of business or organization *(manufacturing, accounting, social service, etc.)*	If Federal employment *(civilian or military)*, list: series, grade or rank, and the date of your last promotion		Your reason for wanting to leave
Museum	GS-1082-07	January 1984	Advancement

Description of work: Describe your specific duties, responsibilities and accomplishments in this job. *If you describe more than one type of work (for example, carpentry and painting, or personnel and budget), write the approximate percentage of time you spent doing each.*

Responsibilities include: plan, research, edit, proofread and monitor production of museum's publications distributed to a readership of nearly 600,000 on an on-going basis; establish and maintain many production schedules, guidelines and procedures; work with contractors and subcontractors, including subject specialists, authors, typesetters, designers and printers; edit rough and finished manuscripts for style, grammar, factual accuracy, readability and tactfulness in the context of the intended audience; assist with design and development of audio-visual programs and television spots.

For Agency Use (skill codes, etc.)

B

Name and address of employer's organization *(include ZIP Code, if known)*	Dates employed *(give month and year)*		Average number of hours per week
Green Associates 1210 El Camino Way Berkeley, CA 94577	From: 5/76	To: 11/80	40
	Salary or earnings Starting $10,200 per year Ending $12,400 per year		Place of employment City Berkeley, State CA

Exact title of your job	Your immediate supervisor			Number and job titles of any employees you supervised
Public Relations Asst.	Name Azalea Jackson	Area Code 415	Telephone Number 555-8935	1 Artist

Kind of business or organization *(manufacturing, accounting, social service, etc.)*	If Federal employment *(civilian or military)*, list series, grade or rank, and the date of your last promotion	Your reason for leaving
Public Relations	N/A	Advancement

Description of work: Describe your specific duties, responsibilities and accomplishments in this job. *If you describe more than one type of work (for example, carpentry and painting, or personnel and budget), write the approximate percentage of time you spent doing each.*

Responsibilities included: writing and re-writing advertising and promotional copy; assisting in conceptualizing campaigns for advertising, public relations, publicity and promotion for a variety of clients; editing advertising and promotional copy; editing client newsletters; coordinating mailings to direct and indirect markets; conducting telephone surveys.

For Agency Use (skill codes, etc.)

Page 2 *FOR MORE EXPERIENCE BLOCKS SEE SF 171-A ON BACK OF INSTRUCTION PAGE*

◄━━━━━━ **ATTACH ANY ADDITIONAL FORMS AND SHEETS HERE** ━━━━━━►

EDUCATION

25 Did you graduate from high school? *If you have a GED high school equivalency or will graduate within the next nine months, answer "YES".*

26 Write the name and location *(city and state)* of the last high school you attended
Napa High School   Napa, CA

YES [X] If "**YES**", give month and year of graduation: 6/72

NO [ ] If "**NO**", give the highest grade you completed:

27 Have you ever attended college or graduate school? YES [X] If "**YES**", continue with **28**
NO [ ] If "**NO**", go to **31**.

28 NAME AND LOCATION *(city, state and ZIP code)* OF COLLEGE OR UNIVERSITY. *If you expect to graduate within nine months, give the **month** and **year** you expect to receive your degree.*

	MONTH AND YEAR ATTENDED		NO. OF CREDITS COMPLETED		TYPE OF DEGREE *(e.g. B.A., M.A.)*	YEAR OF DEGREE
	From	To	Semester Hours	OR Quarter Hours		
1) Napa College Napa, CA	9/72	5/76	124		B.A.	1976
2)						
3)						

29

CHIEF UNDERGRADUATE SUBJECTS *Show major on the first line*	NO. OF CREDITS COMPLETED
	Semester Hours OR Quarter Hours
1) Journalism	24
2) English	18
3)	

30

CHIEF GRADUATE SUBJECTS *Show major on the first line*	NO. OF CREDITS COMPLETED
	Semester Hours OR Quarter Hours
1) N/A	
2)	
3)	

31 Have you completed any other courses or training **related to the kind of jobs you are applying for** *(for example, trade, vocational, Armed Forces, or business)*? YES [X] NO [ ]   If "**YES**", give the information requested below *(More courses?—Use a sheet of paper)*   If "**NO**", go to **32**

MONTH AND YEAR TRAINING COMPLETED	TOTAL CLASSROOM HOURS	SUBJECT(S)	NAME AND LOCATION OF SCHOOL *(City, state, and ZIP code, if known)*	CERTIFICATE, DIPLOMA, etc *(if any)*
1) 6/78	40	Wang Word Processing	Self-taught	
2) 11/79	40	Newsletter Editing	San Francisco State College	
3) 3/73	24	Interpersonal Skills	Queen of the Valley Hospital Napa, CA	

SPECIAL SKILLS, ACCOMPLISHMENTS AND AWARDS

32 List your special qualifications, skills or accomplishments that may help you get a job. *Some examples are: skills with machines; most important publications (do not submit copies); public speaking and writing experience; membership in professional or scientific societies; patents or inventions; etc.*

American Assoc. of PR Professionals: Member and editor of chapter 348 newsletter. Various news and feature stories in assorted newsletters and newspapers. Wang word processor, Mergenthaler Lintotype typesetter, IMB Memory typewriter, all photo-copiers.

33 How many words per minute can you:

TYPE?	TAKE DICTATION?
50wpm	0

Agencies may test your skills before hiring you.

34 List **job-related** licenses or certificates that you have, such as: *registered nurse; lawyer; radio operator; driver's; pilot's; etc.*

LICENSE OR CERTIFICATE	DATE OF LATEST LICENSE OR CERTIFICATE	STATE OR OTHER LICENSING AGENCY
1) N/A		
2)		

35 Do you speak or read a language other than English *(include sign language)*? YES [X] NO [ ]   *Applicants for jobs that require a language other than English may be given an interview conducted solely in that language.*   If "**YES**", list each language and place an "**X**" in each column that applies to you.   If "**NO**", go to **36**.

LANGUAGE(S)	CAN PREPARE AND GIVE LECTURES		CAN SPEAK AND UNDERSTAND		CAN TRANSLATE ARTICLES		CAN READ ARTICLES FOR OWN USE	
	Fluently	With Difficulty	Fluently	Passably	Into English	From English	Easily	With Difficulty
1) French								X
2)								

36 List any honors, awards, or fellowships you have received. For each, give the year it was received.

Student liaison, Queen of the Valley Hospital; Tuition journalism scholarships 1975, 1976 Napa College; Associated Collegiate Press award for best news story of 1974 in a bi-weekly college paper serving a campus of less than 50,000; Bonus Award for error-free newsletters produced for Green Assoc. Dec. 1978.

REFERENCES

37 List three people who are **not** related to you and who know your qualifications and fitness for the kind of job(s) for which you are applying. **Do not** list supervisors you listed under **24**.

FULL NAME OF REFERENCE	PRESENT BUSINESS OR HOME ADDRESS *(Number, street, city, state, and ZIP code)*	TELEPHONE NUMBER(S) *(Include area code)*	BUSINESS OR OCCUPATION
1) Richard Buchsbaum	1000 Esplanade New Orleans, LA	504-555-6509	Editor
2) Mary MacArthur	2100 Pennsylvania Avenue Washington, D.C. 20036	202-555-3971	Arts Manager
3) Scot Lindstrom	4591 Camino del Vista Benicia, CA 94510	707-555-3598	Reporter

Page **3**

BACKGROUND INFORMATION—*You must answer each question in this section before we can process your application*

Place an "X" in the proper column for each question below.

	YES	NO
38 Are you a citizen of the United States? If "NO", write the country or countries you are a citizen of: _____	X	

> **Important note about questions 39 through 44:** We will consider the date, facts, and circumstances of each event you list. In most cases you can still be considered for Federal jobs. However, if you fail to tell the truth or fail to list all relevant events, this failure may be grounds for not hiring you, for firing you after you begin work, or for criminal prosecution [18 USC 1001].

	YES	NO
39 During the last **10 years**, were you **fired from any job** for any reason, did you **quit after being told that you would be fired**, or did you leave by mutual agreement because of specific problems? If "YES", use **47** to write for each job: a) the name of the employer; b) the approximate date you left the job, and c) the reason(s) why you left.....		X

> **When answering questions 40 through 44 you may omit:** 1) traffic fines of $100.00 or less; 2) any violation of law committed before your 18th birthday, if finally decided in juvenile court or under a youth offender law; 3) any conviction set aside under the Federal Youth Corrections Act or similar State law; 4) any conviction whose record was expunged under Federal or State law.

	YES	NO
40 Have you **ever** been convicted of or forfeited collateral for **any felony**? .... *A felony is defined as any violation of law punishable by imprisonment of longer than one year, except for violations called misdemeanors under State law which are punishable by imprisonment of two years or less.*		X
41 Have you **ever** been convicted of or forfeited collateral for any **firearms** or **explosives** violation?		X
42 During the last **10 years** have you forfeited collateral, been convicted, been imprisoned, been on probation, or been on parole? Do **not** include violations reported in **40** or **41** above		X
43 Are you **now** under charges for **any** violation of law?		X
44 Have you **ever** been convicted by a **court-martial**? If no military service, answer "NO".		X

> **IF YOU ANSWERED "YES" TO 40, 41, 42, 43, or 44, GIVE DETAILS IN 47.** For each violation write the: 1) date; 2) charge; 3) place; 4) court; and 5) action taken.

	YES	NO
45 Do any of your relatives work for the United States Government or the United States Armed Forces? Include: *father; mother; husband; wife; son; daughter; brother; sister; uncle; aunt; first cousin; nephew; niece; father-in-law; mother-in-law; son-in-law; daughter-in-law; brother-in-law; sister-in-law; stepfather; stepmother; stepson; stepdaughter; stepbrother; stepsister; half brother; and half sister.* .... If "YES", use **47** to write for each of these relatives, their: a) name; b) relationship; c) department, agency, or branch of the Armed Forces.		X
46 Do you receive, or have you ever applied for retirement pay, pension, or other pay based on military, Federal civilian, or District of Columbia Government service?		X

ADDITIONAL SPACE FOR ANSWERS

47 Write the number to which each answer applies. **If you need more space,** use sheets of paper the same size as this page. On each sheet write your name, Social Security Number, and the announcement number or job title. Attach all additional sheets at the top of page 3.

> 31: Newsletter editing course at San Francisco State was taken during a short period of unemployment while I was laid off from my job at Green Associates while the contract I was working under was renegotiated with the company's major client. I paid for the course myself and have a certificate of completion.

SIGNATURE, CERTIFICATION, AND RELEASE OF INFORMATION

YOU MUST SIGN THIS APPLICATION. Read the following carefully before you sign.

A false statement on any part of your application may be grounds for not hiring you, or for firing you after you begin work. Also, you may be punished by fine or imprisonment (U.S. Code, Title 18, Section 1001).

I **understand** that any information I give may be investigated as allowed by law or Presidential order;

I **consent** to the release of information about my ability and fitness for Federal employment by employers, schools, law enforcement agencies and other individuals and organizations, to investigators, personnel staffing specialists, and other authorized employees of the Federal Government.

I **certify** that, to the best of my knowledge and belief, **all** of my statements are true, correct, complete, and made in good faith.

48 SIGNATURE *(Sign each application in dark ink)*	**49** DATE SIGNED *(Month, day, year)*

☆ GPO : 1984 O - 421-526 (136)

Standard Form 171-A—Continuation Sheet for SF 171

Form Approved:
OMB No. 3206-0012

• Attach all SF 171-A's to your application at the top of page 3.

1. Name *(Last, First, Middle)*	2. Social Security Number
Delich, Marcie D.	490-555-8560

3. Job Title or Announcement Number You Are Applying For	4. Date Completed
#20388	

ADDITIONAL WORK EXPERIENCE BLOCKS IF NEEDED

C

Name and address of employer's organization *(include ZIP Code, if known)*	Dates employed *(give month and year)*	Average number of hours per week
Queen of the Valley Hospital 1000 Silverado Trail Napa, CA 94401	From: 9/72 To: 4/76	20
	Salary or earnings Starting $3.50 per hour Ending $4.75 per hour	Place of employment City Napa, State CA

Exact title of your job	Your immediate supervisor			Number and job titles of any employees you supervised
Editorial Assistant	Name Joanne Marquardt	Area Code 415	Telephone Number 677-9000	None

Kind of business or organization *(manufacturing, accounting, social service, etc.)*	If Federal employment *(civilian or military)*, list series, grade or rank, and the date of your last promotion	Your reason for leaving
Hospital	N/A	Advancement

Description of work: Describe your specific duties, responsibilities and accomplishments in this job. *If you describe more than one type of work (for example, carpentry and painting, or personnel and budget), write the approximate percentage of time you spent doing each.*

Responsibilities included: assisting with gathering and writing employee news for monthly newsletter; editing and proofreading copy; taking photographs for publication; interviewing doctors, union officials and employees; giving visitors tours of the facilities; supervising mass mailings to Napa County residents; assisting with public image campaigns and hospital promotions; making arrangements for annual fund-raising effort; placing newspaper stories; answering queries from outside sources.

For Agency Use (skill codes, etc.)

Name and address of employer's organization *(include ZIP Code, if known)*	Dates employed *(give month and year)*	Average number of hours per week
	From: To:	
	Salary or earnings Starting $ per Ending $ per	Place of employment City State

Exact title of your job	Your immediate supervisor			Number and job titles of any employees you supervised
	Name	Area Code	Telephone Number	

Kind of business or organization *(manufacturing, accounting, social service, etc.)*	If Federal employment *(civilian or military)*, list series, grade or rank, and the date of your last promotion	Your reason for leaving

Description of work: Describe your specific duties, responsibilities and accomplishments in this job. *If you describe more than one type of work (for example, carpentry and painting, or personnel and budget), write the approximate percentage of time you spent doing each.*

For Agency Use (skill codes, etc.)

THE FEDERAL GOVERNMENT IS AN EQUAL OPPORTUNITY EMPLOYER
PREVIOUS EDITION USABLE   NSN 7540-00-935-7157   171-806

Standard Form 171-A (Rev. 2/84)
Office of Personnel Management
FPM Chapter 295

Appendix P
Occupation Groups and Series of Classes on the General Schedule (GS)

GS-000 MISCELLANEOUS GROUP (NOT ELSEWHERE CLASSIFIED)

Correctional Institution Administration Series	GS-006
Correctional Officer Series	GS-007
Institutional Administration Series	GS-008
Institutional Management Series	GS-009
Bond Sales Promotion Series	GS-011
Safety Management Series	GS-018
Safety Technician Series	GS-019
Community Planning Series	GS-020
Community Planning Technician Series	GS-021
Outdoor Recreation Planning Series	GS-023
Park Management Series	GS-025
Park Technician Series	GS-026
Crop Insurance Administration Series	GS-027
Environmental Protection Specialist Series	GS-028
Environmental Protection Assistant Series	GS-029
Sports Specialist Series	GS-030
Funeral Directing Series	GS-050
Chaplain Series	GS-060
Clothing Design Series	GS-062
Fingerprint Identification Series	GS-072
Security Administration Series	GS-080
Fire Protection and Prevention Series	GS-081
United States Marshal Series	GS-082
Police Series	GS-083
Guard Series	GS-085
Guide Series	GS-090
General Student Trainee Series	GS-099

GS-100 SOCIAL SCIENCE, PSYCHOLOGY, AND WELFARE GROUP

Social Science Series	GS-101
Social Science Aid and Technician Series	GS-102
Social Insurance Administration Series	GS-105
Unemployment Insurance Series	GS-106
Economist Series	GS-110
Economics Assistant Series	GS-119

Food Assistance Program Specialist Series	GS-120
Foreign Affairs Series	GS-130
Personnel Management Series	GS-131
Intelligence Series	GS-132
Intelligence Aid and Clerk Series	GS-134
Foreign Agricultural Affairs Series	GS-135
International Cooperation Series	GS-136
Manpower Research and Analysis Series	GS-140
Manpower Development Series	GS-142
Geography Series	GS-140
Equal Opportunity Series	GS-160
History Series	GS-170
Psychology Series	GS-180
Psychology Aid and Technician Series	GS-181
Sociology Series	GS-184
Social Work Series	GS-185
Social Services Aid and Assistant Series	GS-186
Recreation Specialist Series	GS-188
General Anthropology Series	GS-190
Archeology Series	GS-193
Social Science Student Trainee Series	GS-199

GS-200 PERSONNEL MANAGEMENT AND INDUSTRIAL RELATIONS GROUP

Personnel Management Series	GS-201
Personnel Clerical and Assistance	GS-203
Military Personnel Clerical and Technician Series	GS-204
Military Personnel Management Series	GS-205
Personnel Staffing Series	GS-212
Position Classification Series	GS-221
Occupational Analysis Series	GS-222
Salary and Wage Administration Series	GS-223
Employee Relations Series	GS-230
Labor Relations Series	GS-233
Employee Development Series	GS-235
Mediation Series	GS-241
Apprenticeship and Training Series	GS-243
Labor Management Relations Examining Series	GS-244
Contractor Industrial Relations Series	GS-246
Wage and Hour Compliance Series	GS-249

GENERAL ADMINISTRATIVE CLERICAL AND OFFICE SERVICES GROUP

Miscellaneous Administration and Program Series	GS-301
Messenger Series	GS-302
Miscellaneous Clerk and Assistant Series	GS-303
Information Receptionist Series	GS-304
Mail and File Series	GS-305
Correspondence Clerk Series	GS-309
Clerk-Stenographer and Reporter Series	GS-312

Stenographic or Typing Unit Supervisor Series	GS-313
Secretary Series	GS-318
Closed Microphone Reporter Series	GS-319
Clerk-Typist Systems Series	GS-322
Digital Computer Systems Administration Series	GS-330
Computer Operation Series	GS-332
Computer Specialist Series	GS-334
Computer Aid and Technician Series	GS-335
Program Management Series	GS-340
Administrative Officer Series	GS-341
Support Services Administration Series	GS-342
Management Analysis Series	GS-343
Management Clerical and Assistance Series	GS-344
Program Analysis Series	GS-345
Logistics Management Series	GS-346
Equipment Operator Series	GS-350
Printing Clerical Series	GS-351
Bookkeeping Machine Operator Series	GS-354
Calculating Machine Operation Series	GS-355
Data Transcriber Series	GS-356
Coding Series	GS-357
Electric Accounting Machine Operation Series	GS-359
Electric Accounting Machine Project Planning Series	GS-362
Telephone Operating Series	GS-382
Teletypist Series	GS-385
Cryptographic Equipment Operation Series	GS-388
Radio Operating Series	GS-389
Communications Relay Operation Series	GS-390
General Communications Series	GS-391
Communications Specialist Series	GS-393
Communications Clerical Series	GS-394

GS-400 BIOLOGICAL SCIENCES GROUP

General Biological Science Series	GS-401
Microbiology Series	GS-403
Biological Technician Series	GS-404
Pharmacology Technician	GS-405
Agricultural Extension Series	GS-406
Ecology Series	GS-408
Zoology Series	GS-410
Physiology Series	GS-413
Entomology Series	GS-414
Plant Protection Technician Series	GS-421
Botany Series	GS-430
Plant Pathology Series	GS-434
Plant Physiology Series	GS-435
Plant Protection and Quarantine Series	GS-436
Horticultural Series	GS-437
Genetics Series	GS-440
Range Conservation Series	GS-454

Range Technician Series	GS-455
Soil Conservation Series	GS-457
Soil Conservation Technician Series	GS-458
Irrigation System Operation Series	GS-459
Forestry Series	GS-460
Forestry Technician Series	GS-462
Soil Science Series	GS-470
Agronomy Series	GS-471
Agricultural Management Series	GS-475
General Fish and Wildlife Administration Series	GS-480
Fishery Biology Series	GS-482
Wildlife Refuge Management Series	GS-485
Wildlife Biology Series	GS-486
Husbandry Series	GS-487
Fish Hatchery Management Series	GS-488
Home Economics Series	GS-498
Biological Science Student Trainee Series	GS-499

GS-500 ACCOUNTING AND BUDGET GROUP

General Accounting Clerical and Administrative Series	GS-501
Budget and Accounting Series	GS-504
Financial Management Series	GS-505
Accounting Series	GS-510
Internal Revenue Agent Series	GS-512
Accounting Technician Series	GS-525
Tax Technician Series	GS-526
Cash Processing Series	GS-530
Voucher Examining Series	GS-540
Fiscal Auditing (GAO) Series	GS-541
Payroll Series	GS-544
Military Pay Series	GS-545
Benefit-Payment Roll Series	GS-547
Budget Administration Series	GS-560
Financial Institution Examining Series	GS-570
Time and Leave Series	GS-590
Tax Accounting Series	GS-592
Insurance Accounts Series	GS-593

GS-600 MEDICAL, HOSPITAL, DENTAL, AND PUBLIC HEALTH GROUP

General Health Science Series	GS-601
Medical Officer Series	GS-602
Physician's Assistant Series	GS-603
Nurse Series	GS-610
Nursing Assistant Series	GS-621
Autopsy Assistant Series	GS-625
Dietician Series	GS-630
Occupational Therapist Series	GS-631
Physical Therapist Series	GS-633

Corrective Therapist Series	GS-635
Rehabilitation Therapy Assistant Series	GS-636
Manual Arts Therapist Series	GS-637
Recreation/Creative Arts Therapist Series	GS-638
Educational Therapist Series	GS-639
Nuclear Medicine Technician Series	GS-642
Medical Technologist Series	GS-644
Medical Technician Series	GS-645
Pathology Technician Series	GS-646
Medical Radiology Technician Series	GS-647
Medical Machine Technician Series	GS-649
Medical Technical Assistant Series	GS-650
Pharmacist Series	GS-660
Pharmacy Technician Series	GS-661
Optometrist Series	GS-662
Restoration Technician Series	GS-664
Speech Pathology and Audiology Series	GS-665
Orthotist and Prosthetist Series	GS-667
Podiatrist Series	GS-668
Medical Record Librarian Series	GS-669
Health System Administration Series	GS-670
Health System Specialist Series	GS-671
Prosthetic Representative Series	GS-672
Hospital Housekeeping Management Series	GS-673
Medical Clerk Series	GS-679
Dental Officer Series	GS-680
Dental Assistant Series	GS-681
Dental Hygiene Series	GS-682
Dental Laboratory Aide and Technician Series	GS-683
Public Health Dental Hygiene Series	GS-684
Public Health Program Specialist Series	GS-685
Sanitarian Series	GS-688
Industrial Hygiene Series	GS-690
Consumer Safety Series	GS-696
Environmental Health Technician Series	GS-698
Health Aid and Technician Series	GS-699

GS-700 VETERINARY MEDICAL SCIENCE GROUP

Veterinary Medical Science Series	GS-701
Animal Health Technician Series	GS-704
Veterinary Student Trainee Series	GS-799

GS-800 ENGINEERING AND ARCHITECTURE GROUP

General Engineering Series	GS-801
Engineering Technician Series	GS-802
Safety Engineering Series	GS-803
Fire Prevention Engineering Series	GS-804
Materials Engineering Series	GS-806

Landscape Architecture	GS-807
Architecture Series	GS-808
Construction Control Series	GS-809
Civil Engineering Series	GS-810
Surveying Technician Series	GS-817
Engineering Drafting Series	GS-818
Environmental Engineering Series	GS-819
Construction Analysis Series	GS-828
Mechanical Engineering Series	GS-830
Nuclear Engineering Series	GS-840
Electric Engineering Series	GS-850
Electronics Engineering Series	GS-855
Electronics Technician Series	GS-856
Biomedical Engineering Series	GS-858
Aerospace Engineering Series	GS-861
Naval Architecture Series	GS-871
Ship Surveying Series	GS-873
Mining Engineering Series	GS-880
Petroleum Engineering Series	GS-881
Agricultural Engineering Series	GS-890
Ceramic Engineering Series	GS-892
Chemical Engineering Series	GS-893
Welding Engineering Series	GS-894
Industrial Engineering Technician	GS-895
Engineering and Architecture Student Trainee Series	GS-899

GS-900 LEGAL AND KINDRED GROUP

Law Clerk Series	GS-904
General Attorney Series	GS-905
Estate Tax Examining Series	GS-920
Hearings and Appeals Series	GS-930
Administrative Law Judge Series	GS-935
Deportation and Exclusion Examining Series	GS-942
Clerk of Court Series	GS-945
Paralegal Specialist Series	GS-950
Contact Representative Series	GS-962
Legal Instruments Examining Series	GS-963
Land Law Examining Series	GS-965
Passport and Visa Examining Series	GS-967
Legal Clerk and Technician Series	GS-986
Tax Law Specialist Series	GS-987
General Claims Examining Series	GS-990
Workers' Compensation Claims Examining Series	GS-991
Loss and Damage Claims Examining Series	GS-992
Social Insurance Claims Examining Series	GS-993
Unemployment Compensation Claims Examining Series	GS-994
Dependents and Estates Claims Examining Series	GS-995
Veterans Claims Examining Series	GS-996
Civil Service Retirement Claims Examining Series	GS-997
Claims Clerical Series	GS-998

GS-1000 INFORMATION AND ARTS GROUP

General Arts and Information Series	GS-1001
Exhibits Specialist Series	GS-1010
Museum Curator Series	GS-1015
Museum Specialist and Technician Series	GS-1016
Illustrating Series	GS-1020
Office Drafting Series	GS-1021
Translator Series	GS-1045
Clerk-Translator Series	GS-1046
Interpreter Series	GS-1047
Foreign Language Broadcasting Series	GS-1048
Music Specialist Series	GS-1051
Theater Specialist Series	GS-1054
Art Specialist Series	GS-1056
Photography Series	GS-1060
Audio-Visual Production Series	GS-1071
Public Information Series	GS-1081
Writing and Editing Series	GS-1082
Technical Writing and Editing Series	GS-1083
Visual Information Series	GS-1084
Foreign Information Series	GS-1085
Editorial Assistance Series	GS-1087

GS-1100 BUSINESS AND INDUSTRY GROUP

General Business and Industry Series	GS-1101
Contract and Procurement Series	GS-1102
Industrial Property Management Series	GS-1103
Property Disposal Series	GS-1104
Purchasing Series	GS-1105
Procurement Clerical and Assistance Series	GS-1106
Property Disposal Clerical and Technician Series	GS-1107
Public Utilities Specialist Series	GS-1130
Trade Specialist Series	GS-1140
Commissary Store Management Series	GS-1144
Agricultural Program Specialist Series	GS-1145
Agricultural Marketing Series	GS-1146
Agricultural Market Reporting Series	GS-1147
Wage and Hour Law Administration Series	GS-1149
Industrial Specialist Series	GS-1150
Production Control Series	GS-1152
Financial Analysis Series	GS-1160
Insurance Examining Series	GS-1163
Loan Specialist Series	GS-1165
Internal Revenue Office Series	GS-1169
Realty Series	GS-1170
Appraising and Assessing Series	GS-1171
Housing Management Series	GS-1173
Building Management Series	GS-1176

GS-1200 COPYRIGHT, PATENT, AND TRADEMARK GROUP

Patent Technician Series	GS-1202
Copyright Series	GS-1210
Copyright Technician Series	GS-1211
Patent Administration Series	GS-1220
Patent Advisor Series	GS-1221
Patent Attorney Series	GS-1222
Patent Classifying Series	GS-1223
Patent Examining Series	GS-1224
Patent Interference Examining Series	GS-1225
Design Patent Examining Series	GS-1226
Trademark Examining Series	GS-1241

GS-1300 PHYSICAL SCIENCE GROUP

General Physical Science Series	GS-1301
Health Physics Series	GS-1306
Physics Series	GS-1310
Physical Science Technician Series	GS-1311
Geophysics Series	GS-1313
Hydrology Series	GS-1315
Hydrologic Technician	GS-1316
Chemistry Series	GS-1320
Metallurgy Series	GS-1321
Astronomy and Space Science Series	GS-1330
Meteorology Series	GS-1340
Meteorological Technician Series	GS-1341
Geology Series	GS-1350
Oceanography Series	GS-1360
Navigational Information Series	GS-1361
Cartography Series	GS-1370
Cartographic Technician Series	GS-1371
Geodesy Series	GS-1372
Land Surveying Series	GS-1373
Geodetic Technician Series	GS-1374
Forest Products Technology Series	GS-1380
Food Technology Series	GS-1382
Textile Technology Series	GS-1384
Photographic Technology Series	GS-1386
Document Analysis Series	GS-1397
Physical Science Student Trainee Series	GS-1399

GS-1400 LIBRARY AND ARCHIVES GROUP

Librarian Series	GS-1410
Library Technician Series	GS-1411
Technical Information Services Series	GS-1412
Archivist Series	GS-1420
Archives Technician Series	GS-1421

GS-1500 MATHEMATICS AND STATISTICS GROUP

Actuary Series	GS-1510
Operations Research Series	GS-1515
Mathematics Series	GS-1520
Mathematics Technician Series	GS-1521
Mathematical Statistician Series	GS-1529
Statistician Series	GS-1530
Statistical Assistant Series	GS-1531
Cryptography Series	GS-1540
Cryptoanalysis Series	GS-1541
Computer Science Series	GS-1550
Mathematical Science Student Trainee Series	GS-1599

GS-1600 EQUIPMENT, FACILITIES, AND SERVICES GROUP

General Facilities and Equipment Series	GS-1601
Cemetery Administration Series	GS-1630
Facility Management Series	GS-1640
Printing Management Series	GS-1654
Laundry and Dry Cleaning Plant Management Series	GS-1658
Fishery Methods and Equipment Series	GS-1659
General Housekeeping Series	GS-1666
Steward Series	GS-1667
Equipment Specialist Series	GS-1670

GS-1700 EDUCATION GROUP

General Education and Training Series	GS-1701
Education and Training Technician Series	GS-1702
Education and Vocational Training Series	GS-1710
Training Instruction Series	GS-1712
Vocational Rehabilitation Series	GS-1715
Education Research and Program Series	GS-1720
Public Health Educator Series	GS-1725

GS-1800 INVESTIGATION GROUP

General Investigating Series	GS-1810
Criminal Investigating Series	GS-1811
Game Law Enforcement Series	GS-1812
Air Safety Investigating Series	GS-1815
Immigration Inspection Series	GS-1816
Coal Mine Inspection Series	GS-1822
Aviation Safety Officer Series	GS-1825
Securities Compliance Examining Series	GS-1831
Agricultural Commodity Warehouse Examining Series	GS-1850
Alcohol, Tobacco and Firearms Inspection Series	GS-1854
Alcohol Tax Technician Series	GS-1855

Public Health Inspection Series	GS-1860
Consumer Safety Inspection Series	GS-1862
Food Inspection Series	GS-1863
Public Health Quarantine Inspection Series	GS-1864
Import Specialist Series	GS-1889
Customs Inspection Series	GS-1890
Customs Enforcement Officer Series	GS-1891
Customs Appraising and Examining Series	GS-1892
Customs Marine Officer Series	GS-1893
Customs Entry and Liquidation Series	GS-1894
Customs Warehouse Officer Series	GS-1895
Border Patrol Agent Series	GS-1896
Customs Aid Series	GS-1897
Admeasurement Series	GS-1898
Miscellaneous Inspection Series	GS-1899

GS-2000 SUPPLY GROUP

General Supply Series	GS-2001
Supply Program Management Series	GS-2003
Supply Clerical and Technician Series	GS-2005
Inventory Management Series	GS-2010
Distribution Facilities and Storage Management Series	GS-2030
Packaging Series	GS-2032
Supply Cataloging	GS-2050
Sales Store Clerical Series	GS-2091

GS-2100 TRANSPORTATION GROUP

Transportation Specialist Series	GS-2101
Transportation Clerk and Assistant Series	GS-2102
Transportation Industry Analysis Series	GS-2110
Transportation Rate and Tariff Examining Series	GS-2111
Railroad Safety Series	GS-2121
Highway Safety Management Series	GS-2125
Traffic Management Series	GS-2130
Freight Rate Series	GS-2131
Travel Series	GS-2132
Passenger Rate Series	GS-2133
Shipment Clerical Series	GS-2134
Transportation Loss and Damage Claims Examining Series	GS-2135
Cargo Scheduling Series	GS-2144
Transportation Operations Series	GS-2150
Dispatching Series	GS-2151
Air Traffic Control Series	GS-2152
Marine Cargo Series	GS-2161
Aircraft Operation Series	GS-2181

Appendix Q
Occupation Groups and Series of Classes on the Wage Grade System (WG)

Telephone Mechanic, WG-2502

2502	Central Office Telephone Equipment Installing and Repairing Series
2507	Telephone Installing and Repairing Series
2558	Telephone Installing Series
2559	Intercommunication Systems Installing Series

Electronics Mechanic, WG-2614

2604	Radar Equipment Installing and Repairing Series
2607	Electronic Test Equipment Operating Series
2608	Radio Equipment Installing and Repairing Series
2610	Radio Telephone Equipment Repairing Series
2614	Electronic Equipment Making, Installing, and Repairing Series
2620	Television Equipment Installing and Repairing Series
2640	Domestic Radio and Television Receiver Repairing Series
2654	Radio Repairing Series
2655	UHF Radio Repairing Series
2656	Ground Radio Installing Series
2657	Radar Repairing Series
2661	Radio-Radar Equipment Installing Series
2664	Electronic Amplifier Repairing Series
2675	Television Repairing Series
2680	Electronic Amplifier Repairing Series
2683	Electronic Equipment Field Maintaining Series
2688	Electronic Subassembly Repairing Series
2696	Radio Repairing and Installing Series
26100	Electronic Chassis Repairing Series
26101	Microwave and Telemetering Equipment Repairing Series
26103	Television Station Maintaining Series
26119	Ground Radar Trainer Analyzing Series
26121	Training Devices Electronic Components Repairing Series
26126	Meteorological Equipment Repairing Series
2613	Fire Control Instrument Making, Installing and Repairing Series
2617	Electronic Fire Control Systems Making, Installing and Repairing Series
2668	Bombing-Navigational System Analyzing Series
2676	Electronic Instrument and Control System Repairing Series
2687	Experimental Airborne Electronics Systems Analyzing Series
2697	Automatic Checkout Equipment Analyzing Series
26106	Aircraft and Weapons Control System Analyzing Series
26113	Missile Guidance System Mechanical Series
26114	Missile Systems Analyzing Series
26116	Flight Trainer Analyzing Series
26117	Bombing-Navigational Trainer Analyzing Series
26118	Fire Control Trainer Analyzing Series
26119	Ground Radar Trainer Analyzing Series
26127	Flight Trainers Electronic Component Repairing Series
26130	Guided Aircraft Missile Analyzing Series
26131	Airborne Detection and Warning Systems Series

26133 Inertial Guidance System Analyzing Series

Electrician, WG-2805

2803 Electrical Working (Studio) Series
2805 Electrical Installing and Repairing Series
2857 Light Fixture Servicing Series

Electrician (High Voltage), WG-2810

2806 Electrical Line Working Series
2808 Electrical Working (Powerhouse) Series
2810 Electrical Cable Splicing Series

Sewing Machine Operator, WG-3111

3111 Sewing Machine Operating Series
7308 Laundry Mending Series
7357 Laundry Sewing Machine Operating Series

Optical Instrument Repairer, WG-3306

3306 Optical Instrument Repair Series
3308 Photographic Equipment Repair Series
3311 Fire Control Instrument Making, Installing, and Repairing Series
3343 Motion Picture Mechanic Series
3344 Optical Instrument Making Series
3386 Optical Tracker Modifying and Operating Series
3387 System Optical Sight Repairing Series
4008 Optical Instrument Assembly Series

Machinist, WG-3414

3414 Machining, General
3453 Maintenance Machining

Toolmaker, WG-3416

3416 Tool, Die, and Gauge Making Series
3476 Carbide Toolmaking Series

Die Sinker, WG-3428

3428 Die Sinking Series

Machine Tool Operator, WG-3431

3402 Automatic Screw Machine Operating Series
3404 Boring Mill Operating Series
3409 Drill Press Operating Series
3411 Engine Lathe Operating Series
3415 Milling Machine Operating Series
3419 Turret Lathe Operating Series
3421 Planer Operating Series
3423 Broaching Machine Operating Series
3424 Grinding Machine Operating Series
3425 Honing and Lapping Machine Operating Series
3426 Profile Machine Operating Series
3427 Shaper Machine Operating Series
3429 Production Machine Operating Series
3431 Machine Tool Operating Series
3432 Gear Cutting Machine Operating Series
3452 Pantograph Machine Operating Series
3455 General Machine Operating Series
3456 Aircraft Engine Parts Reconditioning Series
3464 Parts Reworking Series
3465 Aircraft Engine Cylinder Reworking Series
3477 Parts Reworking Machine Operating Series

Laborer, WG-3502

3502 Laboring Series
3505 Baggage Handling Series
3544 Freight and Baggage Handling Series
3555 Workhand Series
5209 Refuse Collection, Transfer and Disposal Series

Janitor, WG-3566

3502 Laboring Series (Custodial Laboring Only)
3503 Housekeeping Series
3540 Window Washing Series
3565 Custodial Working Series
3566 Janitorial Series
7555 Nursery Attending Series

Cement Finisher, WG-3602

3602   Cement Finishing Series
3646   Cement Gun Operating Series
3647   Grout Caulking Series
5445   Brick and Cement Products Equipment Operating Series
5711   Mud Jack Operating Series
5747   Concrete Pump Operating Series
5749   Cement Gun Mixing Machine Operating Series

Mason, WG-3603

3603   Masonry Series
3607   Bricklaying Series
3640   Stone Cutting Series
3642   Stone Setting Series

Plasterer, WG-3605

3605   Plastering Series
4645   Lathing Series
4646   Wallboard Taping Series

Roofer, WG-3606

3606   Roofing Series
4655   Roof Maintenance Series

Asphalt Worker, WG-3653

3653   Pavement Repairing Series
5410   Asphalt Plant Operating Series
57252   Oil Distributor Operating Series
57253   Asphalt Spray Equipment Operating Series

Welder, WG-3703

3703   Welding Series
3726   Spot Welding Series
3752   Aircraft Welding Series
3754   Production Welding Series
3755   Welding Machine Operating Series
3788   Experimental Welding Series
3784   Missile Test Facility Welding Series
37905   Combination Welding Series
37906   Electric Welding Series
37907   Gas Welding Series

Electroplater, WG-3711

3711   Electroplating Series
3717   Anodizing Series
3718   Galvanizing Series
3719   Metal Surface Treating
3763   Industrial Electroplating Series
3764   Electroplating Working Series

Sheet Metal Mechanic, WG-3806

3806   Sheet Metal Working Series
3811   Metal Furniture Making and Repairing Series
3853   Aircraft Sheet Metal Working Series
3854   Engine Metal Container Repairing Series
3855   Metal Container Repairing Series
3861   Aircraft Sheet Metal Manufacturing Series
3864   Aircraft Sheet Metal Template Making Series
3865   Aircraft Sheet Metal Parts Repairing Series
3866   Aircraft Engine Sheet Metal Parts Repairing Series
3880   Experimental Sheet Metal Parts Fabricating Series
3881   Project Sheet Metal Fabricating Series
3882   Aircraft Sheet Metal Modifying Series
3883   Aircraft Project Sheet Metal Modifying Series

Boilermaker, WG-3808

3808   Boiler Making Series

Shipfitter, WG-4102

6204   Shipfitting Series

Painter, WG-4102

4102   Painter
4140   Aircraft Painter
4143   Automotive Painter
4153   Industrial Painter
4155   Production Painter

Sign Painter, WG-4104

4104   Sign Painting Series

Pipefitter, WG-4204

4204	Pipefitting Series
4205	Pipefitting (Marine)
4207	Steamfitting Series

Plumber, WG-4206

4202	Automatic Sprinkler System Installing and Repairing Series
4206	Plumbing Series
4240	Water Meter Installing Series
4243	Pipe Caulking Series

Blocker and Bracer, WG-4602

4602	Blocking and Bracing Series

Wood Worker, WG-4604

4604	Boxmaking Series
4609	Crate Making Series
4611	Dunnage Making Series
4615	Nailing Machine Operating Series
4617	Power Saw Operating Series
4621	Crating Series
4659	Production Crating Series
4660	Wood Container Assembling Series
4661	Wood Container Making Series

Wood Craftsman, WG-4605

4605	Cabinetmaking Series
4644	Orthopedic Devices Woodworking Series
4652	Woodworking Series

Carpenter, WG-4607

4607	Carpentry Series
4656	Industrial Carpentry Series

Patternmaker, WG-4616

4616	Patternmaking (Wood) Series

Instrument Maker, WG-4712

2681	Electronic Equipment Fabricating Series
3345	Instrument Making (General)

Model Maker, WG-4714

4748	Model Making (General)

Utilities Systems Repairer-Operator, WG-4742

4742	General Facilities and Equipment Maintaining and Operating Series

Maintenance Mechanic, WG-4749

4707	Preventive Maintenance Working Series
4749	Maintenance Working Series
4752	Building Maintenance Series
4757	Caretaking Series

Medical Equipment Repairer, WG-4805

4805	Medical Equipment Repairing Series
4818	Radiology Equipment Repairing Series

Office Appliance Repairer, WG-4806

4806	Office Appliance Repairing Series

Gardener, WG-5003

3504	Ground Maintenance Series
3562	Gardening Series
3563	Tree Culture Working Series
5003	Gardening Series
5013	Nursery Working Series
5027	Crops Research Helping Series

Pest Controller, WG-5026

3570	Pest Control Series
5026	Pest Controlling Series
5425	Insect and Rodent Control Series

Rigger, WG-5210

3857	Cable Working Series
5207	Submarine and Torpedo Net Rigging Series
5722	Rigging Series
5728	Crane Groundsman Working Series
6205	Ship Rigging Series

Laboratory Worker, WG-3511

7502   Laboratory Worker

Air Conditioning Equipment Mechanic, WG-5306

5306   Refrigeration and Air Conditioning Equipment Repairing Series
5338   Dehumidification Equipment Repairing Series
5358   Evaporative Cooling Servicing Series
5380   Climatic Facility Maintaining Series

Heating and Boiler Plant Equipment Mechanic, WG-5313

5309   Heating Equipment Repairing Series
5327   Powerhouse Equipment Repairing Series

Elevator Mechanic, WG-5313

2808   Electrical Working (Power Plant) Series
5407   Power Plant Operating Series
5463   Electrical Power Dispatching Series

Boiler Fireman, WG-5402

5402   Boiler and Steam Plant Operating Series
5405   Steam Plant Operating Series

Utility Systems Operator WG-5406

5406   Utilities Operating (General) Series

Electric Power Controller, WG-5407

5407   Power Plant Operating Series
5463   Electric Power Dispatching Series

Sewage Disposal Plant Operator, WG-5408

5408   Sewage Disposal Plant Operating Series
5458   Sewage Pumping Station Operating Series
5459   Industrial Waste Plant Operating Series

Water Treatment Plant Operator, WG-5409

5409   Water Treatment Plant Operating Series
5449   Pumping Plant Operating Series
54275   Water Systems Operating Series

Fuel Distribution Systems Operator, WG-5413

5413   Fuel Distribution Systems Operator

Air Conditioning Equipment Operator, WG-5415

5415   Refrigeration and Air Conditioning Equipment Operating Series
5482   Climatic Chamber Operating Series

Sandblaster, WG-5423

5423   Sandblasting Series

Elevator Operator, WG-5438

5438   Elevator Operating Series

Motor Vehicle Operator, WG-5703

5703   Automotive Equipment Operating Series
5714   Staff Car Operating Series
5720   Lumber Carrier Operating Series
5745   Weed Control Equipment Operating Series
5753   Light Vehicle Operating Series
5754   Medium Vehicle Operating Series
5755   Heavy Vehicle Operating Series
5756   Tractor Trailer Operating Series
5757   Ambulance Operating Series

Fork Lift Operator, WG-5704

5704   Fork Lift Operating Series

Tractor Operator, WG-5705

5033   Farm Equipment Operating Series
5705   Tractor Operating Series
5709   Warehouse Tractor Operating Series
5759   Aircraft Light Towing Equipment Operating Series

5760   Aircraft Heavy Towing Equipment
        Operating Series

Engineering Equipment Operator, WG-5716

5716   Engineering Equipment Operating
        Series
5718   Grading Equipment Operating Series
5719   Heavy Duty Earth Hauling Equipment
        Operating Series
5721   Motor Grader Operating Series
5726   Trench Digging Machine Operating
        Series
5739   Ditch Cleaner Operating Series
5741   Loading Equipment Operating Series
5744   Heavy Tractor Operating Series
5746   Roller Operating Series
5761   Earth Refuse Handling Equipment
        Operating Series

Crane Operator, WG-5725

5453   Bridge Crane Operating Series
5471   Gantry Crane Operating Series
5710   Crane-Shovel Operating Series
5712   Electric Bridge Crane Operating
        Series
5717   Gantry Crane Operating Series
5727   Warehouse Crane Operating Series
5763   Light Crane Operating Series
5765   Locomotive Crane Operating Series
5945   Floating Crane Operating Series

Heavy Mobile Equipment Mechanic, WG-5803

5803   Engineer Equipment Repairing Series
5804   Diesel Engine Repairing Series
5805   Fire Protection Equipment Repairing
        Series
5807   Combat Vehicle Repairing Series
5825   Automotive or Engineering Equip-
        ment Repairing (Wheels and Brakes)
        Series (Heavy Mobile Equipment
        only)
5841   Automotive and Engineering Equip-
        ment Repairing Series (Heavy Mobile
        Equipment only)
5853   Industrial Engine Disassembling
        Series
5854   Industrial Engine Assembling Series
5855   Industrial Engine Testing Series

5865   Mobile Equipment Repairing Series
        (Heavy Mobile Equipment only)
5874   Diesel-Electric Locomotive Mechani-
        cal Series
5877   Fire and Crash Truck Mechanical
        Series

Automotive Mechanic, WG-5823

5811   Motorcycle Repairing Series
5816   Automotive Equipment Testing Series
5821   Automotive Equipment Repairing
        (Frame and Wheel Aligning) Series
5822   Automotive Equipment Repairing
        (Engine Rebuilding) Series
5823   Automotive Equipment Repairing
        Series
5828   Warehouse Materials Handling
        Equipment Repairing Series

Braker-Switcher and Conductor, WG-5736

6002   Brakeman Series
6003   Conductor Series

Locomotive Engineer, WG-5737

6004   Locomotive Engineer Series
6005   Locomotive Firing Series
6040   Subway Car Operating Series
6041   Dinkey Engineering Series

Railroad Maintenance Vehicle Operator, WG-5738

6106   Railroad Track Maintaining Series
        (work using self-propelled flanged
        wheel railroad maintenance equip-
        ment only)
6147   Power Ballaster Operator Series
6148   Track Laying Machine Operating
        Series

Artillery Repairer, WG-6605

6605   Artillery Repairing Series

Small Arms Repairer, WG-6610

6607   Small Arms Assembling Series
6608   Small Arms Disassembling Series

6610	Small Arms Repairing Series
6660	Gunsmithing Series
6662	Gun and Cannon Repairing Series
6664	Small Arms Servicing Series

Materials Expeditor, WG-6910

6705	Production Expeditor Series
6956	Supply Processing and Delivery Series
6957	Parts Routing Series
6958	Parts Expediting Series

Tools and Parts Attendant, WG-6904

6904	Tool, Stock, and Parts Keeping Series
6942	Lightman Series
6963	Tool Crib Attending Series
6964	Stock Room Attending Series

Warehouse Worker, WG-6907

6907	Warehousing (General) Series
6959	Stock Handling Series
6960	Warehousing Series
6961	Freight Checking Series
6962	Materials Processing Series

Packer, WG-7002

7002	Packing Series
7008	Strapping and Marking Series
7056	Parcel Post Packing Series
7057	Publications Packing Series
7060	Cryptographic Material Packing Series
7080	Experimental Packaging Series

Equipment Cleaner, WG-7009

3542	Industrial Cleaning Series
3713	Chipping Series
5417	Parts and Equipment Steam Cleaner Operating Series
5418	Parts and Equipment Cleaning Inspecting Series
8858	Aircraft Metal Surfaces Conditioning Series

Laundry Worker, WG-7304

7302	Laundry Marking, Classifying, and Sorting Series

7303	Laundry Receiving and Shipping Series
7304	Laundry Working Series
7353	Marking, Sorting and Checking Series

Laundry Machine Operator, WG-7305

7305	Washing, Extracting, and Tumbling Series

Presser, WG-7306

3156	Pressing Series
7306	Pressing Series
7354	Laundry Press Operating Series
7355	Garment Pressing Series

Baker, WG-7402

7402	Baking Series
7403	Baking (Pastry) Series

Cook, WG-7404

7404	Cooking Series
7452	Diet Cooking Series

Meatcutter, WG-7407

7407	Meatcutting Series

Food Service Worker, WG-7408

7408	Food Service Working Series
7441	Counterwoman (Man) Series
7453	Table Waiting Series
7454	Pantryman Series
7455	Diet Working Series
74252	Pantry Working (Special Diets) Series

Store Worker, WG-6914

7602	Sales Store Working Series
7652	Commissary Stock Handling Series
7655	Produce Attending Series
7667	Meat Market Attendant Series

Animal Caretaker, WG-5048

5029	Poultry Research Helping Series
5030	Livestock Research Helping Series

5032	Laboratory Animal Research Helping Series
5037	Swineherding Series
5038	Beefherding Series
5041	Poultry Farming Series
7701	Miscellaneous Animal Caretaking Series
7703	Stable Hand Series
7706	Animal Caretaking Series
7740	Fish Hatchery Working Series
7741	Poundkeeping Series
7742	Well Working Series

Aircraft Mechanic, WG-8852

6852	Aircraft Mechanical Series
8854	Aircraft Disassembling Series
8855	Aircraft Repairing Series
8857	Airframe Parts Assembling Series
8872	Helicopter Mechanical Series
8875	Flight Line Mechanical Series
8880	Experimental Aircraft Test Mechanical Series

Index

INDEX